CYBARIS®
AN INTELLECTUAL PROPERTY LAW REVIEW

Volume 6   2015   Issue 2

EDITOR-IN-CHIEF
Sarah A. Howes

EXECUTIVE EDITOR
Adam E. Szymanski

NOTES & COMMENT EDITORS
Nadja Baer   Christopher Bayliss   Katherine Boyle

STAFF

Mihajlo Babovic	Joseph W. Dubis	Brian Jarvis
Chelsea Ganske	Kelly Fermoyle	Anthony Marshik
Nodira Ismoilova	Vincent W. Rotty	Anthony Salmo
Caitlin Kowalke	James Ryan	Brian Smith
Molly Littman	Jaime Sekenski	

FACULTY ADVISOR
Ken Port

2015

Cybaris®, an Intellectual Property Law Review, is published two times per year by the students of the Intellectual Property Institute of William Mitchell College of Law at 875 Summit Avenue, Saint Paul, Minnesota, 55105. Telephone: 651-290-6425. E-mail: eic.cybaris@wmitchell.edu.

Manuscripts: Cybaris®, an Intellectual Property Law Review, welcomes unsolicited manuscripts. All manuscripts submitted for consideration should be double spaced, with citations placed in footnotes that conform to THE BLUEBOOK: A UNIFORM SYSTEM OF CITATION (19th ed. 2010). Please forward all submissions to the Cybaris® Editorial Office at the address listed above.

Opinions expressed in Cybaris®, an Intellectual Property Law Review, do not necessarily represent the views of the publication, its editors, the William Mitchell College of Law, or any person connected therewith.

CYBARIS®
AN INTELLECTUAL PROPERTY
LAW REVIEW

Volume 6   2015   Issue 2

Foreword
Daniel L. Bruzzone and Brad D. Pedersen i

Articles
Regionally Based Collective Trademark System in Japan:
Geographical Indicators by a Different Name or a Political
Misdirection
Kenneth L. Port 1

Just Governance or Just War?: Native Artists, cultural
production, and the Challenge of "Super-Diversity"
Rebecca Tsosie 61

Student Articles
Inter Partes Review: A Multi-Method Comparison for
Challenging Patent Validity
Joseph W. Dubis Ph.D. 118

A Short History of Patent Remedies
James Ryan 166

Adapting Alice: How to Formulate a Repeatable Test
Based on Alice v. CLS Bank
Kelly Fermoyle 221

FOREWORD

DANIEL L. BRUZZONE[1] & BRAD D. PEDERSEN[2]

With passage of the America Invents Act (AIA) in 2011, huge changes have been made to the statutes governing patent prosecution in the United States; affecting everything from filing strategies to how the patents are examined to even post-grant challenges. If the AIA itself was the earthquake, the subsequent court rulings have been the aftershocks. The debate and analysis of the issues provided by journals like Cybaris® provide the early warnings for these aftershocks. The reflections of veteran practitioners and the fresh eyes of students come together in one place, informing and persuading policymakers before the law ossifies.

The effects of the AIA were mostly in the area of patent prosecution. Because the AIA was implemented between 2011 and 2013, and because of the lengthy nature of patent prosecution, some of the implications of the AIA with respect to patent prosecution are still being worked out at the U.S. Patent and Trademark Office and in law firms across the country. As patent practitioners, we

---

[1] Daniel L. Bruzzone is an associate attorney at Patterson Thuente IP, practicing patent law. He is a former Editor of Cybaris® and holds a law degree from William Mitchell College of Law. Prior to his legal career, Daniel was a researcher in the product development laboratories at 3M, and he has a Bachelor of Science degree in Physics from the University of Minnesota.

[2] Mr. Pedersen is a shareholder with the law firm of Patterson Thuente Pedersen, PA. He is also an author of "The Matrix For Changing First-To-Invent: An Experimental Investigation Into Proposed Changes in U.S. Patent Law," as found in Volume 4 of Cybaris®. The views expressed in this article are not attributable to the law firm of Patterson Thuente Pedersen, P.A. nor to any clients of the law firm.

think about the effects of the AIA nearly every day. In our opinion, some of the most beneficial changes of the AIA included those very things advocated for in previous editions of this journal, including international harmonization[3] and the availability of patent pro bono services.[4]

Despite the short time since these patent prosecution reforms, commentators and legislators continue to be concerned about deficiencies in the current patent enforcement and litigation mechanisms. An article in this journal, for example, described how the high costs of patent litigation have permitted the reemergence of the "sharks" of the 19th century, now dubbed "patent trolls."[5] The response to this problem of abusive patent litigation tactics, however, cannot be to make patents toothless.[6]

One mechanism for reducing abuses of the system is to provide litigation alternatives, such as those detailed in Joseph Dubis's article. Post-grant

---

[3] Jay A. Erstling et al., *Usefulness Varies by Country: the Utility Requirement of Patent Law in the United States, Europe and Canada*, 3 CYBARIS AN INTELL. PROP. L. REV. 1 (2012).

[4] Amy M. Salmela & Mark R. Privratsky, *Patent Law Pro Bono: A Best Practices Handbook*, 4 CYBARIS AN INTELL. PROP. L. REV. 1 (2012).

[5] Lucas Hjelle, *Case Note: Identifying Indicia of Extortion in Patent Troll Cases: Eon-Net LP v. Flagstar Bancorp*, 3 CYBARIS AN INTELL. PROP. L. REV. 133 (2012).

[6] *See* 114 CONG. REC. S2532 (daily ed. April 29, 2015) (statement of Sen. Chuck Grassley) ("This bipartisan legislation is the result of a careful and deliberative process in which we worked with many stakeholders representing almost every area of the economy, the judiciary, and the administration. Since the process started in the last Congress, we've listened and tried to be responsive to all the concerns raised from the different industries and constituencies. As a result, we have made great strides in addressing issues that have been raised along the way and getting stakeholders comfortable with the bill. So I believe the PATENT Act strikes a good balance. Our intent is to protect the rights of patent holders while addressing the problem of abusive litigation. The PATENT Act does that.").

proceedings before the Patent Trial and Appeal Board can dispatch with claims by patent trolls for a fraction of the cost of litigating at a district court. Understanding the options available and how to use them properly will be crucial in the coming years. J.P. Morgan famously said "If you have to ask the price, you can't afford it." For those involved in patent disputes who find they have less than J.P. Morgan's assets, the sub-heading on Cost for each option will doubtless be appreciated.

Another way to address abusive litigation concerns is by considering the ways damages and attorney fees are awarded. For example, pending legislation is awaiting action by Congress at the time this article was written to provide for fee-shifting in patent cases, among other things.[7] The historical context of remedies in patent litigation provided in James Ryan's article provides not only the current rules, but also the context and recommendations for providing flexibility to courts to modify the rules to be more equitable.

Another area of patent law that has recently been in flux is the very question of what types of inventions are even eligible to be patented. This topic has been addressed by the Supreme Court,[8] and Kelly Fermoyle's article provides guidelines for lower courts to apply the Court's somewhat abstract or nebulous decision, and for litigants to advocate along those lines.

Many of the changes described above harmonize our patent application, prosecution, and enforcement mechanisms with other

---

[7] Innovation Act, H.R. 9, 114th Cong. (2015); PATENT Act, S. 1137, 114th Cong. (2015).
[8] Alice Corp. v. CLS Bank Int'l, 134 S. Ct. 2347 (2014).

countries around the world. As intellectual property law becomes more internationally harmonized, there has been a good deal of discussion relating to the efficiencies and benefits of regional or global filing systems and courts. Rebecca Tsosie's article provides an interesting counterpoint on the downsides of a one-size-fits-all approach, and the benefits of customization of intellectual property protection to the people it is meant to serve. While standardized rules provide benefits of efficiency and predictability, they could come at the cost of failing to protect the creative works of many groups of people, including native artists.

And of course, concerns about regional protection in an era of international commerce are not exclusive to patent law. As outlined in Professor Port's article on regionally based trademarks, collective marks are being increasingly used not only in the United States, but also in countries such as Japan. Implementation of regional or national trademark systems as a type of domestic booster can be difficult to accomplish, and policymakers would be wise to look to the eventual success or failure of the *chiiki* system before attempting to emulate it.

REGIONALLY BASED COLLECTIVE TRADEMARK SYSTEM IN JAPAN: GEOGRAPHICAL INDICATORS BY A DIFFERENT NAME OR A POLITICAL MISDIRECTION?

KENNETH L. PORT[†]

I. Introduction 2

II. Regionally based collective trademarks: the chiiki brand system 5

    A. Collective trademarks generally 7

    B. Japan's experience with chiiki brands 10

    C. Case studies 24

    D. Conclusions from case studies 33

    E. Registration and enforcement data 35

III. Geographic indications 36

    A. Geographic indications generally 36

    B. Chiiki brands as a form of geographic indicators 40

IV. Economic development 42

    A. Connection to economic development generally 42

    B. Will chiiki brands have a positive economic impact? 43

    C. Anti-counterfeit measure 44

V. Chiiki brands as an example of giving in to political pressure toward regionalization and decentralization . 47

VI. Conclusion 51

[†] JD, University of Wisconsin-Madison, 1989; BA, Macalester College, 1983.

I. INTRODUCTION

On April 1, 2006, Japan adopted a new hybrid system to protect regional collective marks.[1] In some ways, these marks are similar to collective marks in the United States, and in some other ways, these marks act like geographic indications that the European Union favors.[2] Although the Japan Patent Office (JPO) promises great economic gains by any association that takes advantage of these marks[3], it is not clear how or why that would happen. Rather, it appears that the Japanese central government is using the regional collective trademark system to gain political favor from an influential lobby: those that favor a decentralized political system focused on regionalism within Japan.[4]

This new type of trademark is referred to as the "regionally based collective trademark system" (*chiiki dantai shōhyō seido* 地域団体商標制度). In Japanese, *chiiki* means "region." The name was abbreviated and thus, the chiiki brand system was born.

On April 18, 2013, the five hundredth such mark was issued to SENDAI ICHIGO (Sendai Strawberries 仙台いちご)[5]:

---

[1] *Regional Collective Trademark System*, JAPAN PAT. OFF., http://www.jpo.go.jp/torikumi/t_torikumi/t_dantai_syouhyou.htm (last visited Mar. 15, 2015).
[2] *Compare id. with* 15 U.S.C. § 1054 (2012) *and Geographical-Indications*, EUROPEAN COMMISSION, http://ec.europa.eu/trade/policy/accessing-markets/intellectual-property/geographical-indications/ (last visited Mar. 15, 2015).
[3] *See Regional Collective Trademark System*, *supra* note 1.
[4] *See* PRADYUMNA PRASAD KARAN, JAPAN IN THE 21ST CENTURY: ENVIRONMENT, ECONOMY, AND SOCIETY 318-19 (2005) (discussing Japan's recent efforts to create more localized regional governmental projects instead of the previously used larger public work projects).
[5] SENDAI ICHIGO (仙台いちご) [Sendai Strawberry] Registration No. 5483902 (Japan); *Sendai Ichigo* (仙台いちご) [*Sendai Strawberry*], JAPAN PAT. OFF.,

Figure 1: Sendai Ichigo

This chiiki brand mark includes descriptive text that is disclaimed and not part of the mark that reads, "ahead, one step at a time" (*ippoippo, mae e* 一歩一歩、前へ).[6] The city of Sendai was eighty miles from the epicenter of the 9.0 magnitude earthquake that started the tsunami that led to the nuclear disaster at Fukushima Daiichi. It is the largest city in the entire tsunami and earthquake zone.[7] The Miyagi Prefecture Strawberry Growers Association seems to be contributing to Japan's attempts to overcome the disaster, encourage economic development, and raise awareness all with one chiiki brand mark.

To mark the occasion of the five hundredth registration, JPO held a special ceremony and awarded a special plaque to the rights-holder.[8] It included this gratuitous explanation of the mark:

> The trademark "Sendai Ichigo" is a brand for promoting the sale of strawberries

---

http://www.jpo.go.jp/torikumi/t_torikumi/tourokushoukai/bunrui/pdf/04-004-5483902.pdf (last visited Mar. 29, 2015) (Japan).
[6] *Id.*
[7] Kenneth Pletcher, *Japan earthquake and tsunami of 2011*, ENCYCLOPEDIA BRITANNICA, http://www.britannica.com/EBchecked/topic/1761942/Japan-earthquake-and-tsunami-of-2011 (last updated Mar. 10, 2015).
[8] *Announcing Registration of the 500th Regionally Based Collective Trademark,*, MINISTRY ECON. TRADE & INDUSTRY (Apr. 11, 2012), http://www.meti.go.jp/english/press/2012/0411_02.html.

from Miyagi Prefecture. As strawberries from Miyagi, "Sendai Ichigo" strawberries are mainly produced in Watari County located in the southern part of Miyagi, which is famous as being the home of the best strawberries in the Tohoku area, taking advantage of the warm climate.[9]

This new system has received significant fanfare in Japan with nearly 1,000 applications and, now, over five hundred registrations.[10] The system has been largely ignored by non-Japanese companies with only three registrations as if the date of this article.[11] As the Japanese search for the magic bullet to jumpstart their lagging economy, which has been burdened with deflation for more than 15 years, the JPO expects the chiiki brand system to encourage significant economic redevelopment.[12] This article tests whether that is likely.

In the end, this article demonstrates that the chiiki brand system is unlikely to produce the positive economic results that the JPO claims it will. Rather, the value of the chiiki brand system will mollify the

---

[9] *Id.*

[10] *JPO Compiled a Booklet Titled "Regional Brands in JAPAN 2015 - Regional Collective Trademarks,"* MINISTRY ECON. TRADE & INDUSTRY (Mar. 6, 2015), http://www.meti.go.jp/english/press/2015/0306_02.html.

[11] *Cf. Chiiki dantai shōhyō jirei-shū 2015 ni tsuite* (地域団体商標事例集2015 について) [*Regional Collective Trademark Case Studies for 2015*], JAPAN PAT. OFF., http://www.jpo.go.jp/cgi/link.cgi?url=/torikumi/t_torikumi/tiikibrand.htm (last visited Mar. 15, 2015).

[12] Of course, now with "Abenomics" in full force, it will be difficult to isolate economic activity on chiiki brands. Abenomics, named after the current Prime Minister of Japan, Shinzo Abe, consists of "a massive fiscal stimulus, more aggressive monetary easing from the Bank of Japan, and structural reforms to boost Japan's competitiveness." *Definition of Abenomics*, FIN. TIMES, http://lexicon.ft.com/Term?term=abenomics (last visited Mar. 16, 2015).

political movement towards Japanese decentralization and internal regionalism.[13] By creating the chiiki brand system, the Japanese central government appears to be responding to movements that encourage the diffusion of government services (and the related industries that tend to follow) away from Tokyo to other parts of Japan.[14] This is politically an astute direction. The chiiki brand system can play into the decentralization movement that pushes some politicians. However, upon closer analysis, it is apparent that the chiiki brand system will fail to encourage economic development and it is, in application, ultimately not a regional system of trademark generation, protection, and enforcement.[15]

This article will show that what appears to be a simple statute to codify the protection of regional collective marks in a hybrid fashion akin to both collective marks from the United States and geographic indications from Europe is actually an attempt to respond to political movements focused on decentralization. As the promised economic benefits have not been recognized by any of the ten most likely associations, and the "regional" part of the chiiki brand system is actually "national" and therefore not responsive to the political voices urging decentralization in the form of regionalism, the chiiki brand system may be a very expensive failure.

II. REGIONALLY BASED COLLECTIVE TRADEMARKS: THE CHIIKI BRAND SYSTEM

The JPO grandly and proudly states that the purpose of the chiiki brand system is to maintain the good faith and credit of businesses to support the revitalization of local economies and strengthen industrial

---

[13] *See infra* Part V.
[14] *See infra* Part V.
[15] *See infra* Part V.

competitiveness.[16] Furthermore, "[i]t is intended to lead to sustained activation of the local economies."[17] This is a vague mantra that is repeated throughout the JPO's publications on the intended consequences of the chiiki brand system. The JPO clearly believes that the chiiki brand system can and will have a positive economic impact on Japan. The objective is not intended to save consumers from confusion, and it is not about encouraging third parties to compete, two parallel objectives to trademark protection in the United States.[18] It is focused on manufacturers and holders of trademark rights, and the JPO believes that the way to a stronger economy is through broadened protection of trademarks.

This goal may, in fact, be possible. The theory the JPO is pursuing is that the chiiki brand system promotes collective action. It encourages entities to cooperate and to raise skill levels of traditional industries. These traditional industries are being lost or forgotten over time. Therefore, the chiiki brand system could play the role of invigorating interest and concern for traditional industries while increasing the skill level of practitioners of these traditional industries. As this type of collective action is inconsistent with Japanese notions of competition and business strategy, it will be interesting to see which side prevails.

One result could be counterproductive. With increased interest in traditional industries and increased

---

[16] *Announcing Registration of the 500th Regionally Based Collective Trademark, supra* note 8.
[17] 商標法の一部を改正する法律について—概要・新旧対照表・附則— [*Overview of an Act to Amend Part of the Trademark Law*], JAPAN PAT. OFF. 2, http://www.jpo.go.jp/torikumi/ibento/text/pdf/houkaisei/01.pdf (last visited Mar. 29, 2015).
[18] David W. Barnes & Teresa A. Laky, *Classic Fair Use of Trademarks: Confusion about Defenses*, 20 SANTA CLARA COMPUTER & HIGH TECH. L.J. 833, 843 (2004).

focus and sale of goods from traditional Japanese industries, it could simply enhance the market for knockoff traditional industry goods. As we will see, there are no meaningful enforcement mechanisms in the chiiki brand system. Those that do exist are not utilized; therefore, it is unreasonable to expect the mere existence of a registration system to deter infringing conduct. In fact, it may encourage it.

At first, it appeared that the chiiki brand system would be quite popular as nearly 700 associations applied to register their marks in the first year. However, by 2010, that number had dropped to just thirty-seven applicants in eleven months between January and November.[19]

A. Collective Trademarks Generally

In the United States, a collective mark is "a trademark or service mark used by the members of a cooperative, an association, or other collective group or organization . . . ."[20] The collective mark has a very limited purpose in the United States and in all nations that recognize such marks.[21] The purpose is to identify membership in some collective or organization. The World Intellectual Property Organization (WIPO) claims that collective marks may serve a positive role in helping small to medium sized entities overcome the challenges brought on by the small size of their operations or isolation in the marketplace.[22] However, even WIPO is devoid of any technical report or study

---

[19] Tetsuya Imamura, *Chiikishudanshyohyoseidotoiu seidosentakuno igito sonomondai* [*The Significance and Problems with the Chiiki Brand System*], 34 NIHON KOGYO SHOYUKENHO GAKKAI NENPO 29, 31 (2010) (Japan).
[20] 15 U.S.C. § 1127 (2012).
[21] *Collective Marks*, WORLD INTELL. PROP. ORG., http://www.wipo.int/sme/en/ip_business/collective_marks/collective _marks.htm (last visited Mar. 4, 2015).
[22] *Id.*

that shows precise economic gain by registering a collective mark. On simple numbers, we do know that there are 3,134 subsisting registrations for collective marks in the U.S. Patent and Trademark Office.[23] Some of these collective marks are quite old, and some are rather new.

In the United States, collective marks are owned by an organization and can be used by members of that organization to show, in addition to some geographic affiliation, that the user complies with certain standards of quality or accuracy or any other criteria set by the organization. The most common example includes the CPA mark to identify membership in the association for Certified Public Accountants. This is very popular in the European Union. For example, the Consorzio del Prosciutto di Parma sued for passing off even their unregistered collective mark.[24] A regulation establishes protection for the Italian ham Prosciutto di Parma, requiring the product to be packaged in the region of production.[25] Asda supermarkets were purchasing ham through the Consorzio del Prosciutto di Parma association, slicing it themselves, and labeling it as "Parma ham."[26] The association brought an action against Asda on the grounds that slicing the ham themselves was contrary to the rules applicable to Parma ham.[27] The court held that the slicing and packaging of ham constituted important operations that

---

[23] Stuart J.H. Graham, Galen Hancock, Alan C. Marco, & Amanda F. Myers, *The USPTO Trademark Case Files Dataset: Descriptions, Lessons, and Insights*, SOC. SCI. RES. NETWORK (Jan. 31, 2013), http://papers.ssrn.com/sol3/papers.cfm?abstract_id=2188621.
[24] Consorzio del Prosciutto di Parma v. Asda Stores, Ltd., Case C-108/01, 2003 E.C.R. I-5121.
[25] *Id.*
[26] *Id.*
[27] *Id.*

can damage the product and the PDO's (protected designation of origin) reputation.[28]

In both the United States and the European Union, collective mark recognition seems to provide real and substantive protection for associations in their attempts to enforce marks and therefore attract membership in the association. There is no data by which one could conclude that the collective trademark systems have any economic impact whatsoever on the United States or the European Union. In fact, to make such an assertion belies the purpose of trademark protection itself in the United States. Although positive economic advantages do inure to the trademark user, that is not why we protect trademarks in the United States. Rather, we protect trademarks in the United States to ensure fair competition. We believe that fair competition leads to furthering the goals of capitalism. We believe that the more players there are in any market, the more competition there will be, and this will translate into lower prices consumers pay for goods and services. This basic rationale has been in place for a very long time.[29] That is, the objective in the United States is fair competition to promote economic development.[30] The goal in Japan is to "contribute to the development of the industry and to protect the interests of consumers,"[31]

---

[28] Ravil SARL v. Bellon Import SARL, Case C-469/00, 2003 E.C.R. I-5053; Consorzio del Prosciutto di Parma & Salumificio S. Rita v. Asda Stores Ltd., Case C-108/01, 2003 E.C.R. I-5121; see Joshua Rozenberg, Nicola Woolcock & Bruce Johnston, *Asda loses battle with Italians over sliced Parma ham*, TELEGRAPH (May 21, 2003, 12:00 AM), http://www.telegraph.co.uk/news/worldnews/europe/italy/1430756/Asda-loses-battle-with-Italians-over-sliced-Parma-ham.html.

[29] Sidney A. Diamond, *The Historical Development of Trademarks*, 73 TRADEMARK REP. 222, 223 (1983).

[30] Karl-Heinz Fezer, *Trademark Protection Under Unfair Competition Law*, 19 IIC 192 (1988).

[31] Shōhyō-hō [Trademark Act], Act No. 27 of April 13, 1959 (as amended up to the revisions of Act No. 63 of 2011), art. 1, *translated in*

and the Japanese believe that that mere investment leads to economic development.[32]

There is some research that indicates that for a newly developing country, having an advanced collective mark system may stimulate growth and investment in such things as tourism, as it may act to internalize values and skills needed to make these industries successful.[33] However, this research applies primarily to post-conflict zones or war zones.[34] Although Japan has been without military conflict for more than sixty years, this might apply to chiiki brands. The economic analysis below pursues the idea of using collective marks to internalize values and skills and the resulting public relations when this is done.

B. Japan's Experience with Chiiki Brands

1. Nature and Scope of Protection—Statutory Scheme

Article 7-2 of the Japanese Trademark Act governs the registration of chiiki brands. In essence, this statutory scheme reads much like the concept of collective marks in the United States.[35] A chiiki brand will be granted to a regional "association" as long as the association allows members to use the mark to indicate membership in the association but does not itself use the mark on or in connection with the sale of any good

---

Trademark Act (Act No. 127 of April 13, 1959), WORLD INTELL. PROP. ORG., http://www.wipo.int/edocs/lexdocs/laws/en/jp/jp180en.pdf (last visited Mar. 15, 2015) (Japan).
[32] KOICHI HAMADA ET AL., MIRACULOUS GROWTH AND STAGNATION IN POST-WAR JAPAN 6 (2011) ("Since the quality of human capital is the key to sustainable development, such inadequate investment in human capital leads to slow economic development.").
[33] Roya Ghafele & Benjamin Giber, *A New Institutional Economics Perspective on Trademarks: Rebuilding Post Conflict Zones in Sierra Leone and Croatia*, 11 J. MARSHALL REV. INTELL. PROP. L. 745, 752 (2012).
[34] *Id.*
[35] *See* 17 U.S.C. § 201(c); Trademark Act, art. 7-2 (Japan).

or service.[36] The chiiki brand contains a place name plus a generic word for a good or service.[37] Furthermore, the chiiki brand will only be worthy of registration if the mark has become "well-known among consumers."[38]

More specifically, the statute provides that a chiiki brand mark should be issued to the applicant

> Provided that the trademark is used by its members and, as a result of the use of the said trademark, the said trademark is well known among consumers as indicating the goods or services pertaining to the business of the applicant or its members, notwithstanding the provision of Article 3 . . . .[39]

The statutory construction of the chiiki brand system has three basic elements. First, the chiiki brand must be widely recognized among consumers.[40] Second, this recognition must be created by use of the mark in commerce.[41] The third element of the statutory construction of the chiiki brand system is that it is "notwithstanding" Article 3 of the Trademark Act.[42] Article 3 of the Japanese Trademark Act prevents marks from being registered that are only of geographic significance.[43] In the language of the statute, a mark that "consists solely of . . . the place of origin in a common manner" shall be denied registration.[44]

---

[36] Trademark Act, art. 7-2 (Japan).
[37] *Id.* at art. 7-2(1).
[38] *Id.*
[39] *Id.*
[40] *Id.* at art. 3.
[41] *Id.*
[42] *Id.*
[43] *Id.*
[44] *Id.* at art. 3(1)(3).

However, this lack of trademark significance for geographically significant marks can be overcome with the Japanese equivalent of secondary meaning.[45] A mark that is initially denied registration for being a geographic place name "may be registered if, as a result of the use of the trademark, consumers are able to recognize the goods or services as those pertaining to a business of a particular person."[46]

In the United States, 17 U.S.C. § 1052(e)(2) denies marks of merely geographic significance from being registered unless the mark has acquired secondary meaning.[47] By statute, the Japanese trademark law addresses marks of geographic significance in the same manner as in the United States.[48] Although the American version is a little tighter in statutory language, the Japanese and the American statutes get to the same point: one may not register a mark of mere geographic significance unless it has secondary meaning.[49]

Therefore, the two most important elements of the Japanese chiiki brand scheme are that there must be an "association" that uses an appellation of source that becomes "well-recognized among consumers."[50] Both are pursued below. In addition, a chiiki brand must consist of a regional name followed by the name of some good or service—as in *Tokyo Ramen*.[51] Only when

---

[45] *Id.* at art. 3(2).
[46] *Id.*
[47] 17 U.S.C. § 1052(e)(2) (2012).
[48] *Compare* Trademark Act, art. 3 (Japan), *with* 17 U.S.C. § 1052(e)(2).
[49] *Compare* 17 U.S.C. § 1052(e)(2) (stating that trademark cannot be registered if the mark is "geographically deceptively misdescriptive") *with* Trademark Act, art. 3 (Japan) (stating that a trademark will be registered unless it "consists solely of a mark indicating . . . place of origin").
[50] *See* Trademark Act, art. 7-2(1) (Japan).
[51] *Overview of an Act to Amend Part of the Trademark Law, supra* note 17.

these elements are established does a registerable chiiki brand come into existence.

To date, the chiiki brand system has been effective in widely granting registrations across all of Japan. The JPO has already granted chiiki brand registrations in many product categories, including fruits and vegetables, meat and seafood, textiles and crafts, as well as services and *onsen* (hot springs).[52]

Chiiki brand registrations represent all forty-seven prefectures in Japan with the majority coming from Hokkaido Prefecture (24) or Hyogo Prefecture (32), which is centered on the city of Kobe.

2. "Association"

An "association" for purposes of the Trademark Act is any business cooperative.[53] Eligible associations may not exclude membership if the applicant entity meets the association's definition of membership.[54] The association must be a registered corporation under Japanese law.[55] And, importantly, these rules apply equally to foreign entities.[56]

The form of incorporation of the association is not relevant. The association simply needs to be a juridical

---

[52] *Regional Collective Trademark Case Studies for 2015*, *supra* note 11. A partial list is included in the Appendix. *See infra* Appendix A.
[53] Trademark Act, art. 7-2 (Japan). For purposes of article 7-2, an association is defined as "[a]ny association established by a special Act, including a business cooperative (those which do not have juridical personality are excluded, and limited to those which are established by a special Act providing, without a just cause, that the association shall not refuse the enrollment of any person who is eligible to become a member or that the association shall not impose on any of its prospective members any condition that is heavier than those imposed on its existing members) . . . or a foreign juridical person equivalent thereto." *Id.*
[54] *Id.*
[55] *Id.*
[56] *Id.*

person.⁵⁷ Incorporating may provide some obstacles to entry for Japanese entities. Compared to the United States, it is difficult and expensive to incorporate in Japan.⁵⁸ In order to respond to fast-growing and fast-paced industries like information technology, in 2006, the Japanese corporate law was amended and consolidated from the Commercial Code to the Company Law.⁵⁹ Although the paid-in capital requirement was abolished in 2006,⁶⁰ there are still only two forms of incorporation that an association would likely choose. One is a stock company, usually chosen by large companies.⁶¹ The other is the limited liability company or a J-LLC (*gōdōkaisha* 合同会社)—a close variant to the American LLC, it is not considered a pass-through entity but a taxable entity by Japanese tax authorities.⁶²

As of this writing, there are no reported court cases in Japan that address the association requirement of the chiiki brand system.

3. *"Well-known among consumers"*

Although the statute does not explicitly require nationwide recognition, it seems on interpretation to mean nationwide or nearly nationwide recognition. The Japanese statute does not say but implies "all"

---

⁵⁷ *Id.*
⁵⁸ *Compare How To Incorporate A Company In Japan*, GAIJINPOT COM. PARTNERS (Oct. 25, 2013), http://blog.gaijinpot.com/incorporating-a-company-in-japan/, *with* CALIFORNIA SECRETARY OF STATE, BUSINESS ENTITIES FEE SCHEDULE, (Jan. 2015), *available at* http://bpd.cdn.sos.ca.gov/pdf/be-fees.pdf.
⁵⁹ Keiko Hashimoto, Katsuya Natori & John C. Roebuck, *Corporations*, *in* JAPANESE BUSINESS LAW (Gerald P. McAlinn, ed. 2007).
⁶⁰ *Id.* at 96.
⁶¹ *How To Incorporate A Company In Japan*, *supra* note 58.
⁶² *Id.*

consumers.[63] It literally says "the consumers."[64] However, the implication is that this is a large group of people because the statute says "widely recognized" (*hiroku ninshiki sa reta* 広く認識された). Whether this means a nationwide audience or some subset thereof, the clear implication is that this is meant to be a large group of people.

The term "widely recognized" is used in multiple places in the Japanese trademark statute.[65] Unfortunately, the meaning is not consistent. The only thing that is consistent in every other instance is that "widely recognized" means of "national reputation."[66] Therefore, although the term "widely recognized" appears in many places in the Trademark Act with disparate meanings, it is relatively clear that a mark that is widely recognized is one with a national reputation.

Interestingly, the JPO claimed in 2006 that national recognition is not necessary for chiiki brands to be registered, only broad recognition in surrounding prefectures.[67] This is a rather odd standard. Japan is a very small country.[68] Geographically, it would fit into the state of California with some room to spare.[69] Additionally, Japan is a highly technical, modern society with Internet and phone capabilities that eclipse the

---

[63] Shōhyō-hō [Trademark Act], Act No. 27 of April 13, 1959 (as amended up to the revisions of Act No. 63 of 2011), art. 7-2 (Japan).
[64] *Id.*
[65] *Id.*
[66] *See* SHOEN ONO, SHOHYOHO (TRADEMARK LAW) 87 (1994) (Japan); KENNETH L. PORT, TRADEMARK AND UNFAIR COMPETITION LAW IN JAPAN 136 (2007).
[67] JAPAN PATENT OFFICE, HEISEI 17 NENDO SHOUHYOU HOU NO ICHIBU KAISEI [INTERPRETATION OF 2005 AMENDMENT OF JAPANESE TRADEMARK ACT] 16 (2005).
[68] *Geography and Climate*, JAPAN FACT SHEET, http://web-japan.org/factsheet/en/pdf/e01_geography.pdf (last visited Mar. 6, 2015).
[69] *Id.*

United States.[70] With the Shinkansen bullet train, travel through and around Japan is fast, reliable, and very common.[71] Mobility in Japan is not an issue. As such, it is hard to imagine a regional collective mark that would be well recognized in the Japanese equivalent of Sacramento, but not known in Los Angeles. This may be a distinction without a difference. For all intents and purposes, a widely recognized mark means one with a national reputation, even though the statute does not expressly state it as such; the JPO seems to allow for something short of national recognition before a chiiki brand is subject to registration; and even though commentators seem to agree that something short of national recognition is sufficient.[72]

The JPO recognized that the mark with the most recognition is one that is nationally known. It makes a clear distinction between nationally known marks and not nationally known marks.[73] However, as stated

---

[70] *Household Download Index*, OOKLA NET INDEX, http://www.netindex.com/download/allcountries/ (last visited Mar. 6, 2015).

[71] All seats on the inaugural run of the Shinkansen in Hokuriku from Tokyo to Toyama sold out in twenty-five seconds on the morning they went on sale on February 14, 2015. *Seats on March 14 Hokuriku Shinkansen Sell Out in 25 Seconds*, JAPAN TODAY (Feb. 14, 2015), http://www.newsonjapan.com/html/newsdesk/article/111387.php. The initial run for the train was at 6:00 AM on March 14, 2015. *Id*. Toyama is a city on the Japan Sea (west) side of Japan and has a population of just over 400,000. *Welcome to Toyama*, TOYAMA PREFECTURE, http://www.pref.toyama.jp/english/ (last visited Mar. 6, 2015). To date, most Shinkansen links have been created to connect much more populous areas or to provide express service to, for example, the Nagano Olympics. *See* INFORMATION SHINKANSEN, http://www.shinkansen.co.jp/jikoku_hyo/en/ (last visited Mar. 6, 2015).

[72] Daisuke Kojo, *The Importance of the Geographic Origin of Agricultural Products: A comparison of Japanese and American Approaches*, 14 MO. ENVTL. L. & POL'Y REV. 275, 29697 (2007).

[73] *Overview of an Act to Amend Part of the Trademark Law*, *supra* note 17, at 9.

above, this seems like a distinction without a difference when applied to Japan. Regionalism has been on the rise in Japan recently. It has become important to some that outsiders do not see Japan as a homogeneous society. Importantly, the Japanese central government has been under pressure to recognize and pay homage to the notion of regionalism. It appears that this concept has bled into the Trademark Act with the chiiki brand system. It would be very unpopular for the Japanese government to require that every chiiki brand be statutorily well-recognized on a national level before registration would be possible. This would reject the now popular notion of Japanese regionalism, of which the chiiki brand system is emblematic. To have a regionally based collective mark system to promote regional growth and then require that all marks thereunder have national recognition would surely be inconsistent with the demands that regionalism be recognized and fostered in Japan. In reality, because the best chiiki brand is one that has national recognition, the JPO is making national recognition the goal of all chiiki brands. That is, this goal implicitly rejects regionalism. While the chiiki brand system is based on marks that derive from regional use on traditional arts, crafts, foodstuffs and services, the best chiiki brand is one with national repute. As such, it appears that the JPO is not serious about supporting Japanese regionalism. As a practical matter, virtually all chiiki brands will have a national reputation; the fact that national fame is not technically required for registration is not a meaningful distinction.

Furthermore, this wide recognition has to be attained through use of the mark in commerce, "as a result of the use of the mark" (*sono shōhyō ga shiyō o sa reta kekka* その商標が使用をされた結果).[74] As a civil law

---

[74] *Id.* at 23.

trademark system, there are very few trademark rights that are gained from use in Japan.[75] Virtually all trademark rights are acquired from registration, not from use. The chiiki brand turns out to be one of the meaningful exceptions to this rule.

In other places in the statute, the Japanese Trademark Act does use the term "fame" (*chomei* 著名). Through normal statutory construction rules, as a specific word is used we should understand that a distinct concept was intended. That is, a widely recognized mark is not a famous mark. Therefore, in determining if a mark is widely recognized, courts look to the nature of actual use of the mark; the duration of use; the geographic scope of use; the volume of sales; and the methodologies and content of advertising.[76]

4. Kitakata Ramen

Figure 2: Kitakata Ramen

---

[75] PORT, *supra* note 66.
[76] ONO, *supra* note 66, at 87.

Perhaps the best example of the application of this standard as it applies to chiiki brands is a Japanese case where the JPO refused registration of "Kitakata Ramen" (喜多方ラーメン) to the Kitakata Ramen Association for use related to a particular type of ramen noodles that come from the city of Kitakata in Fukushima Prefecture. Ramen is a type of wheat noodle, commonly served in a broth. The ramen pictured above is served with slices of pork, scallions, and *kamaboko* (surimi), a white fish cake with a pink swirl.

The JPO refused registration of the mark because it was not "well recognized among consumers" and the Intellectual Property High Court sustained that refusal.[77] The High Court provided a very thorough explication of the chiiki brand system. The court concluded that it was there to invigorate local economies for regional goods and services.[78] The court claimed that the chiiki brand system was created to build brand recognition and identity and thereby stimulate economic growth.[79] The court cites no data or studies to support the notion that the chiiki brand system could contribute to economic growth.

For its part, the Kitakata Ramen Association failed to show that the mark "Kitakata Ramen" was well-recognized by consumers. To register the mark, the court held, would "relax the requirement of showing there is a connection between the goods and services with the association members to an inappropriate level."[80] That is, consumers think of the large city by the name of Kitakata and not of any particular ramen

---

[77] Chiteki Zaisan Kōtō Saibansho [Intellectual Prop. High Ct.] Nov. 15, 2010, 2009 (Gyo-Ke) no. 10433, SAIBANSHO JIHŌ 109 (Japan).
[78] *Id.*
[79] *Id.* at 118.
[80] *Id.* at 119.

producer association when they are confronted with this mark.

In the end, the court's analysis is challenging to follow and it makes one wonder whether any chiiki brand would actually satisfy the IP High Court. The court, however, does state that only 50% of the stores in the city of Kitakata that sell Kitakata Ramen are actually members of the Kitakata Ramen Association. In the stores that are not a member of the Association, the words *Kitakata Ramen* appear in the menus and on advertising for these stores as well as in newspapers and magazines. Therefore, when consumers see the mark Kitakata Ramen, there is no way to tell whether the seller or purveyor is part of the Association or not. As such, the mark failed in the test of being widely recognized by consumers.

In fact, the mark Kitakata Ramen fails to act as a mark indicating the Association as related to the mark. When only 50% of stores that bear the mark are part of the Kitakata Ramen Association, it is difficult to see how, through use (as required by the statute), the mark has come to represent the association.

In terms of the statute, Kitakata Ramen consists "solely of characters indicating, in a common manner, the name of the region and the common name of the goods or services pertaining to the business of the applicant or its members."[81] That is, the mark Kitakata Ramen indicates a commonly recognized place name in a common manner and also refers to a common food from that location and others. As such, it failed to meet the standard of a chiiki brand.

---

[81] Shōhyō-hō [Trademark Act], Act No. 27 of April 13, 1959 (as amended up to the revisions of Act No. 63 of 2011), art. 7-2(1)(i) (Japan).

5. Hakata Ori

Figure 3: Hakata Ori

In the only other substantive chiiki brand case reported in Japan to date, the Fukuoka District Court addressed the enforcement of chiiki brands in a trademark infringement setting. It explained the parameters of a chiiki brand mark in rather clear terms.[82] The Plaintiff was an association of companies that manufactured and sold *Hakata Ori*, textiles from Hakata.[83] These textiles are specially woven and dyed fabrics that are used to make men's neckties, women's

---

[82] Judgment of December 10, 2012, party names not provided in original, Fukuoka Chihō Saibansho [Fukuoka Dist. Ct.] Dec. 10, 2012, *available* *at* http://www.lexis-asone.jp/document/DocView.aspx?id=3297798465&pit=2013-07-11&kw=%E5%9C%B0%E5%9F%9F%E5%9B%A3%E4%BD%93%E5%95%86%E6%A8%99&from=sr (Japan).

[83] *Id.*

purses and kimonos and fabric wrapped around a kimono worn in traditional Japanese style. Figure 3 shows a woman wearing a kimono made from Hakata Ori.

The Hakata Ori has a very long history. The textile manufacturing style was brought from China in the 13th Century.[84] There are very few artisans left in Japan that are able to manufacture the silk and create the clothing in the correct Hakata Ori style. There are currently only 46 members to the Hakata Ori Textile Industrial Association.[85] In the 46 stores, some 450 people are employed as artisans and workers.[86] The stores all exist in and around the city of Fukuoaka in Kyushu, Japan.[87]

The defendant manufactured and sold goods bearing the mark HAKATA OBI (博多帯). An *obi* is the silk sash tied around the waist of a female kimono wearer. The plaintiff claimed that *Hakata Obi* infringed the chiiki brand HAKATA ORI (博多織).[88] The court found no infringement and dismissed the case. There could be no infringement, the court held, because the chiiki brand included the name of a generic item: textiles. The court relied on Section 7-2 of the Japanese Trademark Act for this proposition. As such, the defendant had the right to use the mark as it wished.[89]

---

[84] *See Hakata Ori*, FUKUOKA NOW, http://fukuoka-now.com/article/hakata-ori/ (last visited Mar. 15, 2015).
[85] *Id.*
[86] *See id.*
[87] *See id.*
[88] HAKATA ORI (博多織) [Hakata Textile], Registration No. 5031531 (Japan).
[89] Judgment of December 10, 2012, party names not provided in original, Fukuoka Chihō Saibansho [Fukuoka Dist. Ct.] Dec. 10, 2012 (Japan).

6. Conclusion on Statutory Scheme

The entire chiiki brand system operates as a simple exception to a long held belief in international trademark jurisprudence that restricts trademarks from issuing on purely geographic names.[90] Naturally, the policy in all systems around the world is that people should not be prevented from using geographic terms to describe a product simply because someone else claims it as their trademark. All entities have an equal right to use a place name to denote where the entity is located, to imply that its goods or services are related to that place name, and to share in the goodwill of that place name. Even the European Union, which has broad recognition of geographic indicators, does not grant geographic indicator status arbitrarily to any random claim to a place name.[91] Only when it comes to indicate the location as a unique source of some good or service is it elevated to a geographic indicator.[92]

Japan is no different. Article 3-1 of the Japanese Trademark Act prohibits merely geographically significant trademarks from being registered.[93] As in most systems, this prohibition can be overcome with secondary meaning.[94] Nevertheless, it would act as a bar

---

[90] *See* 1 ANNA GILSON LALONDE, GILSON ON TRADEMARKS § 3.04 (2014).
[91] *See* Xuan-Thao N. Nguyen, *Nationalizing Trademarks: A New International Trademark Jurisprudence?*, 39 WAKE FOREST L. REV. 729, 763–65 (2004).
[92] *See id.* at 764–65.
[93] Shōhyō-hō [Trademark Act], Act No. 27 of April 13, 1959 (as amended up to the revisions of Act No. 63 of 2011), art. 7-3(1) (Japan) (stating that a mark that "consists solely of a mark indicating, in a common manner, in the case of goods, the place of origin" may not be registered).
[94] *See id.* at art. 3(2).

from allowing any chiiki brands from being registered. Japanese courts have well-recognized this fact.[95]

To overcome this problem, a statutory exception was devised to allow for chiiki brands to be registered and, thereby, placate the political movement pushing for more decentralization and more regionalism. Indeed, as we have just seen, the judicial interpretations of the chiiki brand system have led to a national collective marks system, not a regional one.

C. Case Studies

As the chiiki brand system has matured, we might look to specific companies to understand how they fared. In 2007, the popular law magazine, *The Invention* (*Hatsumei* 発明) ran a detailed story about three of the first chiiki brand registrants.[96] This article is presented as a "hot news" type of bulletin and claims that chiiki brands will have a positive effect on the Japanese economy. Most of the source for this article seems to be the Japan Patent Office.

The three Associations featured in the 2007 *Invention* article will be described in some detail. Their financial situations before and after registration will be examined, and a determination will be made as to whether or not the chiiki brand registration had JPO's predicted impact on the Associations' economies.

1. Ogoto Onsen

Located on the shores of Lake Biwa and close to Kyoto, the Ogoto Hot Springs and Ryokan Cooperative/Ogoto Hot Springs Tourist Association ("Ogoto Association") has ten *ryokan* (Japanese inn) or

---

[95] Judgment of Sept. 30, 2009, Intellectual Property High Court, JPO Decision Gazette No. 1208468.
[96] Yuji Osawa, *Hasshin! Chiiki Brand: Looking at Regionally Based Collective Marks*, 2 HATSUMEI (発明) [INVENTION] 6 (2007) (Japan).

hotel complexes. The water that percolates up naturally from the ground is at a constant 36 degrees centigrade or 96.8 degrees Fahrenheit year round, the optimal temperature for hot springs. The actual hot springs are owned and operated by Ostsuki City.[97] The Ogoto Association claims that as a hot springs with alkali dissolved in the water as it comes out of the earth, "Ogoto hot spring water is said to help relieve neuralgia, muscular pain, joint pain, stiff shoulders, paralysis, bruises, chronic gastritis, poor circulation, fatigue, and skin problems."[98]

It can safely be said that the Japanese take their hot springs resorts very seriously.

Ogoto Onsen's history is said to date back more than 1,200 years. It took its name from a combination of a Heian Era (794 to 1195 CE) governor and a classic Japanese harp.[99] It connotes very old, traditional, historic values and sensibilities in the Japanese mindset.

In the 1970s, Ogoto Onsen lost its image as a historical destination. At that time, it gained a national reputation as being a village of Turkish baths— "Soapland" (*sōpurando* ソープランド).[100] That is, it became known for its red-light district and its brothels. In the 1970s, no one would say that they were making Ogoto Onsen a vacation destination. Rather, "Ogoto" became synonymous with "red-light district."

---

[97] *Effects and Origin of Ogoto Hot Springs*, OGOTO HOT SPRINGS TOURIST ASS'N, http://www.ogotoonsen.com/english/history/index.html (last visited Mar. 15, 2015).
[98] *Id.*
[99] *Id.*
[100] *See* Kazutaka Shimanaka, *What's in a Name? Soaplands Still Going Strong 25 Years On*, TOKYO REPORTER (Jun. 26, 2009), http://www.tokyoreporter.com/2009/06/26/whats-in-a-name-soaplands-still-going-strong-25-years-on/.

From the mid-1970s through today, ryokans and hotels, under the slogan "Ogoto Onsen is an Onsen," have worked to change their image. By 2006, the Ogoto Onsen area attracted 443,359 overnight visitors plus 101,571 one-day visits. By 2008, the name of the area's train station was changed from Ogoto Station (*Ogoto-Eki* 雄琴駅), which connoted the red-light district in difficult Chinese characters, to Ogoto Onsen Station (*Ogoto Onsen-Eki* おごと温泉駅), using the simplified Hiragana for the city name—thereby adding to the area's accessibility and attempting to shed the image that Ogoto Onsen was a red-light district.[101]

In 2006, the area went through another image change in an attempt to make it more desirable as a place to live and work. The area is now trying to reproduce the old village from 1200 years ago and live in peace and harmony with the past. In order to realize this, the OGOTO ONSEN (雄琴温泉) chiiki brand was registered.[102] The Association also adopted a new mascot to represent the traditional history melded with current realities.

Figure 4: Ogoton, the Ogoto Onsen Mascot[103]

---

[101] Philbert Ono, *New Train Station Names in Otsu*, SHIGA NEWS (Mar. 31, 2008), http://shiga-ken.com/blog/2008/03/new-train-station-names-in-otsu.

[102] OGOTO ONSEN (雄琴温泉) [Ogoto Hot Springs], Registration No. 5034857 (Japan).

[103] OGOTO ONSEN, http://www.ogotoonsen.com (last visited Mar. 30, 2015).

It took Ogoto Onsen years to shed itself of the red-light-district image. Centered on the chiiki brand OGOTO ONSEN and the accompanying stylized mascot shown in Figure 4, the then-Chairman Harigane of the Association said in 2007, "We worked too hard to have to repeat ourselves."[104] The Ogoto Association has no intention of letting the image slip back into being known as a place where brothels proliferate.

For Ogoto Onsen, there is nothing more important than their brand identity. The OGOTO ONSEN chiiki brand is a weapon to battle the forces that would change Ogoto Onsen back to a red-light district.[105] However, to conclude that the chiiki brand system was or is contributing to the economic development of the area is spurious. It was the Onsen owners' collective desire to shed the red-light-district image as much as the chiiki brand system that brought them economic success. To be sure, tourists and regular vacationers are on the increase. To be sure, the Ogoto Association registered its chiiki brand. However, many factors contributed to the economic success of the area. There are so many factors involved that it is impossible to quantify the role of the chiiki brand system.

---

[104] Osawa, *supra* note 91.
[105] *Id.*

2. Kyo Ningyo

Figure 5: Kyo Ningyo Dolls

Kyo Ningyo dolls are a ubiquitous symbol of Japan. Famous in every Japanese household, the dolls have a very distinguished career. The dolls are, more specifically, a symbol of the Kyoto area of Japan. Artisans make the dolls piece by piece on high quality lathes. The dolls are given facial features and hair and are robed using a process that dates back to the Heian Period of Japan (794 CE–1185 CE),[106] although the current form of the doll dates to the Edo Period (1600–1868).[107] Each doll is said to manifest the maker-craftsman's spirit and skill. Each doll demonstrates a stern, sophisticated charm.[108]

Although there are five poses or shapes of the dolls, the *Hina Ningyo*, pictured in Figure 5, is the most popular. Each Kyo Ningyo doll is manufactured by

---

[106] ANDO-DOLL.COM, http://www.ando-doll.com/english (last visited Mar. 17, 2015).
[107] *See All About Japanese Hina Dolls*, KYOTO NAT'L MUSEUM, http://www.kyohaku.go.jp/eng/dictio/senshoku/hina.html (last visited Mar. 15, 2015).
[108] *Id.* at 8.

hand by individual craftsman or very small enterprises.[109] As such, each doll is said to be brought to life by a single person. The stratified structure of the business model based on the craftsman's skill is an important characteristic of Kyo Ningyo. To be a true Kyo Ningyo craftsman takes years of training and cannot be accomplished by just anyone.

To promote the manufacture and sale of Kyo Ningyo, the Kyo Ningyo Commerce and Industry Cooperative (Kyo Ningyo Association) was created.[110] The chairman of the Kyo Ningyo Association, Bunzo Moriguchi, is "proud of the burden of carrying traditional industry and culture from Kyoto."[111]

The Kyo Ningyo Association applied to register the certification mark KYO NINGYO (京人形)[112] to reaffirm the brand identity.[113] The Kyo Ningyo Association felt that, if it could attain the support of a public agency like the JPO, it would be well on its way to revitalizing and reaffirming the brand on a national scale.

Before it was able to apply for a chiiki brand, its mark, KYO NINGYO, received a designation as a "Traditional Craft" (*den-san shitei* 伝産指定) under the Law on the Promotion of Traditional Craft production.[114] The Director of the Kyo Ningyo Association, Tsuneo Bando, claimed that the designation would give them many more contacts with

---

[109] *See Traditional Industries*, KYOTO PREFECTURE, http://www.pref.kyoto.jp/en/01-02-01.html (last visited Mar. 17, 2015).
[110] *See id.*; KYO-NINGYO.COM, http://www.kyo-ningyo.com (last visited Mar. 17, 2015) (Japan).
[111] *Id.*
[112] KYO NINGYO (京人形) [Kyoto Doll], Registration No. 5003858 (Japan).
[113] Osawa, *supra* note 91, at 8.
[114] Den tōtekikōgeihin-san no shinkō ni kansuru hō [Law on the Promotion of Traditional Craft Production], Law No. 57 of May 25, 1974 (Japan).

the Kyoto City and Prefectural governments. He was told by the government that the designation would mean "a real profit" for his association.[115]

As there are many such designations in and around the Kyoto area, there is keen interest to support such associations. One such group is the Kyoto Brand Trademark Promotion Council. This council supported the Kyo-Ningo Association in their drive to obtain a chiiki brand. Although there was a conflict with another who was using a similar trademark on or in connection with similar goods, with the help of the Council, the KYO NINGYO chiiki brand was finally registered—at least in part because the Kyo Ningyo Association received the designation as a "Traditional Craft" from the Government.[116]

As the Kyo Ningyo Association won the right to register the chiiki brand by that name, many opportunities to partner with the city of Kyoto and the surrounding cities have made the brand well-recognized. As such, the Kyo Ningyo have been used in several temple events and have given the dolls a very positive appeal to Japanese people. In short, the chiiki brand has contributed to this appeal, and this is said to contribute to the profitability of the Kyo Ningyo dolls.[117]

Once again, however, there are too many variables to claim that the chiiki brand system was the catalyst to its economic development. The development may have come with the mere designation as a Traditional Craft. It may have come with simple advertising. It is

---

[115] Osawa, *supra* note 91, at 9.
[116] *See generally Traditional Crafts of Japan*, MINISTRY OF ECON., TRADE & INDUSTRY (Dec. 26, 2013), http://www.meti.go.jp/english/policy/mono_info_service/creative_industries/pdf/Traditional_Crafts_of_Japan.pdf (mapping the Traditional Crafts of Japan).
[117] Osawa, *supra* note 91, at 9.

impossible to quantify and claim that one of the many variables was the only cause for the economic success of the Kyo Ningyo Association.

3. *Odawara Kamaboko*

Figure 6: *Kamaboko*

Kamaboko is a fish paste made into various forms that hold their shape. It is also known as "fish cake." Surimi or fish cake is manufactured by combining several types of white fish.[118] This paste is steamed, formed into blocks, and then served chilled or in soups. Figure 6 shows one common form. In the West, the best-known type of kamaboko is *kanikama*, short for *kanikamaboko*. This is the artificial crabmeat sticks sold in many grocery stores.[119]

Kamaboko is a staple of the Japanese diet and is found in various forms in Japanese dishes. Perhaps the most ubiquitous use is the half-moon shape of pressed

---

[118] SHIZUO TSUJI, JAPANESE COOKING: A SIMPLE ART 68–69 (rev. ed. 2006).
[119] SHIZUO TSUJI, JAPANESE COOKING: A SIMPLE ART (1980). 67 CASSON TRENOR, SUSTAINABLE SUSHI: A GUIDE TO SAVING THE OCEANS ONE BITE AT TIME 52–53 (2009).

white fish with a pink border found in many ramen dishes.

Odawara Kamaboko is distinctive because it is made out of Pacific Croaker rather than Alaskan Pollack.[120] Croaker is considered a higher quality white fish than Pollack, and this gives Odawara Kamaboko an advantage over its considerable competition.[121] Having originated in the 1780s during the Edo Period (1603 to 1868) or possibly in the much earlier Muromachi Period (1337 to 1573),[122] Odawara Kamaboko has now become a favorite New Years' celebratory dish and a significant part of the famous Osechi Ryori served during New Year's meals.[123] In 2007, the Odawara Kamaboko Fish Processors Co-Operative Association (Odawara Association) collectively produced over 83 million pounds of kamaboko.[124]

---

[120] JAE W. PARK ET AL., SURIMI AND SURIMI SEAFOOD 275 (Jae W. Park ed., 3d ed. 2013).

[121] *Id.* at 457 (discussing how the superior quality of the Odawara Kamaboko may be due to the water's high calcium content).

[122] Osawa, *supra* note 91, at 12; *see also History of Kamaboko*, ODAWARA KAMABOKO FISH PROCESSORS CO-OPERATIVE ASS'N, http://en.odawarajibasan.jp/kamaboko/history-kamaboko/ (last visited Mar. 12, 2015).

[123] *100 Dishes From Japan Part 2*, NIHON ICHIBAN, http://nihon-ichiban.com/100-dishes-from-japan-part-2/ (last visited Mar. 12, 2015) (describing kamaboko in food #39).

[124] The ten conditions for a product to be certified as Odawara Kamaboko: "1. The producer must strive to preserve the fine quality of Odawara kamaboko, and the quality should be of the level which is also approved by other producers. 2. The producer must carefully select all ingredients so as not to tarnish the credibility of Odawara kamaboko. 3. The producer should be producing high-protein products by making the most of the fish's natural taste. 4. It must be planked and steamed. (Not including molded kamaboko.) 5. The producer must rigidly uphold the original method, technique and skills involved in producing Odawara kamaboko as well as to continue doing so in the future. 6. The producer's headquarters must be registered in Odawara City and its business bases must also be located in the city. 7. In principle, the producer must have its own factory in

In order to maintain quality, the Odawara Association convenes a special meeting where each producer has to present its kamaboko and the flavor is tested. The registration of the chiiki brand ODAWARA KAMABOKO (小田原蒲鉾)[125] by the Odawara Association has allowed it to identify counterfeit kamaboko and take appropriate measures when disclosed.[126] The chiiki brand system has not been responsible for the already well-established market presence of the Association. Once again, there are too many variables at stake to identify any one as a contributing factor to the already rather developed economic presence of the Association.

D. Conclusions from Case Studies

Several conclusions can be drawn from the three case studies that were held out by the JPO as the poster children of the chiiki brand system when it was first promoted in 2006. Although all three were well-known appellations of source in their own right before chiiki brand registration, each association believes that registration gives it an advantage over the competition. Each association believes that the chiiki brand registration enhances its market power and makes it easier for it to distinguish its members from non-

---

Odawara City. If it is the case that the factory is not located in the city, it can be approved only if the factory is owned by the producer. 8. The producer must have been in business for more than fifty years as a kamaboko producer in Odawara, and must be widely recognised by the public and fellow companies. 9. The management of the producing company must cherish the concepts and traditions of Odawara kamaboko. 10. The producer must be a member of the Odawara Kamaboko Fish Processors Co-Operative Association." *The Ten Conditions – To Be Certified as Odawara Kamaboko*, ODAWARA KAMABOKO FISH PROCESSORS CO-OPERATIVE ASS'N, http://en.odawarajibasan.jp/kamaboko/ten-conditions/ (last visited Mar. 12, 2015).
[125] ODAWARA KAMABOKO (小田原蒲鉾) [Odawara Fish Cake], Registration No. 5437574 (Japan).
[126] Osawa, *supra* note 91, at 13.

member producers of nearly the same product. For example, there are over 900 manufacturers of kamaboko in Japan and only 13 members of the Odawara Association.[127] The chiiki brand allows the members of the Odawara Association to take advantage of historical myths and facts that distinguish their products.

That is, at least in 2006 and 2007 when the concept of chiiki brands was new, the members of the case study Associations believed that membership would add to their bottom lines.

Each member seems to understand brand identity. The Ogoto Onsen Association is especially struggling to keep the area from slipping back into its past reputation as an area for brothels. Each association believes that membership in the chiiki brand system will allow it to have more control over its destiny as the associations actively manage the identity behind the chiiki brand.

As a civil law system, Japanese trademark rights commence with registration,[128] not with use as in the United States.[129] Therefore, registration of the chiiki brand is the beginning of a process. The process includes management of the brand and assurance of quality of the products. This process is made possible by the chiiki brands as associations band together and distinguish themselves. The associations studied here believe that investment in the chiiki brand translates into higher skill and quality, which translates into better

---

[127] *Compare* PARK ET AL., *supra* note 115, at 8 (stating that there were 946 Japanese kamaboko makers in 2011) *with The Ten Conditions – To Be Certified as Odawara Kamaboko*, *supra* note 119.
[128] Shōhyō-hō [Trademark Act], Act No. 27 of April 13, 1959 (as amended up to the revisions of Act No. 63 of 2011), art. 18 (Japan).
[129] Brian G. Gilpin, *Trademarks in Cyberspace: Fulfilling the "Use" Requirement Through the Internet*, 78 J. PAT. & TRADEMARK OFF. SOC'Y 830, 831 (1996).

sales.[180] This is a common understanding by each of the case study associations.

However, there are simply too many variables involved in each industry to accurately claim that it was the chiiki brand system that was responsible for positive economic indicators. It could simply be more attention to the brand in general that contributes to the growth. The growth might be the result of a multitude of other factors as well. It is nice to see such faith placed in a portion of the Japanese trademark system, but whether this faith is misplaced or not is impossible to tell. The present indicators imply that many factors contributed to the growth of the particular economy and that the chiiki brand system alone could not have been responsible.

E. Registration and Enforcement Data

As of March 6, 2015, there were 574 registered chiiki brands.[181] Each one is like the case studies previously discussed, in that an association owns the certification mark and numerous manufacturer association members make goods or services in a certain way that earns each member the right to use the chiiki brand on, or in connection with, the goods or services.

There are a total of eight reported cases that mention chiiki brands since 2006. Only two of these cases, analyzed above, deal with substantive issues in the chiiki brand system. Both chiiki brands failed to be recognized by the court.

Of the other six cases that mention the chiiki brand system, no plaintiff prevailed in asserting its rights.

---

[180] Osawa, *supra* note 91, at 14 (quoting the chairman of the Odawara Association as this idea applies to Odawara Kamaboko).
[181] *JPO Compiled a Booklet Titled "Regional Brands in JAPAN 2015 - Regional Collective Trademarks,"* supra note 10.

Although these cases mention chiiki brands in dicta, it seems to be telling that the Japanese courts may be hostile to the notion of the chiiki brand system. Although clearly too early to tell definitively, this is a fact that needs to be closely watched.

III. GEOGRAPHIC INDICATIONS

A. Geographic Indications Generally

Geographic indications, as defined by the Agreement on Trade Related Aspects of Intellectual Property Rights (TRIPS Agreement), identify goods as originating in the territory of a member where a given quality, reputation, or other characteristic of the goods is essentially attributable to its geographical origin.[132] Geographic indications impart important information about where the products were made, the quality of the products—which is related to the reputation of the geographic region—and the name of the products.[133] The European Union is heavily invested in geographic indicators and insists that other countries respect them;[134] however, the United States has been very hesitant to recognize geographic indicators, as it is inconsistent with U.S. trademark law and policy.[135]

Geographic indications are quite controversial in the United States. United States trademark doctrine and policy have long prohibited geographic indicators from being registered. At least since 1947, registration of

---

[132] Agreement on Trade Related Aspects of Intellectual Property Rights, Apr. 15, 1994, Marrakesh Agreement Establishing the World Trade Organization, Annex 1C, Legal Instruments-Results of the Uruguay Round, 1869 U.N.T.S. 299, 33 I.L.M. 1197 (1994).
[133] *Id.* at art. 22.
[134] Harry N. Niska, Note, *The European Union TRIPs Over the U.S. Constitution: Can the First Amendment Save the Bologna That Has A First Name?* 13 MINN. J. GLOBAL TRADE 413 (2004).
[135] J. THOMAS MCCARTHY, MCCARTHY ON TRADEMARKS AND UNFAIR COMPETITION § 14:21 (4th ed. 2015).

trademarks that are primarily geographic in nature has been prohibited.[136] In 1996, trademark law was amended to allow for geographic marks identifying the source of wines and spirits to be registered. However, the 1996 law only applied to new marks—only those applied for on or after one year after passage of the amendment or January 1, 1996.[137]

The United States has been on a crash course over geographic indicators for a long time.[138] Although the Lanham Act was amended to allow *new* marks of a geographic nature for wines and spirits to be registered, so long as they truly name the place of origin, it did nothing for *old* geographic indicators such as merlot or champagne.[139] In Europe, these are valuable geographic

---

[136] 15 U.S.C. § 1052(e) (2012).
[137] Julia Lynn Titilo, Note, *A Trademark Holder's Hangover: Reconciling the Lanham Act with the Alcohol and Tobacco Tax and Trade Bureau's System of Designating American Viticultural Areas*, 17 J. INTELL. PROP. L. 173, 183 (2009).
[138] *See* Ruth L. Okediji, *The International Intellectual Property Roots of Geographic Indications*, 82 CHI.-KENT L. REV. 1329, 1330 (2007); Justin Hughes, *Champagne, Feta, and Bourbon: The Spirited Debate About Geographical Indications*, 58 HASTINGS L.J. 299, 303 (2006); Tunisia L. Staten, *Geographical Indications Protection Under the TRIPS Agreement: Uniformity Not Extension*, 87 J. PAT. & TRADEMARK OFF. SOC'Y 221, 221 (2005); Eva Gutierrez, *Geographical Indicators: A Unique European Perspective on Intellectual Property*, 29 HASTINGS INT'L & COMP. L. REV. 29, 40 (2005); Stacy D. Goldberg, Comment, *Who Will Raise the White Flag? The Battle between the United States and the European Union over the Protection of Geographical Indications*, 22 U. PA. J. INT'L ECON. L. 107, 110 (2001).
[139] Deborah J. Kemp & Lynn M. Forsythe, *Trademarks and Geographical Indications: A Case of California Champagne*, 10 CHAP. L. REV. 257 (2006); *see* Peter Brody, *Protection of Geographical Indications in the Wake of TRIPs: Existing United States Law and the Administration's Proposed Legislation*, 84 TRADEMARK REP. 520 (1994); *see also* 26 U.S.C. § 5388(c)(2)(B) (2012) (providing a list of geographic indications from Europe that will be considered "semi-generic" for uses by the Alcohol Tobacco and Firearms Department (Angelica, Burgundy, Claret, Chablis, Champagne, Chianti, Malaga, Marsala, Madeira, Moselle, Port, Rhine Wine (syn. Hock), Sauterne, Haut Sauterne, Sherry, and

indicators.[140] For example, only wine from Chianti, Italy may call itself "chianti."[141]

The closest the United States gets to protecting anything like a chiiki brand or a geographical indication is the federal regulation of American Viticultural Areas (AVAs).[142] These regulations allow wine and spirits producers to name a specific geographic area as the source of wine.[143] However, unlike a chiiki brand, these regulations say nothing regarding the exclusive use of the AVA by one specific entity.[144]

The European Union continues to be more and more insistent that the United States change course.[145]

Tokay)). Congress explicitly allowed for the inaccurate uses of these appellations provided that their actual source is clearly labeled on the bottle. *Id.*

[140] Molly Torsen, *Apples Oranges (and Wine): Why the International Conversation Regarding Geographic Indications is at a Standstill*, 87 J. PAT. & TRADEMARK OFF. SOC'Y 31, 31 (2005).

[141] Deborah J. Kemp & Lynn M. Forsythe, *Trademarks and Geographical Indications: A Case of California Champagne*, 10 CHAP. L. REV. 257, 282 (2006).

[142] 27 C.F.R. § 4.25(e) (2012). This regulation provides for five elements that must be established before an AVA is named. The petitioner must show the following: 1) evidence that the name of the viticultural area is locally and/or nationally known as referring to the area specified in the application; 2) historical or current evidence that the boundaries of the viticultural area are as specified in the application; 3) evidence relating to the geographical features (climate, soil, elevation, physical features, and geology) which distinguish the viticultural features of the proposed area from surrounding areas; 4) the specific boundaries of the viticultural area based on features which can be found on United States Geological Survey (U.S.G.S.) maps of the largest applicable scale; and 5) a copy of the appropriate U.S.G.S. map(s) with the boundaries prominently marked. 27 C.F.R. § 9.12 (2011).

[143] 27 C.F.R. § 4.25.

[144] *See id.*

[145] *See* Mary Clark Jalonick, *Europe Wants Its Parmesan Back, Seeks Name Change*, ASSOCIATED PRESS (Mar. 11, 2014), http://bigstory.ap.org/article/europe-wants-its-parmesan-back-seeks-name-change ("The trade negotiations are important for the EU as Europe has tried to protect share of agricultural exports and pull itself

Recently, Italian cheesemakers insisted that American companies stop using the geographic indicator *Parmesan*, as the cheese they produced was not from Parma, Italy.[146] They insisted that Americans change the name to "hard cheese."[147] Needless to say, makers of Parmesan cheese in Wisconsin were not cooperative.[148]

This is the same political environment in which the Japanese find themselves. The chiiki brands system is the way the Japanese are approaching the geographic indicator issue.[149] However, although the system is open to foreigners, virtually no non-Japanese companies have applied for a chiiki brand mark.[150] It will be very interesting to see if chiiki brands are used to protect

---

out of a recession. The ability to exclusively sell some of the continent's most famous and traditional products would prevent others from cutting into those markets.").

[146] *Id.*
[147] *Id.*
[148] *Id.*
[149] Tetsuya Imamura, *Chiikishudanshyohyoseidotoiu seidosentakuno igito sonomondai* [*The Significance and Problems with the Institutional Choice Called the Chiiki Brand System*], 34 NIHON KOGYO SHOYUKENHO GAKKAI NENPO 29, 34 (2010) (Japan); *see also* Anthony Rausch, *Capitalizing on Creativity in Rural Areas*, 4 J. RURAL & COMMUNITY DEV. 65, 68 (2009) ("The Japanese national government has recently emphasized the potential of branding as a means of broadening the image of Japan as a producer of highly specialized and high-quality goods on the global market as well as a means of revitalizing local economics.")
[150] The few exceptions are the registration of chiiki brands to PROSCIUTTO DI PARMA, Registration No. 5073378 (Japan); CANADA PORK (カナダポーク), Registration No. 5129558 (Japan); and ZHENJIANG VINEGAR (鎮江香醋), Registration No. 965547 (Japan). Kaigai (海外), [*Overseas*], JAPAN PAT. OFF. (Mar. 6, 2015), http://www.jpo.go.jp/torikumi/t_torikumi/pdf/tiikibrand/kaigai.pdf (Japan). The marks DARJEELING TEA, applied for by the India Tea Board, and CEYLON TEA, applied for by the Sri Lanka Tea Board, are currently pending. *See Todōfuken betsu chiiki dantai shōhyō shutsugan-chū anken* (都道府県別地域団体商標出願中案件) [*Regional Collective Trademark Pending Case List*], JAPAN PAT. OFF. (Jan. 31, 2015), http://www.jpo.go.jp/torikumi/t_torikumi/pdf/t_dantai_syouhyou/to dofuken_list.pdf (Japan).

things like Merlot wine or Rockford cheese in Japan. To date, no such application has been sought.[151]

B. Chiiki Brands as a Form of Geographic Indicators

Chiiki brands operate very similarly to geographic indicators recognized in most European countries and the European Union. The most obvious distinction is that the use of a chiiki brand inures to the benefit of a specific association affiliated with the brand, while the use of geographic indicators inures to the benefit of any entity that exists in the geographic region.[152]

Chiiki brands have the same association between goods and the region where they are made that is required of geographic indicators in other jurisdictions. The geographic significance of this association might be developed over time in Japan, whereas Europeans believe it is innate to the location. Odawara Kamaboko is a chiiki brand, but it is only by historical accident that Odawara became a place for fish processing that produced kamaboko. There is nothing in the soil or the sea that exclusively indicates that kamaboko from Odawara tastes unique because of its geographic origin.

This is contrast with geographic indicators in the European Union. In France, for example, the belief is that only a grape grown in the Bordeaux region, raised on the right level of rainwater and in soil unique to the Bordeaux region, can produce Bordeaux wine.[153] Any

---

[151] *Cf. Regional Brands in Japan*, JAPAN PAT. OFF. (Aug. 2014), http://www.jpo.go.jp/cgi/linke.cgi?url=/sesaku_e/trademark_system.htm.

[152] For a brief overview of geographic indicators and their differences with trademarks, see *Frequently Asked Questions: Geographical Indications*, WORLD INTELL. PROP. ORG., http://www.wipo.int/geo_indications/en/about.html#difference (last visited Mar. 13, 2015).

[153] Gregory V. Jones & Robert E. Davis, *Climate Influences on Grapevine Phenology, Grape Composition, and Wine Production and Quality for*

wine from that region of France would, theoretically, taste different from "Bordeaux" wines not made in the region. If ODAWARA KAMABOKO were a geographic indication, there would have to be some quality, reputation, or other characteristic essentially attributable to that geographical origin. But Odawara Kamaboko would taste the same if it emanated from Fukuoka instead of Odawara as long as the ingredients and processes used to manufacture the kamaboko were the same. This would not be possible with geographic indication from the European Union.

Japan's attempt to protect marks that look like geographic indicators may, in fact, make the world of trademark harmonization much more difficult. As systems around the world attempt to align their trademark systems to reduce transaction costs and thereby make their goods or services more competitive in world markets,[154] Japan has decided to go it alone. Although it is theoretically possible for a non-Japanese company to take advantage of the chiiki brand system, almost none have so far.[155] This may indicate a lack of knowledge or a lack of interest on the part of all the owners of geographic indicators worldwide, but the fact remains that in the first years of existence, geographic indicator owners have not rushed to Japan to register their marks as chiiki brands.

Bordeaux, France, 51 AM. J. ENOLOGY & VITICULTURE 249, 249 (2000), *available* at http://community.plu.edu/~reimanma/doc/climate-influences.pdf.

[154] *See e.g.*, EUGENIA BARONCELLI, ET AL., TRADEMARK PROTECTION OR PROTECTIONISM? 3, n.3 (2004) ("The Madrid Protocol of 1989 substantially reduce[s] the transaction costs involved in registering trademarks by allowing firms that reside in member states to file a single international application for registration in multiple countries.").

[155] *See supra* text accompanying note 150.

As such, it does not seem that it would be wise to consider the chiiki brand system to be an adequate replacement or substitute for geographic indicators. This seems to be the message owners of geographic indicators are telling us. After all, Japan is the third largest economy in the world.[156] European goods are very popular in all of Japan. As the owners of geographic indicators are an important lobby before the European Union and are constantly calling on the United States to recognize their marks, one would expect that they are paying closer attention to the Japanese market as well. Therefore, it seems the owners of geographic indicators are voting with their feet when it comes to the chiiki brand system. They simply have not gotten involved.

IV. ECONOMIC DEVELOPMENT

A. Connection to Economic Development Generally

It is axiomatic that trademark protection leads to economic development.[157] Without a trademark system, there is no investment in goodwill.[158] With no investment in goodwill, an economy flounders.[159] We

---

[156] *Japan Profile*, BBC NEWS ASIA (Feb. 17, 2015), http://www.bbc.com/news/world-asia-pacific-14918801.

[157] William M. Landes & Richard A. Posner, *Trademark Law: An Economic Perspective*, 30 J.L. & ECON. 265, 265–66 (1987) ("Our overall conclusion is that trademark law . . . can best be explained on the hypothesis that the law is trying to promote economic efficiency.").

[158] Goodwill is the idea that consumers will become loyal to a particular source; therefore, a trademark makes it easier for the consumer to identify that source amongst other similar products. *See* Park 'N Fly, Inc. v. Dollar Park and Fly, Inc., 469 U.S. 189, 198 (1985) (explaining that the goal of the Lanham Act is to "provid[e] national protection of trademarks in order to secure to the mark's owner the goodwill of his business and to protect the ability of consumers to distinguish among competing producers.").

[159] *See* William O. Hennessey, *The Role of Trademarks in Economic Development and Competitiveness*, IPMALL, http://ipmall.info/hosted_resources/Hennessey_Content/RoleofTrad

can look to the economy of Russia for proof of this fact, where in 1993, the government passed advertising restrictions that decreased the effectiveness of trademarks in advertising.[160] Because of this, "Russian entrepreneurs may be less likely to invest in developing their own goodwill and trademark capital, fearing adverse legal and institutional change."[161] Investment in brands begets investment in product lines, competition, and higher quality goods for less money.[162] This is the simple capitalistic calculus that drives our trademark system.

B. Will Chiiki Brands Have a Positive Economic Impact?

The question is whether the protection of chiiki brands can have the same formative impact on an economy that the creation of a trademark system may have. This is simply too difficult to tell. There are too many variables at issue to isolate one chiiki brand and claim that it is responsible for economic development. The JPO and others claim that it will spur economic redevelopment, but they have no data to support this claim.[163] In the cases studied above, there were multiple factors that led to an improved economic outlook.[164]

---

emarksinEconomicDevelopmentandCompetitiveness.pdf (last visited Mar. 15, 2015) ("The *goodwill of the seller* is the bedrock of the traditional consumer economy, where market information was unpredictable and the shopper came to rely upon the good name (or 'goodwill') of the retailer for reliable market information.").
[160] *See* Paul H. Rubin, *Growing a Legal System in the Post-Communist Economies*, 27 CORNELL INT'L L.J. 1, 37 (1994).
[161] Cynthia Vuille Stewart, *Trademarks in Russia: Making and Protecting Your Mark*, 5 TEX. INTELL. PROP. L.J. 1, 16 n.126 (1996) (citing Rubin, *supra* note 160, at 37).
[162] *See* Hennessey, *supra* note 159.
[163] *Id.*
[164] *Id.*

To test this hypothesis, the JPO commissioned a survey in 2012 of chiiki brand associations.[165] This survey is not scientific in the least, has no foundation, and amounts to nothing more than an opinion poll. However, it is telling that the JPO asked what effects were recognized in registering the association's mark as a chiiki brand.[166] Although 48.3% of respondents did say that the registration made it possible to advertise their goods and services and 38.5% responded that it improved the overall image of their chiiki brand-two vital components to any trademark system-only 2.8% said that it increased their sales.[167]

Additionally, the survey failed to ask for data to support the notion of increased sales.[168] Therefore, there is no data being collected to establish the JPO's primary goal of the chiiki brand system-to improve the economic circumstances for regional companies.[169]

C. Anti-Counterfeit Measure

The chiiki brand system is also propounded by the JPO and others as an effective way to combat counterfeit goods.[170] Of course, there is also no reliable

---

[165] Chiiki dantai shōhyō no tōroku-go no katsuyō jōkyō ni tsuite (地域団体商標の登録後の活用状況について) [*Study of Use After Registration of Regional Collective Trademark*], (2012), http://web.archive.org/web/20140813231531/http://www.jpo.go.jp/torikumi/t_torikumi/pdf/tiikibrand/1-6.pdf (Japan).
[166] *Id.*
[167] *Id.* In the survey, the questions were predetermined and the respondents were asked to check off those items that applied. That is, all respondents had the express opportunity to say that as a result of the chiiki brand system, their sales increased; however, only 4.2% did so.
[168] *Id.*
[169] *See Regional Brands in Japan, supra* note 146.
[170] *See id.* ("Thanks to the regional collective trademark system, local business cooperatives, agricultural cooperatives, and other collective groups and organizations are now able themselves to protect, and further develop, their regional brands. The JPO believes that this is a

data regarding how, precisely, this would affect traffic in counterfeit goods. One can theorize that perhaps the ability to label a product as originating from one specific association may play some role in purchasers' decision to buy the product. This might be the most reasonable explanation possible given that no specifics and no data are provided by the JPO. However, this assumes too much.

It assumes that purchasers care where the goods come from. To be sure, Japanese are brand-conscious consumers.[171] However, in tough economic times, they are also price-conscious consumers.[172] It is difficult to say; there is no data to support the notion that Japanese (or other purchasers) would choose brand over price. Some brand-conscious purchasers may make the choice to buy the appropriately branded product; however, some purchasers just want the product and do not care from where it emanates because they cannot afford it.[173] One must have a very refined pallet for Japanese food

---

very useful system to revitalize local industries and promote the betterment and economic development of local communities.").
[171] *Japanese Market*, VENTURE JAPAN, http://www.venturejapan.com/japanese-market.htm (last visited Mar. 15, 2015) ("[T]he Japanese market is a first-mover's market and the Japanese market is a quality conscious, service conscious and brand conscious market."); Debbie Howard, et al., *Japan's Changing Consumer: Drivers of Change for Luxury Brands*, JRMN INSIGHTS BRIEFING (2007).
[172] *See* Eric Pfanner & Megumi Fujikawa, *Japanese Consumers Keep Spending After Sales-Tax Increase*, WALL ST. J. (May 1, 2014, 12:21 PM), http://online.wsj.com/news/articles/SB10001424052702303678404579 535412666350056 ("Though Japanese consumers have been stubbornly price conscious since the bubble economy burst more than two decades ago, a recent tightening in certain parts of the job market and the first widespread wage increases since 2008 have lifted spirits some.").
[173] For an analysis of the kamaboko industry in general and its overall increase in production and value, not just Odawara Kamaboko, *see* Myles Raizin & Lloyd Regier, *Economic Aspects of the Japanese Kamaboko Industry*, 48 MARINE FISHERIES REV. 60 (1986), *available at* http://spo.nmfs.noaa.gov/mfr484/mfr48414.pdf.

to be able, for example, to taste the difference between kamaboko from Odawara compared to kamaboko from anywhere else in Japan. It could be that people just want kamaboko; they do not care where it comes from.[174]

For the system to prevent counterfeiting, it assumes that purchasers know something about the chiiki brand system. Given that applications for chiiki brands have dropped precipitously,[175] it is unrealistic to expect the Japanese public and purchasers in general to know and care about the chiiki brand system. Foreign applicants are not using the system. Japanese association interest in the system has plummeted. To expect purchasers to know the system, look for it on a label, and choose not to buy a product if they do not see a chiiki brand mark on the label is grossly overestimating the sophistication of the average consumer.

Between 2006 and late 2013, there were 1,044 total applications for registration as chiiki brands.[176] Of those, nine have come from countries other than Japan including Jamaica, Canada, Italy, India, China, South Korea, and Sri Lanka.[177] In other words, nine

---

[174] Although Japan was the leading country in the failed international treaty known as the Anti-Counterfeiting Trade Agreement (ACTA), the case for ACTA is grossly overstated by its proponents. *See* Kenneth L. Port, *A Case Against the ACTA*, 33 CARDOZO L. REV. 1131 (2012). As with all alleged counterfeit luxury goods, it is important to have real and reliable data upon which conclusions are based.

[175] *Cf. Regional Collective Trademark Case Studies for 2015*, *supra* note 11.

[176] *Regional Brands in Japan*, JAPAN PAT. OFF. (Aug. 2014), http://www.jpo.go.jp/torikumi/t_torikumi/pdf/regional_brands/chiik i2014.pdf (there were 1,044 applications to register regional brands by Sept. 2013).

[177] Sho gaikoku no chiri-teki hyōji hogo seido oyobi dō hogo o meguru kokusai-teki dōkō ni kansuru chōsa kenkyū (諸外国の地理的表示保護制度及び同保護を巡る国際的動向に関する調査研究) [*Geographical Indications Protections Systems and the Protections of Foreign Countries: Research on International Trends*], JAPAN INT'L ASS'N FOR THE PROTECTION OF INTELL. PROP. (Mar. 2012),

associations from seven different countries have applied to register their purported chiiki brands in Japan. Only one association from a European Union country, where geographic indicators are the strongest, has applied for registration.[178] After nearly ten years, it is safe to say that the non-Japanese users of geographic indicators are not utilizing the chiiki brand system.

The entities in the world that one would expect to have the most to gain by the chiiki brand system are not utilizing it—either because they are ignorant of it or because they find it somehow insufficient. If that is the case, it does not seem realistic to impute knowledge of the system onto average consumers in Japan to know that a product that lacks a chiiki brand label may be a counterfeit good.

V. CHIIKI BRANDS AS AN EXAMPLE OF GIVING IN TO POLITICAL PRESSURE TOWARD REGIONALIZATION AND DECENTRALIZATION

Regionalization or decentralization has been an important movement in Japan for some time.[179] As stated above, this is odd given the relative size of Japan. Japan is a small, mountainous country. All of Japan would fit into the state of California. Only about a third of Japan is not mountainous, not covered with trees, and otherwise arable. In addition to being small, the

---

http://www.jpo.go.jp/shiryou/toushin/chousa/pdf/zaisanken_kouhyou/h23_report_01.pdf (Japan).

[178] *Id.* (Only an association from Italy has applied to register for Japanese chiiki brand protection).

[179] Gilbert Rozman, *Backdoor Japan: The Search for a Way out via Regionalism and Decentralization*, 25 J. JAPANESE STUD. 1 (1999); Hiroshi Ikawa, *15 Years of Decentralization Reform in Japan*, NAT'L GRADUATE INST. FOR POL'Y STUD., Mar. 2008, at 1, *available at* http://www.clair.or.jp/j/forum/honyaku/hikaku/pdf/up-to-date_en4.pdf ("Decentralization has been positively promoted in Japan since the early part of the 1990s.").

population density is quite high.[180] Japan has approximately 125 million people. Considering that only a third of the land is arable, Japan is one of the most densely populated countries in the world.

Yet Japanese people recognize clear regional distinctions. From culture to the taste of food, Japanese people claim great differences between even Tokyo and Osaka,[181] the two most populous cities and the most urbanized.[182] Hokkaido in the north and Okinawa in the south are even more remote.[183]

In addition, all national governmental agencies and services have been in Tokyo for a very long time.[184] Tokyo represents Japan the same way Washington D.C. represents the United States. However, Japan is not a federal state like the United States. Although it has prefectures, the prefectural governments do not have the same authority over their jurisdictions as state governments have authority over their states as in the

---

[180] At 836 people per square mile, Japan is about the thirty-fourth most densely populated country in the world. *Population Density Per Square Mile of Countries*, INFOPLEASE, http://www.infoplease.com/ipa/A0934666.html (last visited Mar. 4, 2015).

[181] *See* Jeffrey Hays, *Osaka Versus Tokyo and Regional Differences in Japan*, FACTS & DETAILS, http://factsanddetails.com/japan/cat18/sub115/item612.html (last updated Mar. 2010).

[182] The population of Tokyo itself is only about nine million people, but the greater metropolitan area is estimated at thirty-five million people. *Tokyo Population 2014*, WORLD POPULATION REV. (Oct. 19, 2014), http://worldpopulationreview.com/world-cities/tokyo-population/. The population of Osaka is approximately three million people. The two cities are separated by a mere 250 miles or roughly the distance between New York City and Rochester, NY.

[183] The distance between Sapporo, Hokkaido and Naha, Okinawa is nearly 1500 miles.

[184] In 1600, the Tokugawa government moved the capitol from Kyoto to Tokyo. At that time, the government imposed a harsh feudal system to control all of Japan from the seat of government in Tokyo. It was very effective. This feudal system lasted until 1868.

United States. Japan acts in most things with one, centralized voice, not fifty-one competing voices as in the United States (the fifty U.S. states plus the U.S. federal government).

These regional differences have led to resentment of the Japanese central government. For example, Tokyo requires Okinawa to use 40% of the arable land in Okinawa for U.S. military bases.[185] There are many other examples less extreme than the contentious situation in Okinawa. Many mayors and prefectures are becoming more and more powerful and independent, not through legislation but through their own initiative.

In 2012, the Governor[186] of Tokyo, Shintaro Ishihara, started an international diplomatic dispute over the Senkaku Islands that gained much attention in the press.[187] Ishihara started to raise money to purchase the Senkaku Islands and make them part of Tokyo. The Senkaku Islands are over 1,000 miles from Tokyo. At least in the popular press, no government official complained that Ishihara did not have the authority to do this. Rather, the Japanese central government quickly preempted Ishihara's plan and bought the islands from the Japanese citizen that owned them before Ishihara could effectuate the plan. This started a diplomatic row with China. Thus the Governor of the Prefecture of Tokyo singlehandedly started one of the

---

[185] Gavan McCormack & Urashima Etsuko, *Okinawa's "Darkest Year"*, 11 ASIA-PACIFIC J. 4 (2014), *available at* http://japanfocus.org/-Urashima-Etsuko/4167 (demonstrating the depth to which Okinawans resent America's bases and blames Tokyo for their existence).
[186] Because the city of Tokyo is its own prefecture, the head of the city is designated the Governor.
[187] *See* Hilary Whiteman, *How a Remote Rock Split China and Japan*, CNN (Jan. 30, 2013, 3:16 PM), http://edition.cnn.com/2012/09/17/world/asia/china-japan-islands-dispute-explained/.

most volatile diplomatic stalemates between China and Japan since the end of World War II.[188]

Tokyo has long paid lip service to the voices calling for decentralization and regionalism.[189] There have been many plans to move specific government functions outside of Tokyo.[190] These plans are specific and well stated but, as of yet, unrealized.

Various smaller steps responsive to the move for regionalism have been realized. The chiiki brand system is one of those steps. By promoting the chiiki brand system as forcefully as it has, the Japanese central government appears to actually be in support of the move for regionalism and decentralization. The promises the central government has made about the chiiki brand system's role in reinvigorating a stagnant Japanese economy are remarkable. The government seems to be quite invested in the chiiki brand system.

But it is quite doubtful that on its own the chiiki brand system could or would produce the economic advantages promised by the Japanese central government. If the economic advantages are not clearly realized and it will not have the promised effect in fighting counterfeit goods, what is the point of the system? If the promised effects cannot and will not be realized, unstated political objectives may actually support the system. This apparent commitment by the Japanese central government to a regional system (that

---

[188] Ivy Lee & Fang Ming, *Deconstructing Japan's Claim of Sovereignty over the Diaoyu/Senkaku Islands*, 10 ASIA-PACIFIC J. 1 (2012), *available at* http://japanfocus.org/-Fang-Ming/3877; Reinhard Drifte, *The Japan-China Confrontation Over the Senkaku/Diaoyu Islands–Between "Shelving" and "Dispute Escalation"*, 12 ASIA-PACIFIC J. 3 (2014), *available at* http://www.japanfocus.org/-Reinhard-Drifte/4154.

[189] *See* Ikawa, *supra* note 174, at 12 ("Decentralization is also indispensable to correct the excessive concentration on Tokyo . . . .").

[190] *Id.* at 1.

defies harmonization and international cooperation) has placated the social movement calling for more decentralization from Tokyo.

The chiiki brand system is working as an elaborate scheme by which the regionalization movement is actually disempowered. The Japanese central government appears to have given the movement much by allowing associations to register and enforce their regional marks. However, given that, almost a decade in, no association has been successful in enforcing their mark, it is appropriate to question what, exactly, the Japanese central government has conceded, if anything?

No law is devoid of politics. The Japanese chiiki brand system makes this abundantly clear. First, the chiiki brand system is an effort to pacify a direct threat to the central government in Tokyo from those who call for stronger and more meaningful regional rights. Second, it is an attempt to marry Japan's ancient traditions to modern European trends. Third, it is a demonstration of Japan's intent to be less dependent upon America and "go it alone" whenever and wherever it can. To be sure, the result of the chiiki brand system, demonstratively, is that Japan has elected to go it alone.

VI. Conclusion

The chiiki brand system is an entirely new way of protecting marks that have primarily geographic significance. This system allows associations to register their interests as collectives in a mark with geographic significance. This new system is something similar to a cross between the EU's geographic indications and the United States' system of collective marks. It makes trademark harmonization of the international community on this point impossible as it is a hybrid system.

Although popular with associations and the JPO, it is difficult to discern what economic effect this new system will have. The JPO claims that the system will be the catalyst by which the stagnant Japanese economy will be saved.[191] This has encouraged over 500 associations all across Japan to register their geographic marks.[192]

The JPO is also expecting non-Japanese owners of significant geographic indicators to take advantage of the chiiki brand system; however, to date, almost none have. Of the over 1,000 applications the JPO has received to register a chiiki brand, only nine of the applications have come from non-Japanese associations and only one has come from a European Union country. This may be all the proof that is necessary to show that Japan's attempts to go it alone with its new hybrid system are doomed to failure.

There are simply too many variables to determine what one economic factor contributed, or not, to the economic growth of an entity or association. The JPO offers no data to support its claim that the chiiki brand system would have a positive effect on the economic condition of its participants. Any positive stories that do exist are anecdotal at best. If the stated goals are unattainable, one must consider unstated goals.

One unstated goal has to do with a contentious political movement in Japan calling for regionalization and decentralization from Tokyo. The chiiki brand system plays well into the narrative of support for such voices. In supporting the chiiki brand system, the Japanese central government appears to be supporting regionalization and thereby conceding to this political

---

[191] Hennessey, *supra* note 154.
[192] *JPO Compiled a Booklet Titled "Regional Brands in JAPAN 2015 - Regional Collective Trademarks," supra* note 10.

movement; however, as the chiiki brand system will not have the claimed economic effects, it is difficult to tell what was conceded, if anything.

A possible explanation for the chiiki brand system is that it is a response by the Japanese central government to lax intellectual property practices of surrounding East Asian countries and the impact it has had on Japanese consumerism. The JPO indicated in a survey report on "losses caused by counterfeiting" that the average loss a Japanese company due to counterfeiting totaled 100.1 billion Yen.[193] From September 1st through the 5th, the fifth round of negotiations on a free-trade agreement among Japan, China and the Republic of Korea took place in Beijing. Intellectual property was discussed among various topics at this negotiation.[194]

Japan is in the process of establishing free-trade agreements between various East Asian countries in order to improve international business activity.[195] In preparation for this change to the international trade market, the Japanese central government is attempting to improve its control over sales functions, including the marketability of its products. One of the primary concerns Japan has in doing business with China is

---

[193] *See* Japan Patent Office, *2013-Nendo mohō higai chōsa hōkoku-sho chōsa bunseki kekka no gaiyō* (2013 年度模倣被害調査報告書 調査分析結果の概要) [*Survey Report on Losses Caused by Counterfeiting*], MINISTRY OF ECON., TRADE & INDUSTRY (Mar. 17, 2014), http://www.meti.go.jp/press/2013/03/20140317001/20140317001-2.pdf (Japan) (providing a summary of the results of the survey).
[194] *Fifth Round of China-Japan-Korea Free Trade Area Negotiations Held in Beijing*, CHINA FTA NETWORK (Sept. 3, 2014), http://fta.mofcom.gov.cn/enarticle/enrelease/201411/18880_1.html.
[195] *See* Chris Buckley, *East Asian Powers Set to Push Trade Pact Talks*, REUTERS (May 12, 2012, 10:43 PM), http://www.reuters.com/article/2012/05/13/us-china-summit-idUSBRE84C00V20120513 (noting that the Japanese Prime Minister has stated that Japan is pursuing cooperation as an economic strategy).

protecting intellectual property rights.[196] In anticipation of these business risks, the Japanese central government is implementing internal infrastructure that attempts to mitigate foreseeable risks and improve international business activity.[197] The chiiki brand system could be a means for the Japanese central government to strengthen the regulation of its own products in order to combat problems associated with counterfeit goods such as loss of markets, loss of potential profits, and a declining brand image.[198]

The chiiki brand system harmonizes business practices among the different regions of Japan, which the Japanese central government hopes will lead to a more efficient business model, and provide the Japanese central government with a means of protecting staple products from loss due to counterfeiting. Whether it will or not seems uncertain. The various regional governments of Japan act as subsidiaries to the Japanese central government in implementing these public expenditures. This structure promotes a top down model of government, effectively relegating regional governments to the role of administrative limbs for the Japanese central government. Although the regional governments do have some discretion in how these funds are

---

[196] *See White Paper on International Economy and Trade 2007*, MINISTRY OF ECON., TRADE & INDUSTRY, 244 (2007),
http://www.meti.go.jp/english/report/data/gWT2007fe.html
(discussing how Japanese companies are hesitant of entering into business with China due to increased business risks. The primary risks include problems with Chinese laws, taxation, and protection of intellectual property.).

[197] *See id.* at 252 (explaining how Japanese companies are deepening their ties to business networks within Japan to increase the growth of regional economies.).

[198] *See id.* at 248 (describing how Japan is taking steps to improve the financial environment in East Asia by stabilizing financial exchange markets.).

distributed, the requirement for a brand to be well recognized gives the Japanese central government the power to determine which products qualify for the chiiki brand trademark.

The chiiki brand system is an interesting way to encourage cooperation among regional producers; however, its uniqueness is its undoing. No country can or would harmonize to this standard and there are virtually no non-Japanese entities that have applied for registration. As such, this may prove to be another failed attempt by Japan of going it alone.

Appendix A

The following is a listing of categories in which chiiki brands have been registered:[199]

Vegetables	49
Rice	7
Fruit	38
Meat	55
Seafood	38
Processed food	50
Milk and dairy	5
Spices	15
Confectionary	11
Noodles, grain	11
Tea	15
Liquor	13
Soft Drinks	1
Plants	3
Textiles	52
Bags, crafts	78
Pottery	28
Toys, dolls	15
Buddhist alters and furniture	36

---

[199] *Regional Collective Trademark Case Studies for 2015, supra* note 11.

Precious metal products, cutlery and tools 9
Wood, coal, charcoal 14
Onsen (hot springs) 41
Services (other than Onsen) 14

Appendix B

In the run up to implementation of the chiiki brand system, the JPO used the following companies as poster children for the effort.[200] It will be interesting to watch whether these companies experience the economic benefit the JPO has claimed they will.

1. Long potatoes (TOCHACHIKA NISHINAGAIMO 十勝川西長いも).

> **Owner:** 帯広市川西農業協同組合 (Obihiro Kawanishi agricultural cooperative)
>
> **Address:** 〒089-1182北海道帯広市川西町西2線61番地の1 (2-61-1 West Kawanishi, Obihiro, Hokaido 089-1182)
>
> **Website:** http://www.jaobihirokawanisi.jp

2. Green tea (SHIZUOKA CHA 静岡茶).

> **Owner:** 1静岡県経済農業協同組合連合会 (Shizuoka Economic Federation of Agricultural Cooperatives) and 2 静岡県茶商工業協同組合 (Shizuoka tea commerce and industry cooperative)
>
> **Address:** 〒422-8006静岡県静岡市駿河区曲金3丁目8番1号 (3-8-1 Magarikane, Suruga-ku, Shizuoka-shi, Shizuoka Prefecture 422-8006)

---

[200] Katsuyō jirei no go shōkai (活用事例のご紹介) [*Case Studies*], JAPAN PAT. OFF. (2008), http://www.jpo.go.jp/torikumi/t_torikumi/pdf/tiikibrand/2008katuyoujirei.pdf (Japan).

〒420-0005静岡県静岡市葵区北番町81番地 (81 Kitabancho, Aoi-ku, Shizuoka-shi, Shizuoka Prefecture 420-0005

Website: http : //jashizuoka-keizairen.net/, http : //www.siz-sba.or.jp/kencha

3. Transam Wood Art (OSAKA RANMA 大阪欄間).

   Owner: 大阪欄間工芸協同組合 Osaka transom crafts cooperative

   Address: 〒564-0001大阪府吹田市岸部北5丁目30-1 (5-30-1 Kishibekita, Suita-shi, Osaka 564-0001)

   Website: http://www.kougei.or.jp/ranma/

4. Sponge cake (NAGASAKI KASUTERA 長崎カステラ).

   Owner: 長崎県菓子工業組合 (Nagasaki confectionary industry union)

   Address: 〒850-0801長崎県長崎市八幡町4番26号 (4-26 Nagasaki-shi Nagasaki 850-0801)

   Website: http : //www1.cncm.ne.jp/〜nagakasi

5. Hot springs (KUROKAWA ONSEN 黒川温泉).

   Owner: 黒川温泉観光旅館協同組合 (Kurokawa Onsen Ryokan tourism cooperative)

   Address: 〒869-2402熊本県阿蘇郡南小国町大字満願寺6594番地の3 (6594-3 Ozamanganji, Minami Oguni-cho, Aso-gun, Kumamoto Prefecture 869-2402

   （権利者のウェブサイト）

   Website: http://www.kurokawaonsen.or.jp

6. Soba noodles (OKINAWA SOBA 沖縄そば).

Owner: 沖縄生麺協同組合 (Okinawa raw noodles cooperative)

Address: 〒901-0152沖縄県那覇市小禄1831番地1 (1831-1 Koroku, Naha-shi, Okinawa) 沖縄産業支援センター203-3号室

Website: http://www.oki-soba.jp

JUST GOVERNANCE OR JUST WAR?: NATIVE ARTISTS, CULTURAL PRODUCTION, AND THE CHALLENGE OF "SUPER-DIVERSITY"

REBECCA TSOSIE[†]

I. Introduction 63
II. Colonialism, Cultural Imagery,
 and Native Peoples 74
III. National Identity, Tribal Identity,
 and Identity Harm 80
 A. Stereotyping and Identity Harm 83
 B. Native American Mascots and Identity Harm 88
IV. Cultural Production and the Rights
 of Native Artists 93
 A. The Historic Framing of Art as
 Cultural Production 94

[†] Regents' Professor of Law and Associate Vice Provost for Academic Excellence and Inclusion, Arizona State University College of Law. This essay was inspired and enhanced by the contributions of the author's colleague, Luke Dorsett, a Technical Systems Analyst at ASU and also one of the featured artists of the "What Tribe Project," a Native/Chicano arts collaborative directed toward eradicating the negative images of Native peoples and other diverse cultures, and promoting the voice of contemporary Indigenous artists. The author thanks him for his intellectual and artistic contributions to this essay. The author is very grateful to Adam Szymanski and the exceptional editorial staff of Cybaris for their excellent contributions with this article. Finally, the author thanks her research assistant, Kristyne Schaaf-Olson, and David Gay, Tara Mospan, and Beth DiFelice, librarians at the Ross-Blakely Law Library, for their assistance with the research for this article.

B. Indigenous Perspectives on Art as Cultural
   Production 97

V. The Role of International Law in Regulating
   Indigenous Cultural Expression 103

   A. Traditional Cultural Expression 105

   B. The Human Rights Approach to Indigenous
      Goverance of Cultural Heritage. 112

V. Conclusion 116

I. INTRODUCTION

> If you know the enemy and know yourself, you need not fear the result of a hundred battles. If you know yourself but not the enemy, for every victory gained you will also suffer a defeat. If you know neither the enemy nor yourself, you will succumb in every battle.[1]

You might ask what an ancient text, written by a Chinese philosopher over 2,500 years ago, could possibly have to do with the topic of my essay, which concerns the rights of Native American artists to their creative works and the rights of tribal governments to protect tribal cultural art forms, such as quill work, bead work, and basketry. Indigenous artists and tribal communities are actively engaged in a fight to protect their cultures and art forms from appropriation and misuse. As Walter Echo-Hawk observes, there has been little legal protection for the cultural rights of Indigenous peoples, and consequently, "indigenous heritage has been appropriated, pirated and misused."[2] According to Echo-Hawk:

> The theft of culture is part of the one-way transfer of property from indigenous to non-indigenous hands seen in colonies and settler states around the world—it includes not only the taking of land, natural resources, personal property, but even the heritage of indigenous peoples

---

[1] SUN TZU, THE ART OF WAR 18 (James Clavell ed. 1983).
[2] WALTER R. ECHO-HAWK, IN THE LIGHT OF JUSTICE: THE RISE OF HUMAN RIGHTS IN NATIVE AMERICA AND THE U.N. DECLARATION ON THE RIGHTS OF INDIGENOUS PEOPLES 198 (2013).

and their very identities, plucking them as clean as a Safeway chicken.³

Of course, many non-Indians fail to appreciate that Indigenous peoples hold a form of property right to aspects of their cultures, namely the right to exclude others from particular uses or condition such use by requiring a license (for example, for the commercial use of the tribal name).⁴ The U.S. laws regulating intellectual property rights (copyright, patent, trademark) provide a poor fit for the interests of Indigenous nations in protecting the intangible aspects of their cultural heritage.⁵ There have been limited victories by federally recognized American Indian and Alaska Native nations seeking to prevent consumer confusion about what an "Indian product" is for purposes of the federal Indian Arts and Crafts Act,⁶ which protects the right of American Indian and Alaska Native artists to market their art as an authentic Indian product.⁷ However, the appropriation of tribal art forms continues, as design guru Ralph Lauren and commercial marketers such as J.C. Penney have demonstrated by transforming the intricate silver and turquoise jewelry of Southwest Indian tribes into mass-market products for trendy fashionistas trying to "play Indian."⁸ If appropriately

---

³ *Id.*
⁴ Angela R. Riley, *"Straight Stealing": Towards an Indigenous System of Cultural Property Protection*, 80 WASH. L. REV. 69, 71-72 (2005) (describing the use of Native American cultural practices in the entertainment industry without any social response to the appropriation of Native American culture.)
⁵ *Id.*
⁶ *See* Indian Arts and Crafts Act of 1990, Pub. L. No. 101-644, 104 Stat. 4662.
⁷ *See id.*
⁸ *See* John Hartman, *Under Turquoise Skies – Ralph Lauren*, DURANGO SILVER (Mar. 6, 2011), http://www.durangosilver.com/blog/tag/ralph-lauren-turquoise/; *See* Megan Finnerty, *Stepping into a Cultural Conundrum*, THE ARIZONA REPUBLIC, Apr. 25, 2015,

labeled to avoid consumer confusion, the non-Indian design world will continue to capture the greatest share of commercial value of tribal art forms, and most consumers and producers will overlook the impact on tribal cultural identity.

Many, if not most, non-Indians fail to understand the significance of cultural identity to Indigenous peoples, nor do they understand the concept of cultural harm.[9] Consequently, the battle over cultural appropriation continues as Dan Snyder, owner of the Washington team, proclaims that the "Redskins" logo and team name actually honors Indians, ignoring the protests of Native leaders and tribal members who assert that the mascot disparages and degrades them.[10] The battle continues over sacred symbols as pop music giant Pharrell Williams and countless other celebrities wear garish "war bonnets"[11] in a caricature of the ceremonial headdress that is culturally authorized for use only by esteemed and worthy tribal leaders from the Indigenous nations of the Southern and Northern Plains. But is this really a desecration or is it a permissible act of artistic appropriation? If there is no

---

http://www.azcentral.com/story/entertainment/arts/2015/04/25/appropriation-cultural-conundrum-native-american/26334281/
[9] *See* Rebecca Tsosie, *Cultural Challenges to Biotechnology: Native American Genetic Resources and the Concept of Cultural Harm*, 35 J. L. MED. & ETHICS 396, 405–09 (2007) (articulating multiple examples of cultural harm against Indians by non-Indians due to their failure to recognize or understand the significance of cultural identity and the unique nature of Tribal claims).
[10] *Daniel Snyder Defends Redskins*, ESPN (Aug. 6, 2014), http://espn.go.com/nfl/story/_/id/11313245/daniel-snyder-redskins-term-honor-respect. This essay refers to that entity as "the Washington Team" in the text that follows.
[11] *See* ELLE (July 2014) (UK edition) (picturing Williams on the cover in a headdress); Shan Li, *Victoria's Secret Apologizes For Use of Native American Headdress*, LA TIMES (Nov. 13, 2012), http://articles.latimes.com/2012/nov/13/business/la-fi-victorias-secret-native-american-20121113.

legal right to stop these appropriations, why should it matter? Perhaps most vexing of all, it seems to outsiders that not "all Indians" agree on the terms of the debate. Team owner Dan Snyder pointed this out as he hosted his VIP guests, then-Navajo Nation President Ben Shelly and First Lady Martha Shelly, during a 2014 football game in Glendale, Arizona, all wearing hats with the infamous Washington Team logo.[12]

If one reads Sun Tzu's words carefully, it is abundantly clear that identity is of paramount importance in times of war, as in the context of a battle.[13] One must know oneself and also one's enemy. Similarly, one must differentiate the rules of governance that hold a civil society together, from the principles that govern a war between enemies. Sun Tzu also wrote that "[h]umanity and justice are the principles" by which states must govern their affairs.[14] In comparison, "opportunism and flexibility" govern armies as they go to war with the enemy, and these are "military rather than civic virtues."[15] Are we in a time where just principles of governance will define the respective boundaries between Native rights and those who want to profit from Native culture? Or do the terms of the debate suggest that cultural production is yet another battleground between Native governments and the nation-states that now encompass them?

This essay is intended to facilitate a dialogue about who possesses the authority to use tribal designs, symbols and motifs within the contemporary sphere of

---

[12] *See* Andrew Joseph, *Navajo Nation President Ben Shelly Sits in Box With Dan Snyder*, ARIZ. CENT. (Oct. 13, 2014, 10:39 AM), http://www.azcentral.com/story/sports/heat-index/2014/10/13/navajo-nation-president-ben-shelly-sits-in-box-with-dan-snyder/17188935/.

[13] *See* TZU, *supra* note 1 and accompanying text.

[14] *Id.* at 17.

[15] *Id.*

cultural production.¹⁶ I will explore why U.S. copyright and trademark law often do not adequately protect the interests of Native artists or tribal governments, and why tribal governments should be concerned about the international dialogue concerning ownership of traditional cultural expression. This essay builds on Walter Echo-Hawk's argument that securing adequate legal protection for the cultural rights of Native artists and tribal governments is pivotal to the realization of their human rights within domestic society.¹⁷ Echo-Hawk's argument embodies a complex array of issues, and this essay maps those issues for future discussion and analysis. In my view, Echo-Hawk appropriately describes the protection of Indigenous cultural rights as the most important issue for the future because if the law cannot intervene to protect Indigenous peoples from cultural harm, the final phase of colonialism will proceed unabated. I use the term "colonialism" to describe the power dynamics of European settlement on the lands that ultimately became the United States.¹⁸ That dynamic alternately engaged policies of war and peace with Native peoples, but always employed the use of power and dominance to subordinate Native peoples and appropriate land, resources, and rights from them. This was done to build the empire of the British Crown and then to build the new nation that emerged as the United States.

Colonialism in the United States has proceeded through three phases. The first phase involved the

---

¹⁶ Finnerty, *supra* note 8.
¹⁷ ECHO-HAWK, *supra* note 2 at 198.
¹⁸ *See* CAROLE GOLDBERG, REBECCA TSOSIE, KEVIN WASHBURN & ELIZABETH WASHBURN, AMERICAN INDIAN LAW: NATIVE NATIONS AND THE FEDERAL SYSTEM 3 (6th ed. 2010) (describing Federal Indian law as "a doctrinal, historical vestige of the legal regime that tried to rationalize, legitimate, and regulate American colonialism over Indian tribes.").

destruction of Native peoples through outright military action from the date of European contact until the "Indian Wars" were deemed officially concluded in the United States at the close of the nineteenth century.[19] The battleground was tangible and the cost of defeat was loss of life. There was no confusion over who was Indigenous and who was not. The conversation was about who was an ally and who was an enemy. During this first phase, the United States used its military power to subdue Indigenous Nations who were deemed to be the enemies of the United States, and the U.S. sought political alliances with Indigenous Nations who were willing to be its allies.[20] There are over 500 treaties between American Indian Nations and the United States government, dating from 1778 until 1871, when Congress ended making treaties with Indian nations.[21] Each of those documents acknowledges the sovereignty of the Indian nations, as well as their rightful claims to their traditional lands and resources. Most of those treaties were subsequently breached,[22] in whole or in part, due to the actions of the United States, as well as its failure to protect treaty-guaranteed lands from encroachment by settlers.[23] Today, that brutal past exists in monuments that mark the sites of the massacres at Wounded Knee, Sand Creek, and other places where Native peoples experienced genocide as they fought to protect their homelands and peoples. Of course, the past also lives on in the memory of their descendants.

---

[19] *See id.*, at 1–121 (recounting the history of Federal Indian law in great detail).
[20] *Id.* at 14–20.
[21] *Id.* at 4; Helen Oliff, *Treaties Made, Treaties Broken*, NAT'L RELIEF CHARITIES BLOG (March 3, 2011), http://blog.nrcprograms.org/treaties-made-treaties-broken/.
[22] Oliff, *supra* note 21.
[23] GOLDBERG ET AL., *supra* note 18 at 15–16.

The second phase of colonialism involved the appropriation of Native lands and cultural objects for use of Euro-American settlers in the guise of efforts to civilize Indians so that they could eventually be incorporated into society as American citizens. During this era, all Indians were treated alike, whether they had been friends or enemies of the United States during the prior interval. Federal civilization policy relied on the notion of a "wardship" under which the benevolent civilized government maintained virtually absolute control over the "savage" wards, who were deemed to lack the fundamental capacity to maintain rights to ownership of property or ability to contract for goods and services, as "civilized" peoples could. Until the late 1930s, the Indian Agent assigned to each reservation assumed direct control over tribal members on the reservation, and the Indian ward had no right to leave the reservation or enter the larger society, except with the approval of the Agent or his designees. The battleground became both tangible and intangible because control was exercised over the physical body and at the level of the mind to break down the freedom of Native peoples and their ability to maintain their historical and separate cultural and political identities. Federal law and policy converted the political relationship between Nations into a hierarchical relationship between the dependent ward and the benevolent master as "trustee."[24]

During this second era of colonialism, the United States government used its political power to appropriate vast amounts of Native land and tangible tribal cultural heritage, including sacred objects, objects

---

[24] Rebecca Tsosie, *Reclaiming Native Stories: An Essay on Cultural Appropriation and Cultural Rights*, 34 ARIZ. STATE L.J. 299, 317-332 (2002) (describing the relationship between historical policies and the use of native images by outsiders.).

of cultural patrimony, and human remains.[25] At the same time, the U.S. government endeavored to erase tribal cultural identity through a mandatory civilization program that featured the federal boarding school policy; federally-supported efforts to convert Indians to Christianity; the federal allotment policy, which was designed to break down tribal landholdings and inculcate an individual ethic of property ownership, as well as other nineteenth and twentieth century equivalents. Policymakers touted the civilization program as being "beneficial" to Indians because it would prepare them for a future in which they might transcend the limitations of their status as wards and become U.S. citizens.[26] Initially, Congress selectively naturalized American Indians to citizenship if they demonstrated successful assimilation.[27] In 1924, Congress enacted the Indian Citizenship Act, which extended U.S. citizenship to all American Indians, but specified that they would retain their treaty rights and political rights under federal law, as members of federally recognized tribal governments.[28]

Indigenous peoples survived the first two waves of colonialism and today, federally recognized tribal governments exist as separate nations, with recognized legal rights of self-governance and the moral and political right to self-determination.[29] Tribal governments possess executive, legislative, and judicial powers, and they exercise jurisdiction over their lands

---

[25] *See generally* Rebecca Tsosie, *Who Controls Native Cultural Heritage? "Art," "Artifacts," and the Right to Cultural Survival*, CULTURAL HERITAGE ISSUES: THE LEGACY OF CONQUEST, COLONIZATION, AND COMMERCE (2009); *see also* Tsosie, Reclaiming Native Stories, *supra* note 24, at 317–332.
[26] *See* Tsosie, Reclaiming Native Stories, *supra* note 24 at 317–332.
[27] GOLDBERG ET AL., *supra* note 18, at 30.
[28] Indian Citizenship Act of 1924, ch. 233, 43 Stat. 253 (1924) (codified at 8 U.S.C. § 1401(b) (2012)).
[29] GOLDBERG ET AL., *supra* note 18 at 13–39, 111–12.

and their members.[30] American Indian and Alaska Native peoples are members of their tribal Nations, as well as full citizens of the United States and the states where they reside. They are free to practice the religion of their choice, can attend public or private schools, and may reside on or off the reservation. Some would say that we are no longer in an era of colonialism because citizenship guarantees the same autonomy of choice that all members of U.S. civil society possess. However, I argue that we are currently in a third and perhaps final phase of colonialism, which is quite insidious because it operates at the level of consciousness. We all possess beliefs that are deeply programmed into our subconscious minds and these beliefs inform our actions and our beliefs about what is "possible." As collectives and as individuals, who do we think that "we" are and who do we think that "they" are? Have "we" become "them"? Do we mirror who "they" think that "we" are? Clearly, identity matters. But who decides the rules? And as we address the issue of Indigenous cultural rights, do we operate by the principles of just governance in a civil society? Or do we operate by the principles of war?

These are complex questions and they merit sustained attention. This essay will frame the components of the debate as a way to expand the dialogue about the rights of Native artists and the role of Indigenous rights in "cultural production," which is a process that involves many different dynamics, including social media, the entertainment industry, the art industry, the marketplace, the laws that govern the rights of "individuals" to their creations (intellectual

---

[30] *See generally* GOLDBERG ET AL., *supra* note 18, at 382-94 (discussing tribal governmental structures and functions in the modern era); 1–18 COHEN'S HANDBOOK OF FEDERAL INDIAN LAW § 4.04 (Nell Jessup Newton ed., 2012).

property law), and the laws that govern the rights of tribal governments to their cultures (Federal Indian law). In discussing "American" cultural production, I will build on an insight made by Kevin Gover, Director of the National Museum of the American Indian, at a recent lecture given at Arizona State University.[31] Gover discussed an upcoming exhibit at the National Museum of the American Indian (NMAI) entitled "Americans," noting that until the 1700s, the term was used exclusively to reference Indigenous peoples in the Americas. However, over time, the term "Americans" has become synonymous with the people of the United States. The United States was birthed from British colonies and presumably built upon a British cultural tradition. This is clearly illustrated by our categories of law and philosophy, which continue to inform the discussion about rights and what is a legal issue, versus a moral issue. However, the United States has constructed itself as a multicultural democracy through a mode of cultural production that draws heavily upon its "Indigenous" heritage. Does the cultural heritage of Indigenous peoples belong to the United States? Or is this appropriation of Indigenous cultural identity the final act of colonialism in a centuries-long struggle to claim victory over the Indigenous Nations of this land?

That question is of increasing importance since technology can enhance our capacity to generate creative expression, but it can also further confuse cultural identity. This essay highlights the contemporary policy issues and argues for Indigenous nations to develop their own governance systems for "traditional cultural expression," which is the term used by nation-states to describe a default category of

---

[31] Kevin Gover, Dir., Nat'l Museum of the Am. Indian, Lecture at the Sandra Day O'Connor College of Law Indigenous Stereotypes in Sports Symposium (Jan. 30, 2015).

cultural heritage that contains anything that is not formally protected under existing intellectual property laws.[32] In addition, individual Native artists should be active participants in the dialogue about the relationship between art and cultural identity and what falls within the category of permissible cultural production, as a system of voluntary and appropriate cultural sharing and exchange. This must be contrasted with what falls within the category of cultural misappropriation, meaning the involuntary and exploitive transfer of value and benefit from the Indigenous group to the dominant producers and consumers of the global arts economy.[33] Currently, public policy is unable to differentiate the permissible use of Indigenous cultural expression from its misuse, and Indigenous peoples are the only ones who can speak to this.[34] I will argue that the rules of civil society should govern this debate in a spirit of just and respectful intercultural exchange between Indigenous

---

[32] In 2013, the World Intellectual Property Organization (WIPO) sought comment on a draft Treaty dealing with the Protection of Traditional Cultural Expression. In that draft, Traditional Cultural Expression is defined as "any form of artistic and literary expression, tangible and/or intangible, or a combination thereof, . . . in which traditional culture and knowledge are embodied . . . [and] which is intergenerational, . . . including, but not limited to phonetic and verbal expressions, musical and sound expressions, expressions by action, tangible expressions, and adaptations of these expressions." The notes to the text clarify that the category encompasses stories, epics, legends, poetry, narratives, songs, rituals, dance, plays, ceremonies, and games, as well as "material expressions of art, handicrafts, ceremonial masks or dress, handmade carpets, architecture and sacred places." Intergovernmental Committee on Intellectual Property and Genetic Resources, Traditional Knowledge and Folklore, *The Protection of Traditional Cultural Expressions: Draft Articles*, WIPO/GRTKF/IC/27/5 (Jan. 22, 2014) [hereinafter "Draft Articles"], *available at* http://www.wipo.int/edocs/mdocs/tk/en/wipo_grtkf_ic_27/wipo_grtkf_ic_27_5.pdf.
[33] Finnerty, *supra* note 8 (distinguishing the two sets of cases).
[34] *Id.*

peoples and the various national and global governance systems. However, if this is not possible, we should at least understand the rules of the war that we are engaged in, and we should acknowledge the battlegrounds that exist at the level of consciousness and in the material world that drives our economic system.

In the text that follows, I will sketch my ideas in a chronological form, so that the reader can understand the relationship of Indigenous cultural identity to the rights of cultural production in the modern era. Part II of the paper discusses the context for the debate by examining the historical and modern context of cultural imagery, as it has affected Native peoples. Part III discusses identity harms and the role of tribal governments in regulating the protection of Native culture under existing domestic law. Part IV of the paper focuses on the rights of Native artists to their creations and the principles that U.S. law invokes for determining rights claims. In Part V, the paper discusses the broader implications of these issues for Indigenous peoples, focusing on international human rights law as a tool to define Indigenous governance over cultural identity.

II. COLONIALISM, CULTURAL IMAGERY, AND NATIVE PEOPLES

As Professor Robert Williams notes in his brilliant critique of Western civilization, *Savage Anxieties*, Western European peoples have, for centuries, employed the cultural imagery of the "savage" to divest other peoples (including Indigenous peoples) of their rights and to reinvent their own governments and societies in the process.[35] Williams argues that "without

---

[35] ROBERT A. WILLIAMS, JR., SAVAGE ANXIETIES: THE INVENTION OF WESTERN CIVILIZATION 1 (2012).

the idea of the savage to understand what it is, what is was, and what it could be, Western civilization, as we know it, would never have been able to invent itself."[36] In particular, Western philosophers and jurists relied on the notion of an "irreconcilable difference between civilization and savagery" to shape and direct the nature of the policies that would govern their interaction with these peoples.[37]

Building on his prior work, Williams demonstrates how the cultural imagery of the "savage" justified the Doctrine of Discovery, under which Western European nations appropriated lands in the Americas for their "ownership" and control during the colonial era; the same cultural imagery was invoked to birth a new nation, the United States, and to justify its claims for land acquisition during the nineteenth and early twentieth centuries.[38] Today, Williams claims, this dynamic reprises in stereotypes of Native peoples and legal justifications for policies that would otherwise reflect an illegitimate form of racism under

---

[36] *Id.*
[37] *Id.*
[38] *See id.* at 224–25. The Doctrine of Discovery was first applied under international law to vacant lands in order to validate the ownership of the first Nation to discover such lands. However, it was then extended during the era of European colonialism to validate the claims of civilized Christian nations to colonize areas inhabited by uncivilized and non-Christian peoples (heathens and infidels in India and the Middle East, as well as Native peoples throughout the Americas). Chief Justice John Marshall imported the Doctrine of Discovery into Federal Indian law in the famous case of *Johnson v. McIntosh*, which held that Great Britain and its successor, the United States, retained the fee interest in the lands that they discovered and settled, except for the "right of occupancy" (aboriginal title), which allowed Native people to remain in possession of their lands until their title of occupancy was extinguished by the European sovereign by purchase or conquest. *See* 21 U.S. 543 (1823). The Doctrine of Discovery thus established a hierarchy of authority that subordinated Indigenous governance systems.

contemporary law.[39] Native stereotypes continue while the overt caricatures of Black, Latino, and Asian peoples have disappeared from the contemporary marketplace.[40] Thus, in the twenty-first century, the Western world's "most advanced nation-states continue to perpetuate the stereotypes and clichéd images of human savagery that were first invented by the ancient Greeks to justify their ongoing violations of the most basic human rights of cultural survival belonging to indigenous tribal peoples."[41]

Williams identifies these doctrines as the most dangerous threat to the continuing survival of the world's indigenous peoples because it normalizes the hierarchical and exploitive relationship created by colonialism.[42] As Williams and Echo-Hawk point out, the failure to recognize adequate legal rights to tribal cultural protection constitutes a compelling human rights problem in this country. This battle is intangible, and therefore it remains unseen and unacknowledged by most citizens in contemporary society, even by some of those who are Indigenous. The battle involves identity, power, and the right to claim the essence of an Indigenous people as belonging to the European-derived nations that claim rights through discovery. This mode of engagement served the European nations as they appropriated Native lands, through the concept of the "public domain," and it continues to serve descendants of European nations today as they appropriate Native identities.[43]

---

[39] WILLIAMS, *supra* note 35, at 225.
[40] *See* Marty Westerman, *Death of the Frito Bandito*, AM. DEMOGRAPHICS Mar. 1989, at 28.
[41] *Id.* at 9.
[42] *Id.*
[43] *See* statement by Professor James Anaya, Special Rapporteur on the rights of Indigenous peoples, twenty-third session of the World Intellectual Property Organization, Intergovernmental Commission,

There is clearly an element of racism at work, given the cultural imagery of the savage. However, Federal Indian law neatly sidesteps the issue of racism by affirming that federally-recognized American Indian and Alaska Native governments are political, rather than racial, groups, and that their rights are governed by the unique rules of Federal Indian law, as opposed to the rules that govern equality of citizenship for members of racial minorities. With limited exceptions, contemporary U.S. civil rights law disclaims the need to treat citizens differently based upon their status as members of "racial or ethnic minority groups."[44] Today, all laws that create race-based classifications, whether beneficial (i.e., affirmative action) or harmful, are evaluated under strict scrutiny for purposes of the equal protection clause.[45] In comparison, the United States routinely passes special legislation to secure the political rights of the Native Nations that are in a trust relationship with the United States.[46] These laws are treated very deferentially, applying only the minimal level of review to determine whether they are rationally related to the government's trust responsibility.[47]

Today, tribal attorneys build on the Federal Indian law framework to argue for Indigenous cultural rights

---

Feb. 4, 2013, at 3 (comparing notion of the public domain with the Terra Nullius doctrine) [hereinafter Professor Anaya statement].
[44] *See, e.g.,* 42 U.S.C. §§ 300u-6, 2000e-16 (2012) (government employment is free from discrimination on the basis of "race, color, religion, sex, or national origin").
[45] *See* Adarand Constructors, Inc. v. Pena, 515 U.S. 200 (1995) (holding that all racial classifications authorized by any governmental actor must be analyzed by the reviewing court under strict scrutiny).
[46] Title 25 of the U.S. Code is devoted to the rights of tribal governments. *See* 25 U.S.C. §§ 1–44 (2012).
[47] *See, e.g.,* Morton v. Mancari, 417 U.S. 535, 555 (1974) ("As long as the special treatment can be tied rationally to the fulfillment of Congress' unique obligation toward the Indians, such legislative judgments will not be disturbed.").

under the guidance of the political right to self-determination. As Professor James Anaya points out, the norm of self-determination encompasses a right to cultural integrity for Indigenous peoples.[48] The self-determination argument works well with tangible resources such as land and cultural patrimony. It is less successful as applied to intangible resources because the relationship of Native culture to self-determination is much more nuanced and complex. This is due to the historical legacy of cultural imagery that was employed to divest Indigenous peoples of their rights to land and cultural identity, as well as the modern trend to normalize "cultural borrowing" as a means to contemporary cultural production.[49] After 500 years of contact, the line between European and Indigenous culture is blurred and any attempt to fence out an intrusion or appropriation meets resistance unless it falls within a classic case of copyright or trademark violation.

Furthermore, in the case of stereotyping, it is not always obvious that the political status of tribal governments can insulate them from the multiple harms that stereotyping causes to tribal identity, and individually to tribal members.[50] Indeed, as philosopher Miranda Fricker points out, our basic social interactions tend to have profound impacts upon particular groups, and epistemic injustice can arise when individuals are harmed in their ability to convey knowledge to others

---

[48] S. JAMES ANAYA, INDIGENOUS PEOPLES IN INTERNATIONAL LAW 111 (2d ed. 2004).
[49] *See* Christine Hoff Kraemer, *Cultural Borrowing/Cultural Appropriation: A Relationship Model For Respectful Borrowing*, 2 THORN MAG. 36 (2009).
[50] *E.g.*, CNN Wire Staff, *Native Americans Object to Linking Geronimo to bin Laden*, CNN (May 6, 2011, 5:55 AM), http://www.cnn.com/2011/US/05/05/bin.laden.geronimo/index.html.

or to make sense of their own experience.[51] In such cases, the "politics of epistemic practice" determine how social power operates to produce injustice in everyday social practices. A group can be harmed in its ability to participate equally in creating a given social experience, including defining what constitutes art.[52] Is art the individual creation of an artist? Does it comprise the tribe's own form of culturally authorized cultural production; through songs, designs, ceremonies, symbols, and the like? According to Fricker, when a group is excluded from exerting power within an institution, such as legislative or judicial bodies, which controls the terms of their own experience, injustice arises.[53] Similarly, when individuals who object to the dominant system are targeted as militants or not representative of the group itself, they suffer a further injustice that impairs their ability to convey valid or relevant information because they have been labeled as unreliable or not meriting credibility. Indigenous peoples have been affected by epistemic injustice in many categories of public policy and these dynamics exist in the current debates over Native control over culture and art.[54]

The next section will discuss the impact of stereotyping as a form of identity harm, arguing that certain forms of cultural production are employed to negate the ability of tribal governments to control intangible aspects of cultural heritage.

---

[51] *See* MIRANDA FRICKER, EPISTEMIC INJUSTICE: POWER AND THE ETHICS OF KNOWING 1 (2007).
[52] *Id.* at 153–54.
[53] *Id.*
[54] *See generally* Rebecca Tsosie, *Indigenous Peoples and Epistemic Injustice: Science, Ethics, and Human Rights*, 87 WASH. L. REV. 1133 (2012).

III. NATIONAL IDENTITY, TRIBAL IDENTITY, AND IDENTITY HARM

The law is a social institution that broadly involves power relations between the national government and its citizens, and between the United States and Native Nations. In the former case, the government and its citizens share a political identity within civil society, although pluralistic democracies must manage diverse cultural identities. Modern pluralistic democracies, such as the United States, tend to do this under the project of "multiculturalism," which Professor Steven Vertovec describes as a diversity management strategy that promotes "tolerance and respect for collective identities" associated with specific cultural groups.[55] This requires an overall understanding of the dominant identity of the national government, as well as the careful management of racial and ethnic minorities to ensure that they enjoy equal citizenship, meaning equal access to political and civil rights. Notably, under this model, religion and other forms of cultural differences are tolerated and accommodated to the extent possible, consistent with other national objectives.[56] However, there is no right to culture within the United States, and therefore, attributes of minority cultures, such as language and other cultural practices, are not affirmatively protected or preserved, unless they are part of the national culture, such as designated historic sites.[57]

The question of what belongs within the dominant cultural identity of the national government, and what

---

[55] *See* Steven Vertovec, *Super-Diversity and Its Implications*, 30 ETHNIC & RACIAL STUD. 1024, 1027, 1047 (2007).
[56] *Id.* at 1027.
[57] *See* Tsosie, Reclaiming Native Stories, *supra* note 24 at 332-46 (identifying the arguments for and against legal protection for a "right to culture").

belongs within the minority group's cultural identity, may be clear in Great Britain and other European countries. However, it is a difficult question in settler nations, such as the United States, Canada, and New Zealand, at least in relation to Indigenous peoples. In the quest for a separate national identity, the United States, like many other settler countries, appropriated Indigenous land and cultural imagery as a way to establish its own identity separately from its British forebears. This is clearly demonstrated by the role of the museum in settler states, such as Canada, the United States, New Zealand, and Australia, which focused on "creating a common identity for the new nation, pluralistic in nature, descended from Europe, but located on new lands separated from Europe."[58] Throughout its history, the United States has appropriated Indigenous names and symbols to build federal power, including use of Native images and identities on U.S. currency, and military operations and equipment (e.g. the Apache helicopter, "Operation Geronimo").[59] Similarly, the United States has built a national creation mythology around the encounter of Europeans with Indians (e.g. Pocahontas and John Rolfe, Sacajawea and Lewis and Clark).[60] Even if the images portray Native people positively, they are invoked to build the country's national identity.

Conversely, the negative stereotypes of the Indian as a "savage" that Professor Williams discusses were used

---

[58] Rebecca Tsosie, *Native Nations and Museums: Developing an Institutional Framework for Cultural Sovereignty*, 45 U. TULSA L. REV. 3, 6 (2000).
[59] 'Geronimo': Native Americans Blast Bin Laden Code Name, NBCNEWS.COM, http://www.nbcnews.com/id/42897871/ns/world_news-death_of_bin_laden/t/geronimo-native-americans-blast-bin-laden-code-name/#.VVMIWkaGNqw (last updated May 4, 2011).
[60] Gover, *supra* note 31.

to justify federal paternalism to take Indian land, children, religions, and cultural objects for the "good of the Indians" in the nineteenth century.[61] Although modern policymakers disclaim any continuing intent to invoke cultural racism, stereotypes about Native peoples persists in American culture, politics, and sports, thus perpetuating the historical consciousness about Native identity within contemporary society. It is important to note that this national consciousness undermines the ability of Indigenous peoples to participate as equals in the construction of their contemporary identities, labeling such exercises as mere efforts to establish what is politically correct. In this world, the "good" Indian still passively relies on the non-Indian benefactor to create value for tribal existence, as demonstrated by Dan Snyder's attempt to gain the support of nationally recognized tribal leaders and organizations for the Washington Team's mascot. The "bad" Indians who demonstrate and voice opposition are dismissed as troublemakers and malcontents, as were the nineteenth century Indigenous patriot leaders, such as Sitting Bull, Crazy Horse, and Geronimo. The end result is that the United States government maintains the power to use Native identities for its purposes without being accountable for the harms to Native peoples. In fact, the use of cultural imagery is often protected as freedom of expression for purposes of the U.S. Constitution.[62]

Clearly, American Indian and Alaska Native peoples have been affected by stereotypes throughout history. For purposes of this essay, it is necessary to examine who controls the image of the "Indian" in

---

[61] *See* Rebecca Tsosie, Cultural Challenges to Biotechnology, *supra* note 9 at 403.
[62] Rebecca Tsosie, *Reclaiming Native Stories: An Essay on Cultural Appropriation and Cultural Rights*, 34 ARIZ. ST. L.J. 299, 347-49 (2002).

contemporary society. Are cultural images and identities considered property, in the sense that they can be owned and commercialized? Or are these images merely ideas that are beyond government regulation and are available for appropriation by others?

A. Stereotyping and Identity Harm

Stereotyping is a primary source of prejudice in which a biased attitude can manifest in legally prohibited behavior, such as discrimination, but is not, itself, actionable.[63] For this reason, the case against stereotyping is best made by identifying its function. Miranda Fricker describes stereotypes as "widely held associations between a given social group and one or more attributes."[64] Fricker asserts that stereotyping is one of the primary ways in which members of a society make "credibility judgments" about other members, to include them, privilege them, or exclude them from a given social practice.[65] In this way, stereotyping is linked to other forms of injustice and can serve as a means of invoking identity power.

Identity power is of particular importance because many social interactions depend upon the participants' mutual understanding of their social power.[66] Feminist scholars, for example, point out that men can use their male identity to influence a woman, perhaps by patronizing or intimidating her.[67] These subtle forms of domination, sometimes framed as

---

[63] Kerri Lynn Stone, *Clarifying Stereotyping*, 59 U. KAN. L. REV. 591 (2011) (discussing how stereotyping becomes actionable as discrimination).
[64] FRICKER, *supra* note 51, at 30.
[65] *Id.*
[66] *Id.* at 14 ("Whenever there is an oprtaion of power that depends in some significant degree upon...shared imaginative conceptions of social identify, then *identity power* is at work.").
[67] Tsosie, Indigenous Peoples and Epistemic Injustice, *supra* note 54, at 1154 (citing *id.* at 17).

"microaggressions," are not actionable under the law as gender discrimination, and yet, they may have a very harmful impact upon women's rights to equality under the law.[68] Similarly, tribal governments should care deeply about forms of cultural imagery that are used to portray Native peoples, because those stereotypes link up to a variety of harms, including economic exploitation, or, in the case of Native women, interpersonal violence.[69]

As Professor Anita Bernstein demonstrates in her article *What's Wrong With Stereotyping?*, contemporary stereotyping represents a struggle between liberty and equality.[70] Those who maintain that they have a constitutionally protected right to engage in symbolic speech, such as the use of mascots and other forms of negative cultural imagery about other groups, are asserting a degree of liberty that has adverse consequences for other groups, such as racial minorities and women. Stereotyping adversely affects those groups by constraining their opportunities, but the law does not acknowledge this harm. Instead, proponents of liberty often point out that all groups stereotype each other (Republicans and Democrats, Yankees and

---

[68] Robin Lukes & Joann Bangs, *A Critical Analysis of Anti-Discrimination Law and Microaggressions in Academia*, 24 RES. HIGHER EDUC. J. 1, 3 (2014) ("By their very nature, many microaggressions are not legally prohibited, because they are 'everyday verbal, nonverbal, and environmental slights, snubs, or insults.'" (quoting DERALD WING SUE, MICROAGGRESSIONS IN EVERYDAY LIFE: RACE, GENDER, AND SEXUAL ORIENTATION 7 (John Wiley & Sons, Inc. 2010)), *available at* http://www.aabri.com/manuscripts/141824.pdf); *see* Derald Wing Sue, *Microaggressions: More than Just Race*, MICROAGGRESSIONS IN EVERYDAY LIFE (Nov. 17, 2010), https://www.psychologytoday.com/blog/microaggressions-in-everyday-life/201011/microaggressions-more-just-race.

[69] Shan Li, *supra* note 11 (cultural imagery sexualizes native women and promotes sexual violence).

[70] *See* Anita Bernstein, *What's Wrong with Stereotyping?*, 55 ARIZ. L. REV. 655 (2013).

Southerners, Texans and New Yorkers, French and English, Catholics and Protestants) because all groups have a "type" (a set of characteristics and mannerisms) which is invoked, often humorously (e.g. the "redneck") to poke fun at one's own group or others. In other words, this is just what people do. What is the harm?

Bernstein responds by noting that if groups operate on an equal basis of power in their social interactions, stereotyping is not harmful and it quite frequently *is* humorous.[71] However, she points out that there are several stereotypes that we should care about because they affect vulnerable groups and perpetuate harm by painting the vulnerable group as stupid, crazy, irrational, violent, predatory, brutish, or subhuman.[72] In these cases, there is a historical pattern to the use of stereotypes that identify traits associated with the group that (1) denigrates the group, (2) substantiates the dominant consciousness that the trait is actually true, and therefore (3) justifies a negative assertion of social power to control the group.[73] This dynamic was also invoked by the Framers of the Constitution to justify the assertion that African peoples, who were imported into the United States to serve as slaves, should be counted as three fifths of a person[74] while white persons were counted as full persons. This diminished status was justified by the view, expressed most overtly in the infamous *Dred Scott* case, that Africans, as a race, possessed a set of inferior traits that made enslavement the best destiny for them.[75] Justice Taney wrote that Africans had, for more than a century, been "regarded as beings of an inferior order, and altogether unfit to

---

[71] *Id.* at 664.
[72] *Id.* at 665.
[73] *Id.* at 720.
[74] U.S. CONST., art. I, § 2, cl. 3, *amended by* U.S. CONST. amend. XIV.
[75] *See* Dred Scott v. Sandford, 60 U.S. (19 How.) 393 (1856), *superseded by constitutional amendment*, U.S. CONST. amend. XIV.

associate with the white race."[76] He found that they had been regarded as having "no rights which the white man was bound to respect; and that the Negro might justly and lawfully be reduced to slavery for his benefit."[77]

Even after the passage of the Fourteenth Amendment, this form of dehumanizing imagery justified the social subordination of African American people under the distorted logic of *Plessy v. Ferguson*, which described racism as a social problem, rather than a legal problem, thereby justifying official government policies of segregation as a permissible form of social management.[78] The separate-but-equal doctrine established by *Plessy*[79] was ultimately overruled in the realm of K-12 public school education by the 1954 Supreme Court case of *Brown v. Board of Education*,[80] followed by the more comprehensive reforms of the Civil Rights Act of 1964[81] and subsequent civil rights legislation. However, racial equality remains elusive in the United States. Today, our society espouses "formal equality," meaning that we resist most overt racial classifications. Yet, implicit racial biases are deeply embedded, and today the negative assertion of power

---

[76] *Id.* at 407.
[77] *Id.*
[78] Plessy v. Ferguson, 163 U.S. 537 (1896) *overruled by* Brown v. Bd. of Ed. of Topeka, Shawnee County, Kan., 347 U.S. 483 (1954).
[79] *Id.* at 551, 561 (upholding Louisiana law segregating public transportation by restricting railway carriages for "white" and "colored" citizens on the theory that "separate but equal accommodations" regulate social norms and are therefore consistent with the Fourteenth Amendment's call for political equality).
[80] *Brown*, 347 U.S. 483 (1954) *supplemented sub nom.* Brown v. Bd. of Educ. of Topeka, Kan., 349 U.S. 294 (1955) (holding that racially segregated public schools are "inherently unequal" because they deny equal educational opportunity to children and impede their development as citizens in a democratic society).
[81] Civil Rights Act of 1964, Pub. L. No. 88-352, 78 Stat. 241 (1964) (codified as amended in scattered sections of 2 U.S.C., 28 U.S.C., and 42 U.S.C.).

can manifest as prejudice, which is generally not actionable because it is a private state of mind, or as discrimination, which is actionable if it violates a civil rights statute, for example, a landlord's refusal to rent property based on the tenant's racial status.

Within contemporary society, the overt racism of the past has evolved into covert racism, a shadow form of disparate treatment that remains unseen by many members of society.[82] These negative assertions of power can be masked as "neutral" policies (e.g., sentencing laws that have disparate impacts upon racial groups), and can also undergird racial profiling and disparate use of force to subdue African American "suspects," most recently demonstrated by the recent events in Ferguson, Missouri.[83] Months after the fatal shooting of Michael Brown, an eighteen-year-old black man, by Officer Darren Wilson, a white law enforcement officer, the U.S. Department of Justice released a report demonstrating that the Ferguson Police Department engaged in "a broad pattern of racially biased enforcement . . . including the use of unreasonable force against African American suspects."[84] Specifically, the report documents that 88% of the cases involving use of force in Ferguson concerned African American suspects.[85] The statistics

---

[82] *See* William Y. Chin, *The Age of Covert Racism in the Era of the Roberts Court During the Waning of Affirmative Action*, 16 RUTGERS RACE & L. REV. 1, 1–2 (2015).
[83] James B. Comey, Dir., Fed. Bureau Investigation, Address at Georgetown University (Feb. 12, 2015) (presenting on the role of implicit bias in criminal justice system), *available at* http://www.fbi.gov/news/speeches/hard-truths-law-enforcement-and-race; *see also* Kevin Johnson & Yamiche Alcindor, *DOJ: Ferguson PD Engaged In Racially Biased Policing*, USA TODAY (Mar. 3, 2015), http://www.usatoday.com/story/news/2015/03/03/ferguson-justice-report/24320987/.
[84] Johnson & Alcindor, *supra* note 83.
[85] *Id.*

may speak for themselves, but they also align with a history of cultural imagery depicting African American males as violent and given to criminal behavior, which has consistently resulted in a violation of the human rights and civil rights of African American people.

B. Native American Mascots and Identity Harm

Similarly, the use of cultural imagery as a mechanism to subordinate the rights of Native American peoples has been operative throughout history. Professor Williams' work highlights the impact of the construction of Indigenous peoples as "savages."[86] The contemporary use of Indian images as sports mascots illustrates the continuing nature of the problem. The use of these images originated at a time in American history when overt racism and bigotry was the norm in American society.[87] However, today these images are worth millions of dollars as a property interest in the hands of sports franchises such as the Washington Team, the Kansas City Chiefs, the Cleveland Indians, the Atlanta Braves, and the Chicago Blackhawks.[88] Because the use of Native American cultural imagery has been normalized within American society, generations of Americans have grown up with their own ideas about what they ought to be able to do, which includes the use of Indian mascots, even though they would no longer be willing to use overt cultural imagery to mock African Americans, Latinos, or Asians.[89] Although two-thirds of Indian sports images

---

[86] WILLIAMS, *supra* note 35, at 1.
[87] *See* NAT'L CONGRESS OF AM. INDIANS, ENDING THE LEGACY OF RACISM IN SPORTS AND THE ERA OF HARMFUL "INDIAN" SPORTS MASCOTS 2 (October 2013) [hereinafter NCAI REPORT], *available at* http://www.ncai.org/resources/ncaipublications/Ending_the_Legacy_of_Racism.pdf.
[88] *Id.*
[89] The "Frito Bandito" and "Little Black Sambo," for example, disappeared from commercial use during the 1970s. *Frito Bandito,*

and mascots have been eliminated from use during the past thirty-five years, following a course of activism by Native peoples and support by the U.S. Commission on Civil Rights, as well as a host of other professional organizations and associations, there are still over 1,000 Indian sports images in active use, and the Washington Team continues to litigate its right to trademark the "Redskins" team name and image.[90]

What accounts for the disparity between the treatment of these other groups and Native Americans? African Americans, Latinos, and Asians constitute much larger groups within U.S. society, wielding significant economic and political clout, while Native Americans continue to represent less than 2% of the U.S. population.[91] But, the fact that the team owners continue to profit from the use of Native American images as sports mascots means that it is palatable to most Americans to consider these images to be the property of non-Native people. Native images have economic value to American society, demonstrating that the third phase of colonialism is actively in progress. In addition, the use of these images aligns with the intuition of Americans that cultural imagery is a form of constitutionally protected expression (symbolic speech)[92] that merits protection as a liberty interest.

WIKIPEDIA, http://en.wikipedia.org/wiki/Frito_Bandito (last visited Apr. 7, 2015); Marty, Westerman, *Death of the Frito Bandito*, AMERICAN DEMOGRAPHICS (Mar. 1989); Marjorie Rosenthal, *Banned From American Bookshelves: The Story Of Little Black Sambo*, LONG ISLAND BOOK COLLECTORS (Aug. 11, 2013), http://longislandbookcollectors.com/2013/%EF%BB%BFbanned-from-american-bookshelves-the-story-of-little-black-sambo.
[90] NCAI REPORT, *supra* note 87, at 6, 10–15.
[91] *Id.* at 5.
[92] Examples of protected symbolic speech can be found in *Virginia v. Black*, 538 U.S. 343 (2003) (cross burning), *United States v. Eichman*, 496 U.S. 310 (1990) (flag burning), and *United States v. O'Brien*, 391 U.S. 367 (1968) (burning a draft card), among others.

And finally, the use of Native American cultural imagery is not cast as racism, but as a way to "honor" the Native American people. In other words, Americans have created themselves, through the use of Native American cultural imagery, a continuation of the dynamic that Williams describes in relation to the mythology of the "savage" as means to construct Western civilization.

Within the third phase of colonialism, the commercial value of "Indian identity" belongs to non-Indians. This is being litigated right now in federal court, following a recent ruling by the U.S. Patent and Trademark Office Trademark Trial and Appeal Board in *Blackhorse v. Pro-Football, Inc.*, which cancelled six active trademark registrations for the "Redskins" on the grounds that this symbol disparages Native American people within the meaning of the federal Trademark laws.[93] This ruling is currently being challenged by the Washington Team in a federal district court lawsuit that seeks to protect the right of the team to profit from the name.[94] If the Native American petitioners prevail, the use of the term "Redskins" will lack Trademark protection, meaning that Pro-Football, Inc. will have no federally protected property interest in the team name. This ruling, of course, does not affect the ability of individuals or corporations to use the term in other

---

[93] Blackhorse v. Pro-Football Inc., 111 U.S.P.Q.2d 1080 (T.T.A.B. 2014); *see also* Zoe Tillman, *Judge Rules Redskins Trademark Case Can Move Forward*, LEGALTIMES (Nov. 25, 2014 12:09 P.M.), http://www.nationallawjournal.com/legaltimes/id=1202677398589/Judge-Rules-Redskins-Trademark-Defense-Can-Move-Forward?slreturn=20150228133911 (discussing ruling of U.S. District Court Judge Gerald Bruce Lee which denied motion of Native American petitioners to dismiss the appeal, finding that Pro-Football has a significant economic interest in the Trademarks which justifies appeal).
[94] Tillman, *supra* note 93.

ways that would be offensive to Native American people.

For example, several years ago, the Hornell Brewing Company used the name of a revered nineteenth century Lakota leader, Crazy Horse, to market a Malt Liquor product: "Crazy Horse Malt Liquor."[95] At the request of outraged tribal leaders, Congress held hearings on the matter and concluded that the name should be cancelled because the company was intentionally marketing the product to Native youth and creating further social problems for these impoverished communities with high rates of alcoholism, traffic related fatalities, and youth suicides.[96] The federal court disagreed, holding that the company's use of the name was constitutionally protected commercial speech, and that the government had impermissibly acted by banning the speech.[97] When the descendants of Crazy Horse attempted to sue Hornell Brewing Company in tribal court for a cultural tort, based upon defamation of their ancestor's spirit and the family by unauthorized use of the leader's name to market liquor, the federal courts held that the tribal court lacked jurisdiction over the Hornell Brewing Company, which was not doing business on the reservation.[98]

The above cases demonstrate that harms to a name or cultural identity are not actionable unless they can be tied to a specific violation of existing law. So, for example, tribal governments have a legal right to

---

[95] Nell Jessup Newton, *Memory and Misrepresentation: Representing Crazy Horse in Tribal Court*, BORROWED POWER: ESSAYS ON CULTURAL APPROPRIATION 195, 201 (Bruce Ziff & Patima V. Rao eds. 1997).
[96] 102 CONG. REC. S13, 420 (daily ed. Sept. 14, 1992).
[97] Hornell Brewing Co. v. Brady, 819 F. Supp. 1227, 1228 (E.D.N.Y. 1993).
[98] Hornell Brewing Co. v. Rosebud Sioux Tribal Court, 133 F.3d 1087, 1093 (9th Cir. 1998).

regulate the use of their tribal name through trademark law. As an aspect of their authority, they can license use of the tribal name to third parties (as the Seminoles have done) or they can prosecute unauthorized uses of the tribal name, as the Navajo Nation did with Urban Outfitters.[99] Contemporary Native artists and tribal governments can invoke the provisions of the Indian Arts and Crafts Act to prevent non-Indians from falsely marketing their goods as "Indian made" or the product of a specific Indian tribe.[100] Both actions constitute a form of deceptive advertising that causes consumer harm.[101] Tribal governments do not generally retain the exclusive right to produce particular art forms, such as rugs or baskets, even if there are distinctive design qualities to these traditional arts. So long as the producer of an item is, in fact, "Indian" for purposes of the Indian Arts and Crafts Act, he or she has the right to freely produce "Indian" art. Conversely, so long as a producer of an item correctly labels his or her art as "inspired by Native American designs," he or she may freely appropriate Indigenous art forms. Individual

---

[99] The Seminole Tribe of Florida has authorized Florida State University to retain the "Seminoles" Team name. *See* Robert Andrew Powell, *Florida State Can Keep its Seminoles,* THE NEW YORK TIMES (Aug. 24, 2005), http://www.nytimes.com/2005/08/24/sports/24mascot.html?pagewanted=all&_r=0. The Navajo Nation successfully challenged the use of the term "Navajo" on Urban Outfitters clothing designs. Navajo Nation v. Urban Outfitters, Inc., 935 F.Supp.2d 1147 (D.N.M. 2013); *see also* Caroline Jamet, *Urban Outfitters Sued for Trademark Infringement by Navajo Nation,* INTELL. PROP. BRIEF: AM. U. WASH. C. L. (June 18, 2012), http://www.ipbrief.net/2012/06/18/urban-outfitters-sued-for-trademark-infringement-by-navajo-nation/.
[100] Indian Arts and Crafts Act of 1990, 25 U.S.C. §§ 305–305e (2012).
[101] False advertising is defined as "[t]he tortious and sometimes criminal act of distributing an advertisement that is untrue, deceptive, or misleading; esp. under the Lanham Act, an advertising statement that tends to mislead consumers about the characteristics, quality, or geographic origin of one's own or someone else's goods, services, or commercial activity." BLACK'S LAW DICTIONARY 719 (10th ed. 2014).

Native American artists generally have the same rights as any artist to obtain protection for their own unique creations under the U.S. copyright laws,[102] and they have the additional right under the Indian Arts and Crafts Act to label their cultural productions as an "Indian product."[103] However, as the next section demonstrates, individual artists and tribal governments generally lack the right to control the use of traditional cultural expression beyond these specific legal categories.[104]

IV. Cultural Production and the Rights of Native Artists

There is a profound conceptual problem at the heart of debates about art as a means of cultural production, which is, that "art" is a category defined by Western views about the relationship of persons to objects, and the categories of legal protection that are available to artists are aligned with that conception.[105] Western philosophy and law worked in tandem to construct the categories of "art" and "artifacts" to differentiate the

---

[102] *See* 17 U.S.C. § 102(a) (2012) (listing copyrightable subject matter). *See also* The Visual Artists Rights Act of 1990, 17 U.S.C. § 106(a) (expanding rights of orators of visual art to include the rights of "attribution" and "integrity."); see Tsosie, Who Controls Native Cultural Heritage, *supra* note 25 at 3-5 (discussing conceptual problems within the law that regulates protection of Indigenous cultural heritage due to the inability of the law to adequately distinguish "objects of art" from "cultural objects"); see also Dr. Jane Anderson, "Access and Control of Indigenous Knowledge in Libraries and Archives: Ownership and Future Use," (May 5-7, 2005) at p. 9 (quoting Australian Indigenous leader Mick Dodson, who stated that "our laws and customs do not fit easily into the pre-existing categories of the Western system. The legal system does not even know precisely what it is in our societies that is in need of protection. *The existing legal system cannot properly embrace what it cannot define and that is what lies at the heart of the problem*.") (emphasis added by Anderson).
[103] 25 U.S.C. §§ 305–305e.
[104] *See* Tsosie, Who Controls Native Cultural Heritage, *supra* note 25.
[105] *Id.*

rights of Western authors who create works of "art" from those of non-Western cultures who produce "artifacts." Today, individual Native artists are actively engaged in cultural production, and there are also significant repositories of tribal art and art forms in the archives of museums and libraries throughout the nation and the world. Indigenous art forms are intergenerational expressions of culture. However, because of the continuing conceptual problems that relate to the categories of "art" and "artifacts," as well as what merits protection under U.S. copyright or trademark law, there is significant confusion about what rights, if any, exist in these tangible and intangible expressions of culture.[106]

A. *The Historic Framing of Art as Cultural Production*

In contemporary America, "art" is perceived as a commodity in the hands of consumers, and creators have limited rights to their original expression, which are defined by copyright law.[107] Our domestic legal system regulates the economic aspects of art as an enterprise by offering a limited incentive to creators to produce original art for the market. However, ideas are freely exchanged and therefore a robust public domain

---

[106] See Olivia J. Greer, *Using Intellectual Property Laws to Protect Indigenous Cultural Property*, 22 NYSBA 27 (discussing the inability of U.S. intellectual property law to "prevent the unauthorized exploitation of tangible and intangible indigenous cultural property"); Anderson, Access and Control of Indigenous Knowledge in Libraries and Archives, *supra* note 102 at 33 (concluding that the failure of existing law to protect Indigenous cultural knowledge and art forms is promoting the institutional development and use of "protocols" which can "prescribe modes of conduct through emphasizing or normalizing particular forms of cultural engagement"); Kimberly Christen, *Opening Archives: Respectful Repatriation*, 74 AM. ARCHIVIST 185 (2011) (discussing a "collaborative archival project aimed at digitally repatriating and reciprocally curating cultural heritage materials of the Plateau tribes in the Pacific Northwest").
[107] 17 U.S.C. § 106 (2012).

is perceived as necessary to serve the public interest in innovation and free expression. Traditional Indigenous art forms are largely seen as part of the public domain because they are ancient "tribal" cultures and there are many "creators" who share this tradition, rather than one individual "artist." In addition, many outsiders see tribal designs as "generic" because they are disassociated from their original cultural context and the meaning of the symbols is not understood by contemporary consumers.[108] In other words, the entire conception of "art" is defined by the relationship of the viewer/consumer to the object, which has been created by the artist. This set of relationships is embedded within the Western philosophy of aesthetics.[109]

Within the philosophy of aesthetics that constructed the category of art, the individual artist is understood to create a work (painting, novel, sculpture, musical arrangement) that evokes a specific response from the viewer. According to Western philosophers, "aesthetic judgment" in the observer is premised on an attitude of "disinterested contemplation," in which the viewer focuses on the item's intrinsic, non-relational, and immediately perceptible properties.[110] Thus, the Western concept of art encompasses objects and things that are susceptible of aesthetic appreciation and the more sophisticated and original the work is, the more it

---

[108] *See* Rebecca Tsosie, Who Controls Native Cultural Heritage, *supra* note 25 at 5-7 (discussing Native and Western cultural views about "art" and "artifacts").

[109] *See* Stephen Davies, *Aesthetic Judgments, Artworks and Functional Beauty*, 56 PHIL. Q. 224–41 (2006) (explaining the historic construction of aesthetics and the ways in which non-Western cultures were excluded from the framework governing art and the rights of creators); *see generally* STEPHEN DAVIES, THE ARTFUL SPECIES: AESTHETICS, ART, AND EVOLUTION (2012) (discussing the possibility of how aesthetics may be partly determined by human biology).

[110] *See* Stephen Davies, *Non-Western Art and Art's Definition*, THEORIES OF ART TODAY 199, 201–02 (Noël Carroll ed., 2000).

is protected by the law as an original work. Original authorship is the key to earning rights within the Western copyright system. The artist is rewarded with certain rights to incentivize his or her creation, and after a specific duration of time, the work will fall into the public domain to serve as inspiration for other artists.[111]

Of course, the philosophy of aesthetics represents a distinctively Western experience. Under the philosophy of aesthetics, tribal art is generally placed within the category of "artifacts," which is a vast repository of "primitive" and "non-Western" cultural expression. "Artifacts" are not considered "art" *even if* they contain elements that inspire aesthetic appreciation. This is why so much "tribal art" ended up in museums of natural history in the nineteenth century, rather than art museums.[112] Western aesthetics also excluded from the cultural category of art "phenomena" that lack significant aspects of "human design" and appeared to largely reflect "objects of nature" (arrangements of shells on a string, for example). To the Western "observer," tribal cultural expression generally falls into the category of "artifacts" or "phenomena." The creator(s) are not considered to have rights of authorship, and therefore tribal designs and symbols are freely appropriated by others as merely "design" elements.[113]

---

[111] 17 U.S.C. §§ 302–03 (2012) (stating the duration of a copyright in a work).

[112] *See* Tsosie, Native Nations and Museums, *supra* note 58, at 7.

[113] *See generally* Kathy M'Closkey, *Up for Grabs: Assessing the Consequences of Sustained Appropriations of Navajo Wavers' Patterns, in* NO DEAL!: INDIGENOUS ARTS AND THE POLITICS OF POSSESSION 128, 129–132 (Tressa Berman ed., 2012) (discussing how the Navajos' rug market was flooded by cheap "knock-off" rugs because the Navajos could not protect their weaving patterns under U.S. law).

Because modern art collectors often trade in "primitive art," the art market must regulate what is the cultural patrimony of nations (for example, Mexico claims a national right to pre-Columbian art), as well as the private property of museums, which are constantly embattled by theft of original works and fraudulent reproductions. Native American cultural patrimony is regulated by statutes such as the Archaeological Resources Protection Act, which protects archaeological resources that are 100 years of age or older on federal and tribal lands,[114] and the Native American Graves Protection and Repatriation Act, which criminalizes trafficking of tribal cultural patrimony and sacred objects.[115] However, there is no domestic law regulating the intangible category of tribal cultural expression. There are countless images on the internet that reflect Native American people, including individuals in photographs; and tribal symbols, songs, designs, and art forms.[116] The question is how to regulate the use of these images. Who owns tribal images and identities in the modern era?

B. Indigenous Perspectives on Art as Cultural Production

The late Elouise Cobell, a Blackfeet woman who was an acclaimed tribal leader, activist, and entrepreneur, said, "Art is the greatest asset Indian people have in our

---

[114] Archaeological Resources Protection Act, 16 U.S.C. §§ 470aa–470mm (2012).
[115] Native American Graves Protection and Repatriation Act, 25 U.S.C. §§ 3001–13 (2012).
[116] See Kimberly Christen, Opening Archives *supra* note 106 at 193 (noting that "Digital technologies and the Internet have combined to produce both the possibility of greater indigenous access to collections, as well as a new set of tensions for communities" who seek to enforce cultural protocols for dealing with circulation of those materials).

communities, yet it is the most underdeveloped."[117] A recent study on the economic value of art to Native communities found that "an estimated 30% of all Native peoples are practicing or potential artists and most live below the poverty line."[118] The same study examined the situation of emerging Native artists and found that they reported an annual household income of less than $10,000.[119] Native artists living on reservations are largely working through home-based enterprises for a cash income.[120] They often live hundreds or even thousands of miles from the urban art markets. They may lack access to electronic markets[121] and they may instead rely upon non-Native gallery owners and agents to market their work to collectors. Clearly, as a group, Native artists lack direct access to a significant portion of the market[122] Because of their disadvantaged status, they are also likely to lack the resources to obtain legal advice on how to use existing intellectual property law to protect their rights as individual artists. In that sense, Native artists are "underserved" by the contemporary legal structure.

As Ms. Cobell noted, however, cultural expression has always been of vital importance to Native peoples.[123] Language and art are linked to tribal, cultural, and spiritual identity.[124] And Native art reflects the

---

[117] ARTSPACE, KATHLEEN PICKERING SHERMAN, FIRST PEOPLES FUND, LEVERAGING INVS. IN CREATIVITY, NW AREA FOUND., ESTABLISHING A CREATIVE ECONOMY: ART AS AN ECONOMIC ENGINE IN NATIVE COMMUNITIES 9 (Marianna Shay, 2013), *available at* https://www.firstpeoplesfund.org/assets/uploads/documents/document-market-study.pdf.
[118] *Id.* at 7.
[119] *Id.* at 17.
[120] *See id.* at 8–9.
[121] *See id.* at 11–12.
[122] *See id.*
[123] *See id* at 1.
[124] *Id.* at 5.

expression of living cultures, which are linked intergenerationally to their ancestors and the generations yet to be born.[125] Because Native art forms often embody traditional practices, including notions of stewardship and appropriate transmission of knowledge, it is incumbent upon Native communities to have the power to regulate cultural art forms. This is the genesis of movements to establish a "cultural trademark" to identify authentic Indigenous art and protect against misappropriation. For example, the Office of Hawaiian Affairs funded a Native Hawaiian Cultural Trademark study, which culminated in a 2007 report recommending the use of a cultural trademark program to protect the authenticity of Native Hawaiian art and the cultural transmission of knowledge that Native Hawaiian arts embody.[126] The Report documented the many issues that arise with any form of cultural certification, but recommended a process that would be consistent with Native Hawaiian practices of cultural transmission of knowledge and the genealogy of Native Hawaiian peoples.[127]

The Maori "Toi Iho" Cultural Trademark program in Aotearoa (New Zealand) is cited by the authors of this report as a model.[128] The Maori "Toi Iho" Certification Trademark was created by a statute passed by the New Zealand parliament "to assist Maori to retain control over their cultural heritage and maintain the integrity of their art culture in an increasingly commercialized

---

[125] *Id.*
[126] *See* HO'OIPO KALAENA'AUAO PA, HALE KU'AI STUDY GRP., NATIVE HAWAIIAN CULTURAL TRADEMARK STUDY: FINDINGS AND RECOMMENDATIONS 38–40 (2007), *available at* http://hawaiiantrademarkstudy.com/Media/TrademarkStudyReport.pdf.
[127] *Id.*
[128] *Id.* at 37–43.

world."[129] The legislation specified that the Certification Mark would be administered through the Arts Council of New Zealand in consultation with a parallel Maori arts agency, Te Waka Toi Cultural Arts Board."[130] The Maori Arts Board is pivotal to the implementation of the program, and the actual Certification Mark is premised on the "Iho," which is the essence of creation and the origin of Maori knowledge and tradition, representing the core of Maori arts.[131] From this core symbol, emanate the "whakapapa" or genealogy lines of past, present and future generations, and there are colored spires in the design, which represent the creativity, innovation, and the dynamism of Maori artists.[132]

Through the use of the Maori cultural trademark, the Maori people have assumed governing authority over their culture and its expression in authentic Maori art that is genealogically and culturally tied to Aotearoa.[133] This includes the traditional art forms of Maori people, which have a rich tradition of transmission of knowledge. But, it also includes the

---

[129] *Id.* at 37.
[130] *Id.*
[131] *Id.*
[132] *Id.* at 39.
[133] *Id.* at 39. *But see* Jessica C. Lai, *Maori Culture in the Modern World: Its Creation, Appropriation, and Trade* 24 (Int'l Commc'ns & Art Law Lucerne, Working Paper No. 02, 2010), *available at* http://papers.ssrn.com/sol3/papers.cfm?abstract_id=1961482 ("On its inception, toi iho was considered to be a world-leading initiative, often cited as a model to be used by other Indigenous peoples. However, the current National Government has decided to cease investment, management, licensing and promotion of toi iho. Creative New England stated that market research showed that it had not achieved increased sales of Maori art by licensed artists or retailers."); LAW LIBRARY OF CONGRESS, GLOBAL LEGAL RESEARCH CTR., NEW ZEALAND: MAORI CULTURE AND INTELLECTUAL PROPERTY LAW (2010), *available at* http://www.loc.gov/law/help/nz-maori-culture/nz-maori-culture-and-intellectual-property-law.pdf.

modern creations and innovations of contemporary Maori artists, who are engaged in a process of cultural production that reflects modern cultural identity. This is a very powerful example of what could happen for Native artists in the United States as a means to exert governance authority over Native American cultural production.

In the United States, inequities extend beyond the level of the individual artist to the level of the Indigenous group as a collective. Many American Indian and Alaska Native Nations continue to possess cultural methods of regulating tribal art forms. However, with a few exceptions, the idea of a "cultural trademark" for specific Indigenous nations has not received sustained attention. In the United States, the Indian Arts and Crafts Act is the only law that protects tribal governments and artisans from overt attempts by non-Indians to falsely market their goods as "Indian-made."[134] However, the federal law is designed to avoid consumer confusion and not to substantiate tribal claims to cultural identity.[135] There are 566 federally recognized tribal governments in the United States, representing many distinctive cultures and language groups.[136] But the cultural distinctiveness of American Indian and Alaska Native Nations is often not seen. Rather, symbols such as the "dream catcher" become part of a generic Indian identity, which is widely appropriated by others. As of 2015, there is no domestic law in the United States regulating the appropriation of

---

[134] *See* 25 U.S.C. § 305a (2012); *see also* Kelly Mauceri, Note, *Of Fakes and Frauds: An Analysis of National American Intangible Cultural Property Protection*, 5 GEO. J. L. & PUB. POL'Y 263, 268 (2007).
[135] Mauceri, *supra* note 134.
[136] INDIAN ENTITIES RECOGNIZED AND ELIGIBLE TO RECEIVE SERVICES FROM THE UNITED STATES BUREAU OF INDIAN AFFAIRS, 80 Fed. Reg. 1942 (Jan. 14, 2015), *available at* http://www.gpo.gov/fdsys/pkg/FR-2015-01-14/pdf/2015-00509.pdf.

intangible tribal cultural heritage. Rather, the discussion of what rights Indigenous peoples have to their "traditional cultural expressions" is largely taking place in the international arena through the agencies of the United Nations and the World Intellectual Property Organization.[137]

The nation-states possess governing authority within those structures and the dominant system of international trade depends upon a robust public domain to serve the commercial interests of consumers and producers in a global economy.[138] Today, intangible cultural heritage is increasingly stored in electronic databases.[139] These archives of "traditional cultural expressions" currently lack clear definition of ownership. Does ownership go to the person or persons who created the database or archive? Does it go to the individuals who produced the recorded expression? Does it go to the Indigenous communities these individuals belong to? Or are these archives part of the "common heritage of all mankind," an open-access resource and creative commons from which others may liberally borrow for their own purposes?

The policy discussion about cultural production will benefit from careful thinking and planning. Indigenous

---

[137] Draft Articles, *supra* note 32.

[138] *See generally* INTERNATIONAL TRADE IN INDIGENOUS CULTURAL HERITAGE: LEGAL AND POLICY ISSUES (CHRISTOPHER B. GRABER, KAROLINA KUPRECHT, & JESSICA C. LAI eds., 2012). *See also* Intergovernmental Committee on Intellectual Property and Genetic Resources, Traditional Knowledge and Folklore, *Note by the Secretariat: Note on the Meanings of the Term "Public Domain" in the Intellectual Property System with Special Reference to the Protection of Traditional Knowledge and Traditional Cultural Expression/Expressions of Folklore*, WIPO/GRTKF/IC/17 (Nov. 24, 2010) [hereinafter Intergovernmental Committee on IP] ("Maintaining a rich and robust public domain is commonly put forward as an important public policy goal.").

[139] *See* Anderson, *supra* note 102, and Christen, *supra* note 106, and accompanying text.

nations should develop their own governance for traditional cultural expression and should be actively involved in the dialogue about the relationship between art and cultural identity.

V. THE ROLE OF INTERNATIONAL LAW IN REGULATING INDIGENOUS CULTURAL EXPRESSION

As this essay has demonstrated, the protection of Indigenous cultural heritage in the United States is limited and largely depends upon the existence of a federal law, such as NAGPRA or the Indian Arts and Crafts Act, which validates specific rights of Indigenous peoples, although the underlying right is often grounded upon Indigenous customary law.[140] To some extent, Indigenous customary law may be incorporated into specific federal laws. For example, under NAGPRA, the very definition of categories, such as "sacred objects" and "objects of cultural patrimony" depends upon the cultural construction given to a particular item by the Native American group under its traditional law.[141] The federal laws protecting Indigenous cultural heritage are exceptional in relation to the general statutory and Constitutional laws of the United States, and the fact that they exist at all is directly related to the advocacy of Native leaders for redress of egregious historical conduct by the United States toward Indigenous peoples.[142]

---

[140] See *infra* note 142 and accompanying text.
[141] *See* 25 USC section 3001 (3) (C) (defining "sacred objects" with reference to traditional Native American religious practices) and (D) (defining "cultural patrimony" with reference to the value accorded under Native American cultural traditions).
[142] See Senator Daniel K. Inouye, "Repatriation: Forging New Relationships," 24 Ariz. St. L. J. 1-3 (1992) (describing the "dark picture of mistreatment" of Native American people and their deceased relatives that led to the enactment of NAGPRA).

Traditional cultural expression is not currently regulated by U.S. domestic law, and international organizations have struggled to define the term in a meaningful way, as illustrated by the 2013 effort of WIPO to create a draft treaty on the governance of traditional cultural expression.[143] If the term is defined broadly as an expansive "cultural commons" which is not protected by existing intellectual property law, then the presumption will be that the nation-states control the overarching governance of Indigenous cultural expression and have the power to include these groups within certain "exceptional" forms of domestic statutory protection (such as the Indian Arts and Crafts Act), or exclude them from protection, enabling the appropriation of Native cultural expression at will by innovative Westerners. In his role as the U.N. Special Rapporteur on the Rights of Indigenous Peoples, Professor James Anaya counseled against such an approach, recommending instead that nation-states should recognize Indigenous peoples' rights to traditional knowledge and other aspects of their cultural heritage in alignment with the standards of international human rights law.[144]

In the text that follows, I will sketch out the existing approach of international law to traditional cultural expression and compare the approach that might be generated under the international human rights law relevant to Indigenous peoples. The choice of approaches will likely be informed by the contemporary dialogue on cultural production and international trade, and I will draw on that dialogue in my discussion, acknowledging that there is no global consensus on the outer boundaries of this dynamic.

---

[143] *See* WIPO treaty, *supra* note 32; Intergovernmental Committee on IP, *supra* note 32.

[144] See Anaya, *supra* note 48 at 7.

A. Traditional Cultural Expression

The effort to create an equitable set of policies for the governance of traditional cultural expression has been ongoing for several decades. In 1989, UNESCO defined "traditional cultural expression" as:

> The totality of tradition-based creations of a cultural community, expressed by a group or individuals and recognized as reflecting the expectations of a community insofar as they reflect its culture and social identity; its standards and values are transmitted orally, by imitation or by other means. Its forms are, among others, language, literature, music, dance, games, mythology, rituals, customs, handicrafts, architecture and other arts.[145]

In 2005, UNESCO adopted the Convention on the Protection and Promotion of the Diversity of Cultural Expressions with the stated objective of encouraging an intercultural dialogue that would promote respectful interchange among diverse cultural groups.[146] The 2005 Convention noted the link between culture and

---

[145] 1 UNITED NATIONS EDUCATIONAL, SCIENTIFIC AND CULTURAL ORG., Records of the General Conference, 25th Session 239 (1989), *available at* http://unesdoc.unesco.org/images/0008/000846/084696e.pdf#page=242.

[146] *See* Rebecca Tsosie, *International Trade in Indigenous Cultural Heritage: An Argument for Indigenous Governance of Cultural Property*, INTERNATIONAL TRADE IN INDIGENOUS CULTURAL HERITAGE: LEGAL AND POLICY ISSUES (CHRISTOPHER B. GRABER, KAROLINA KUPRECHT, & JESSICA C. LAI eds., 2012) 233-34 and footnote 37 (discussing 2005 UNESCO Convention on the Protection and Promotion of the Diversity of Cultural Expressions. 2440 UNTS 311 (adopted on 20 October 2005, entered into force 18 March 2007).

development as a common interest of global nations and called for an ethic of "partnership" among the nation-states, indicating that this would best serve their collective interest in promoting productive international trade. Significantly, this Convention upholds the sovereignty of the nation-states to implement the measures that they deem necessary to foster the diversity of cultural expressions within their territorial boundaries. Nation-states are encouraged to be sensitive to the special needs and circumstances of particular groups and cultures, while promoting an overall ethic of productive collaboration around the use of traditional cultural expression.

In the hands of the communities of origin, traditional cultural expression is a mechanism to transmit culture across multiple generations and to ensure the cultural survival of these cultural communities. Therefore, some commentators argue for a strong theory of group rights to traditional cultural expression, equivalent to standard categories of intellectual property rights, but situated in cultural communities rather than particular individuals.[147] However, traditional cultural expression is often contained in the databases and archives of museums and libraries, and there are no uniform policies on governance of these resources.[148] Libraries and museums play an important role in preserving and providing access to cultural heritage throughout the world, and some commentators argue against validating

---

[147] *See, e.g.*, Angela R. Riley, *Recovering Collectivity: Group Rights to Intellectual Property in Indigenous Communities*, 18 CARDOZO ARTS & ENT. L.J. 175 (2000).
[148] Anderson, *supra* note 102 at 4 (noting that "in most cases, Indigenous people are not the legal copyright owners of the material," which means that they cannot control how the material is used and accessed, and further noting that much of what they seek to protect "is already in the public domain").

cultural rights in the communities of origin on the theory that libraries, archives, and museums have a duty to safeguard this knowledge as the "common heritage of all mankind."[149] Under this view, the purpose of the institution is to catalogue and distribute information about global cultures and to build repositories of this knowledge, which is potentially valuable for many purposes.[150]

It is clear that the communities of origin have legitimate concerns about facilitating public access to parts of their culture and the associated harms that can result from misappropriation and misuse of their cultures. These harms are even more likely to occur given technological advances, which enable libraries to collect, store, preserve, and digitize cultural works, and then transmit those digital representations broadly through the Internet where they can be downloaded and even modified without any authorization from the community of origin. As commentators note, some institutions are dealing with these issues on a case-by-case basis, developing institutional protocols and best practices to involve Indigenous peoples in collaborative management of repositories and archives of cultural heritage.[151] For example, Kimberly Christen described three principles that were vital to a collaborative endeavor involving several Indigenous nations from the Plateau region of the Pacific Northwest.[152] The first principle involved developing an inclusive approach to

---

[149] *See, e.g.*, Amy Hackney Blackwell & Christopher William Blackwell, *Hijacking Shared Heritage: Cultural Artifacts and Intellectual Property Rights*, 13 CHI. KENT. J. INTELL. PROP. 137, 143 (2013) (arguing for open sharing of data from any object or resource that does not fall under the protection of intellectual property rights laws).
[150] *Id.*
[151] *See* Anderson and Christen, *supra* notes 102 and 106 and accompanying text.
[152] Christen, *supra* note 106 at 195-96.

institutional holdings that comprised Native perspectives on the resources. The second principle was to respect and act on both Native American and Western approaches to "caring for archival collections."[153] The third principle was to "consult with culturally affiliated community representatives to identify those materials that are culturally sensitive and develop procedures for access to and use of those materials."[154]

Similarly, experts within the fashion industry are counseling designers to work with Indigenous artists and communities to ensure respectful collaboration and avoid exploitive forms of cultural appropriation.[155] This effort also involves a set of best practices, including involving Native peoples at the outset of "ideation and design processes," welcoming their "influence and control" throughout the production and marketing process, and offering "financial or resource-based compensation."[156] In addition, cultural outsiders are encouraged to respect the views of Indigenous governments, such as the Hopi Tribe, which oppose the commercial use of Hopi culture by any outside entity based on their belief that cultural knowledge is sacred and that "only certain people can have access to certain kinds of information."[157]

At this point, these standards and best practices are considered voluntary and optional in many cases, precisely because the Indigenous artist or tribal government may not have a recognized legal right under existing law. The expansion of technology and

---

[153] *Id.* at 195.
[154] *Id.* at 196.
[155] *See* Finnerty, *supra* note 8.at 2F.
[156] *Id.*
[157] *Id.* at 3F (discussing comments of Leigh Kuwanwisiwma, who leads the Hopi Tribal Cultural Preservation Office).

global markets offers an additional challenge, as does the reconfiguration of contemporary cultures due to the transnational migration of peoples and cultures.

The harms of cultural misappropriation are accentuated in the contemporary era by politics of "super-diversity," which Steven Vertovec describes as a mechanism, which shapes national identity in the wake of new forms of immigration and transnationalism.[158] As applied to cultural production, super-diversity suggests that "culture" and "cultural difference" (diversity) will be used to construct, maintain, transform, or undermine national identities given the diverse forms of human migration and social organization that characterize the modern world.[159] Vertovec claims that "immigrant cultures are routinely posed as threats to national culture," and therefore issues surrounding migration "stimulate, manifest, and reproduce cultural politics."[160] Within this matrix, policymakers manipulate "popular notions of national versus alien culture" by invoking a notion of "difference" premised upon "particular images, narratives, and symbols of national culture."[161]

As American identity is transformed through the politics of super-diversity, cultural production will increasingly be used to sustain a particular national identity. Where will Indigenous identity fit within this new politics? It is unclear how the politics of super-diversity will affect cultural production. It is possible that tribal cultures could be inadvertently associated with foreign cultures for purposes of exclusionary laws

---

[158] Steven Vertovec, *The Cultural Politics of Nation and Migration*, 40 ANN. REV. ANTHROPOLOGY 241 (2011).
[159] *Id.*
[160] *Id.* at 242.
[161] *Id.* at 242; *see also Griffith v. Caney Valley Pub. Sch.*, 2015 U.S. Dist. LEXIS 66059 (N.D. Okla. May 20, 2015).

designed to uphold the dominant culture, such as the recent effort of legislators in Oklahoma to ban state courts from invoking any "alien" or "foreign law," with a specific reference to Sharia law,[162] but clearly implicating tribal law systems as well. It is also possible that the national governments will further accentuate the construction of an "American" culture that draws heavily upon its "Indigenous" past, as a way to encompass Native cultures within the dominant narrative, in contrast to the "immigrant" cultures of Asians and Latinos. Significantly, the media has a prominent role in developing "national narratives" and in the construction of imagined (national and transnational) communities.[163] This is an additional reason why media images employing Native stereotypes have such a profound influence on the construction of identity.

I would argue that the project of super-diversity should include attention to the political movement of Indigenous self-determination, which rejects multiculturalism in favor of what Professor Duane Champagne terms "multinationalism," that is the construction of a new consensual political order in which indigenous peoples are included as sovereign governments and treated with equal respect.[164] Within this matrix, it is imperative that Indigenous peoples

---

[162] H.R.J. Res. 1056, 52d Leg., 2d Sess. (Okla. 2010), *available at* https://www.sos.ok.gov/documents/legislation/52nd/2010/2R/HJ/105 6.pdf; *see also* Awad v. Ziriax, 670 F.3d 1111 (10th Cir. 2012) (affirming issuance of a preliminary injunction of the state constitutional amendment as there was a likelihood of success that the provision would be unconstitutional).

[163] Isabelle Rigoni, *Intersectionality and Mediated Cultural Production in a Globalized Post-Colonial World*, 35 ETHNIC AND RACIAL STUD. 834, 835 (2012).

[164] Duane Champagne, *Rethinking Native Relations with Contemporary Nation States*, *in* INDIGENOUS PEOPLES AND THE MODERN NATION STATE 3–23 (Duane Champagne et al., eds. 2009).

have the ability to control their cultural identity. The right of self-determination depends upon the ability of a people to define themselves autonomously as separate cultural groups with distinctive ties to territory, distinctive forms of social organization (clans/kinship groups), separate languages, and the ability to govern themselves under their own laws and institutions. Indigenous political identity will always depend, to some extent, upon the group's ability to use its core cultural identity to designate itself as separate from the nation-state and other groups. This means that cultural production must be consistent with indigenous norms about what is appropriately shared, and what must be retained within the group (or even, more narrowly, for example by certain clans or societies within the group).

This mode of governance may be a challenge for future generations, given the prevalence of many forms of shared cultural expression. So, for example, young Native artists have begun to explore synergies with hip-hop culture and rap music, as well as skateboard culture.[165] Professor David Martinez explores the work of Doug Miles, an Apache artist and creator of Apache Skateboards, who observes that skateboarding absorbs all nationalities and cultures, but also encourages Native artists to "take back the discourse on their work and redirect the discussion away from the mythical pristine lens of the past toward how Indigenous artists actually see themselves."[166] Native identity is fluid and changing, but also stable and enduring. Native artists and tribal governments are engaged in cultural production, just as the dominant society is. However, it is necessary to see what their respective goals and purposes are, and also understand where the conflicts are located.

---

[165] *See* David Martinez, *From Off the Rez to Off the Hook! Douglas Miles and Apache Skateboards*, 37 AM. INDIAN Q. 370, 370 (2013).
[166] *Id.* at 373.

B. The Human Rights Approach to Indigenous Goverance of Cultural Heritage.

As Professor James Anaya has explained, there are several composite norms embedded within the concept of Indigenous self-determination, including the norm of cultural integrity.[167] In my prior work, I have argued that the human rights approach should be used to reshape the domestic and international law governing intangible cultural heritage as it pertains to Indigenous peoples.[168] The U.N. Declaration on the Rights of Indigenous Peoples (UNDRIP) offers the most comprehensive treatment of the norm of cultural integrity in its many provisions, and Article 31 specifically articulates the right of Indigenous peoples to protect their cultural heritage:

> Indigenous peoples have the right to maintain, control, protect and develop their cultural heritage, traditional knowledge and traditional cultural expressions, as well as the manifestations of their sciences, technologies and cultures, including human and genetic resources, seeds, medicine, knowledge of the properties of fauna and flora, oral traditions, literatures, designs, sports and traditional games and visual and performing arts. They also have the right to maintain, control, protect and develop their intellectual property over such cultural heritage, traditional knowledge and traditional cultural expressions.

---

[167] *See* Tsosie, International Trade in Indigenous Cultural Heritage, *supra* note 146 at 225.
[168] *See Id.*

> In conjunction with indigenous peoples, States shall take effective measures to recognize and protect the exercise of these rights.[169]

As Article 31 recognizes, most Indigenous peoples do not separate the tangible and intangible components of their cultural heritage. Indigenous knowledge gives meaning to cultural symbols and songs, and that meaning must be articulated and governed by Indigenous peoples. Any other outcome would perpetuate the forms of "epistemic injustice" that have characterized the process of colonization.

In my view, the right of tribal governments to protect their intangible cultural heritage constitutes the core of their inherent sovereignty as Indigenous nations. This "cultural" form of sovereignty cannot be limited by the same artificial construction of "sovereignty" that informs the characterization of federally-recognized Indian tribes as "domestic dependent governments." This construction emerged out of the Doctrine of Discovery that was used to justify European claims to land and sovereignty during the colonial era. It cannot now serve as the basis to appropriate the core of Indigenous culture as belonging to the United States or any other contemporary nation-state which purports to act on behalf of the Indigenous peoples that were subsumed within its borders. Rather, as Professor Anaya observes "the same basic arguments that have resulted in the rejection of the *terra nullius* doctrine also speak for a reformation of the public domain, as it applies to indigenous knowledge."[170] Under this logic, Native people have always been the

---

[169] Declaration on the Rights of Indigenous Peoples, art. 31, G.A. Res. 61/295, Annex, U.N. Doc. A/RES/61/295 (Sept. 13, 2007).
[170] Professor Anaya statement, *supra* note 43 at 5.

custodians of their traditional knowledge and traditional cultural expressions. They never ceded their governance rights and there is no justifiable basis to find that the nation-state somehow assumed the right to appropriate these aspects of Indigenous identity.

Thus, the only challenge for contemporary policymakers is to recognize how existing jurisdictional limitations constrain the ability of Indigenous governments to protect their intangible cultural heritage from being misappropriated for commercial gain or other uses. Tribal governments currently have the power to enact laws to govern their members and their resources, but they may be hampered in their ability to apply this law outside reservation boundaries to non-members of the tribe. This is the area where federal law could prove useful, if there is an appropriate set of consultations between the United States and Indigenous nations, and if there is a way to achieve a political consensus about the terms of such protection, which will necessarily require modifications of the domestic law.

At the international level, the nation-states that participate in WIPO are differentiating the categories of "traditional knowledge," "traditional cultural expressions," and "genetic resources" for potential action through a multilateral treaty process. The United States is participating in this effort even though it has not conducted a formal consultation on this topic with the elected leaders of the 566 Federally-recognized Indian tribes, which reprises the dynamic of colonial governance. The political leaders of the nation-states view Indigenous traditional knowledge and genetic resources as vital to the appropriate development of natural resources in an era of climate change.[171] For example, the study of Indigenous seed stocks and farming practices may promote the development of drought-resistant crops by biotech companies seeking to patent new products and enable the commercial transfer of adaptive technologies to countries likely to suffer from warming trends and drought in the years to come.[172] Expanding innovation in science and technology is the driving force behind the current effort to reach global consensus on the use of traditional knowledge and genetic resources.

In comparison, the use of traditional cultural expressions is often allocated less importance due to the view that this is related to "art," rather than "science and technology." Indigenous governments should pay close attention to this effort by the nation-states to create new categories and hierarchies that replicate the same Western cultural assumptions that were used to divest Indigenous nations of their lands and cultural resources. Will "traditional cultural expressions" be considered a resource like property (or intellectual property)? Or are they merely ideas, free for appropriation by cultural outsiders? The public benefit argument has always been employed by the colonial nations and their descendants to justify appropriation from Native peoples. This argument continues to be made in the contemporary era in the context of a robust public domain.

Indigenous peoples must take back the power to define the terms of the debate within their own cultural frameworks and argue for a form of governance that

---

[171] See Rebecca Tsosie, *Climate Change, Sustainability, and Globalization: Charting the Future of Indigenous Environmental Self-Determination*, 4 ENVTL. & ENERGY L AND POL'Y J. 188, 250 (2009) (discussing role of Indigenous knowledge in sustainability planning).

respects and protects the core of Indigenous culture. This process must begin internally, within each Indigenous group, because only tribal law can adequately reflect the categories and interests at stake. Professor Angela Riley and Professor Kristen Carpenter describe the process of using traditional norms and practices to generate new frameworks of tribal law in their article "Indigenous Peoples and the Jurisgenerative Moment in Human Rights."[173] Building on their insights, I would argue that tribal law on the protection of traditional knowledge and cultural expression can be used to generate a dialogue with the United States and potentially national legislation that adequately protects the interests of tribal governments. With participation from Indigenous governments, the United States would be able to engage in a discussion with other nation-states about the terms of a multinational convention or treaty that would protect Indigenous rights. Without such collaboration, the United States will likely take actions that will further impair Indigenous rights. Through an intercultural process of dialogue and collaboration among Indigenous peoples and the nation-states that encompass them, it may be possible to generate new categories of law that can overcome the mythology of discovery and effectively protect the rights of indigenous peoples.

V. CONCLUSION

The fundamental challenge for the future is to develop equitable governance structures that facilitate respect and responsibility for the important values and interests at stake. There are likely various potential models of governance, depending upon the nature of

---

[173] Kristen A. Carpenter & Angela R. Riley, *Indigenous Peoples and the Jurisgenerative Moment in Human Rights*, 102 CALIF. L. REV. 173, 175 (2014).

the community. A "one size fits all" approach to protecting the rights of an Indigenous community to traditional cultural expression may not be feasible because these communities are not equally situated. For many Indigenous peoples, traditional cultural expression is imbued with sacred value and this must be acknowledged and respected.[174] Within the United States, the federal government should engage a consultation with tribal governments to assess the possibility of issuing statutory protection for tribal "cultural trademarks" as a first step toward protecting traditional cultural expression. For American Indian, Alaska Native, and Native Hawaiian peoples within the United States, the overall issue of governance must be addressed through international, domestic, and tribal structures of law and policy. The principles of "humanity and justice" should inform the contemporary dialogue on cultural production, and tribal governments should have an equal voice in creating a workable structure for governance of traditional cultural expression.

---

[174] *See* Finnerty, *supra* note 8 (quoting the Director of the Hopi Tribal Preservation Office who stated that the Hopi have chosen not to trademark their designs because they are sacred and must be protected in perpetuity).

INTER PARTES REVIEW: A MULTI-METHOD COMPARISON FOR CHALLENGING PATENT VALIDITY

JOSEPH W. DUBIS, PH.D.[†]

I. Introduction 120

II. Inter Partes Review: The Details 126

   A. Filing the inter partes review petition 126

   B. Standard to institute a trial proceeding 127

   C. Trial proceedings 128

   D. Duration 131

   E. Cost 132

III. Inter Partes Reexamination: The Details 133

   A. Filing the inter partes reexamination petition 134

   B. Standard to institute a reexamination 134

   C. The reexamination 135

   D. Duration 138

   E. Cost 138

[†] Joseph W. Dubis, Ph.D. is a *Juris Doctor* Candidate at William Mitchell College of Law, expected to graduate in 2016. He received a Bachelor of Science in Biology from the University of St. Thomas and a Ph.D. in Biological and Medical Sciences with an emphasis in Neurosciences from Washington University in St. Louis. He would like to thank Andrew J. Lagatta and Christopher C. Davis at Merchant & Gould, P.C. for sharing their knowledge of and experience with inter partes review.

F. Rates of institution and claim invalidation 139

IV. Patent Litigation: The Details 140

    A. Patent litigation defenses 141

    D. Cost 144

    E. Rates of patent litigation and patent
       invalidation 145

V. Comparing Inter Partes Review, Inter Partes
   Reexamination, and Patent Litigation 146

    A. Procedural comparison 147

    B. Durational comparison 154

    C. Cost comparison 155

    D. Rates of institution and claim cancelling 157

    E. Conclusions of method comparison 160

VI. Conclusion 161

    A. If patents are going to be invalidated, what
       is the best method to use? 161

    B. The future of inter partes review 164

I. INTRODUCTION

On September 16, 2011, President Obama signed the Leahy-Smith America Invents Act into law.[1] The most transformative feature of the America Invents Act (AIA), the most significant patent reform legislation since the original patent legislation of 1790,[2] shifts priority for patent applications from first to invent to first-to-file.[3] Since this change took effect on March 16, 2013,[4] judging the shift's impact, at the time of writing this article, is difficult; however, other components of the AIA have already made a considerable first impression.[5]

In particular, a new form of patent litigation before the United States Patent and Trademark Office[6] ("Patent Office") has arguably had the most dramatic and immediate impact.[7] This new patent litigation procedure is the inter partes review.[8] When

---

[1] Bruce Y.C. Wu & Stephen B. Maebius, *Examining AIA's High-Speed* Inter Partes *Review System*, LAW360 (Nov. 15, 2011, 12:17 PM), http://www.foley.com/files/Publication/1d2e694e-555e-4fed-9248-8a3b73d2f8ee/Presentation/PublicationAttachment/6782af99-2360-4c7b-ab59-8cea5de06ae8/IPL360Nov15.pdf.

[2] *See* David Kappos, *Re-Inventing the U.S. Patent System, Director's Forum: A Blog from USPTO's Leadership*, USPTO (Sept. 16, 2011, 5:45 PM), http://www.uspto.gov/blog/director/entry/re_inventing_the_us_patent.

[3] *See* Richard G. Braun, Note, *America Invents Act: First-to-File and a Race to the Patent Office*, 8 OHIO ST. ENTREP. BUS. L.J. 47, 47 (2013).

[4] Examination Guidelines for Implementing the First Inventor to File Provisions of the Leahy-Smith America Invents Act, 78 Fed. Reg. 11059, 11059 (Feb. 14, 2013) (codified at 37 C.F.R. pt. 1).

[5] *See* Robert M. Siminski et al., *6 Reasons* Inter Partes *Review Was Popular In 2013*, LAW360 (Dec. 17, 2013, 11:24 PM), http://www.law360.com/articles/495709/6-reasons-inter-partes-review-was-popular-in-2013.

[6] *Id.*

[7] *Id.*

[8] *Id.*

implemented on September 16, 2012,[9] inter partes review replaced inter partes reexamination, a similar, yet distinct, Patent Office proceeding.[10] Inter partes review provides certain grounds for a petitioner to challenge the validity of a patent before the Patent Trial and Appeal Board, a recently formed adjudicative body replacing the Board of Patent Appeals and Interferences, which is composed of judges with vast experience in dealings of patent law and technology.[11] Inter partes review was designed to be a speedy and relatively inexpensive mechanism to prove a patent's invalidity based on the use of a different legal standard than is used during district court proceedings.[12]

Given some of the similarities between inter partes reexamination and inter partes review[13] combined with the historically slow rate at which clients have adopted new procedures which risk their intellectual property,[14]

---

[9] Alison J. Baldwin & Aaron V. Gin, *Inter partes Review and Inter partes Reexamination: More Than Just a Name Change*, INTELL. PROP. TODAY (Feb. 2014), http://www.iptoday.com/issues/2014/02/inter-partes-i-review-and-inter-partes-i-reexamination-more-than-just-name-change.asp.

[10] Robert A. Kalinsky & Linhda Nguyen, *Obtaining Your Stay During InterPartes Review*, LEXOLOGY (Sept. 18, 2013), http://www.lexology.com/library/detail.aspx?g=fc6627c9-8ba3-4707-8322-11df1861083d.

[11] Ryan Davis, *5 Tips for Killing Patents In AIA Reviews*, LAW360 (Apr. 17, 2014, 7:57 PM) [hereinafter Davis, *Tips for Killing Patents*], http://www.law360.com/articles/525242/5-tips-for-killing-patents-in-aia-reviews.

[12] Aarti Shah, *Choosing Wisely: Practical Considerations for Choosing Venues for IP Disputes*, INSIDE COUNS. (July 2014), http://www.insidecounsel.com/2014/07/07/choosing-wisely-practical-considerations-for-choos.

[13] Andrew J. Lagatta & George C. Lewis, *How Inter Partes Review Became a Valuable Tool So Quickly*, LAW360 (Aug. 16, 2013, 12:01 PM), http://www.law360.com/articles/463372/how-inter-partes-review-became-a-valuable-tool-so-quickly.

[14] *See id.* (noting only twenty-six inter partes reexaminations were filed in the first four years).

many individuals thought that the use of inter partes review would be initially slow.[15] Furthermore, some practitioners believed that the perceived inflation of the burden of proof required to initiate a proceeding in inter partes review compared to under inter partes reexamination would deter the use of the new patent litigation proceeding.[16] They were wrong.

Inter partes reviews are being filed at an extraordinary rate. In the first ten months that inter partes review was available, 377 inter partes review petitions were filed.[17] This is more inter partes review petitions filed than the 374 inter partes reexamination petitions filed in the 2011 fiscal year.[18] In 2013, 514 inter partes review petitions were filed.[19] In 2014, 1,310 inter partes review petitions were filed.[20] AIA petitions, which are composed of inter partes review and a small percentage of covered business method petitions, have been especially popular for electrical/computer technologies (63.8% of petitions) and mechanical technologies (24.1% of petitions).[21] A few individuals have been especially active in inter partes review proceedings.[22] It is unclear whether inter partes review

---

[15] *Id.*
[16] *See id.* (discussing the shift from the "substantial new question" of patentability standard used in inter partes reexamination to the "reasonable likelihood" of prevailing standard used in inter partes review).
[17] *Id.*
[18] *Id.*
[19] U.S. PATENT & TRADEMARK OFFICE, PATENT TRIAL AND APPEAL BOARD AIA PROGRESS STATISTICS 1 (Feb. 5, 2015) [hereinafter AIA STATISTICS], *available at* http://www.uspto.gov/sites/default/files/documents/aia_statistics_02-05-2015.pdf.
[20] *Id.*
[21] *Id.*
[22] Ryan Davis, *Apple, Samsung Top Filers of AIA Review Petitions*, LAW360 (July 03, 2014, 7:40 PM),

can continue with such unchecked popularity[23] or whether a cap on inter partes review petitions will need to be implemented.[24]

Despite inter partes review's early popularity, some major concerns regarding the Patent Trial and Appeal Board's findings have developed.[25] To date, an inter partes review trial has been instituted for 78% of the

---

http://www.law360.com/articles/554393/apple-samsung-top-filers-of-aia-review-petitions (noting the top ten filers were involved in more than twenty-five percent of the proceedings); Ryan Davis, *Intellectual Ventures Not Top of AIA Hit List*, LAW360 (June 10, 2014, 6:09 PM), http://www.law360.com/articles/546488/intellectual-ventures-not-top-of-aia-hit-list (noting Zond Inc. has been the patent owner in sixty-two inter partes reviews and most of the top ten patent owners of inter partes reviews are non-practicing entities).

[23] *See* 37 C.F.R. § 42.102(b) (2014) ("The Director may impose a limit on the number of inter partes reviews that may be instituted during each of the first four one-year periods in which the amendment made to chapter 31 of title 35, United States Code, is in effect by providing notice in the Office's Official Gazette or Federal Register. Petitions filed after an established limit has been reached will be deemed untimely.").

[24] To date, no limits have been placed on the number of inter partes reviews that may be filed in a fiscal year; however, some believed the limit was 270, the number of inter partes reexaminations filed in 2010, the fiscal year prior to the signing of the AIA. Robert G. Sterne et al., *America Invents Act: The 5 New Post-Issuance Procedures*, 13 SEDONA CONF. J. 27, 37 (2012); *see also* Wu & Maebius, *supra* note 1.

[25] The primary concern is that the method is too harsh on patent owners. *See* David A. Prange & Cyrus A. Morton, *Experts Rule in Rare Patent Owner IPR Wins*, INTELL. PROP. TODAY, June 2014, *available at* http://www.iptoday.com/issues/2014/06/experts-rule-in-rare-patent-owner-ipr-wins.asp; *see* Ryan Davis, *In Rare Feat, 2 Patents Emerge Unscathed From AIA Reviews*, LAW360 (Apr.15, 2014, 9:44 PM) [hereinafter *Experts Rule*], http://www.law360.com/articles/528526/in-rare-feat-2-patents-emerge-unscathed-from-aia-reviews; Cyrus Morton & David Prange, *Patent Owners Beware, Your Patent Has a 15 Percent Chance (or Less) of Surviving the PTAB*, INSIDE COUNS. (Mar. 2014) [hereinafter *Patent Owners Beware*], http://www.insidecounsel.com/2014/03/19/patent-owners-beware-your-patent-has-a-15-percent.

filed petitions,[26] down from roughly 93% after the first ten months[27] and 96% after the first six months.[28] When a final written decision is then issued, patent claims are being found invalid at a rate of roughly 91%.[29] Few final written decisions have been published without canceling at least one claim.[30] The high mortality rate of patent claims in inter partes review proceedings caused then-Chief Judge Randall Rader of the Federal Circuit, to equate the Patent Trial and Appeal Board judges with "death squads,"[31] a characterization the judges refuted.[32]

The United States Constitution set out the goal of "promot[ing] the progress of science and useful arts, by

---

[26] *See* AIA STATISTICS, *supra* note 19.
[27] *See* Lagatta & Lewis, *supra* note 13.
[28] David O'Dell & Thomas King, *Inter Partes Review: How Is It Going So Far?*, INTELL. PROP. TODAY (Sept. 2013), http://www.iptoday.com/issues/2013/09/inter-partes-review-how-it-going-so-far.asp.
[29] *See* Prange & Morton, *supra* note 25.
[30] Those final written decisions that have published without cancelling any claims include: Avaya Inc. v. Network-1 Sec. Solutions, Inc., IPR 2013-00071, 2014 WL 2175370 (P.T.A.B. May 22, 2014); ABB Inc. v. ROY-G-BIV Corp., IPR2013-00063, 2014 WL 2112556 (P.T.A.B. May 16, 2014); Corning Inc. v. DSM IP Assets B.V., IPR2013-00045, 2014 WL 1917394 (P.T.A.B. May 9, 2014); Corning Inc. v. DSM IP Assets B.V., IPR2013-00049 (P.T.A.B. May 9, 2014); Corning Inc. v. DSM IP Assets B.V., IPR2013-0043, IPR2013-0044, 2014 WL 1783277 (P.T.A.B. May 1, 2014); Corning Inc. v. DSM IP Assets B.V., IPR2013-0047, 2014 WL 1783279 (P.T.A.B. May 1, 2014); ABB Inc. v. ROY-G-BIV Corp., IPR2013-00062, 2014 WL 1478218 (P.T.A.B. Apr. 11, 2014); ABB Inc. v. ROY-G-BIV Corp., IPR2013-00282 (P.T.A.B. Apr. 11, 2014); ABB Inc. v. ROY-G-BIV Corp., IPR2013-00074, IPR2013-00286, 2014 WL 1478219 (P.T.A.B. Apr. 11, 2014).
[31] *See* Prange & Morton, *supra* note 25.
[32] Erica Teichert, *PTAB Says It's Not A 'Death Squad' For Patents*, LAW360 (Apr. 15, 2014, 8:16 PM), http://www.law360.com/articles/528519/ptab-says-it-s-not-a-death-squad-for-patents (quoting Chief Judge James Donald Smith of the Patent Trial and Appeal Board in response to then-Chief Judge Randall Rader's characterization of the Patent Trial and Appeal Board judges as "death squads").

securing for limited times to authors and inventors the exclusive right to their respective writings and discoveries."[33] Given this goal, one must question whether the new inter partes review proceeding is too harsh on patent owners to accomplish the Constitution's worthy goal. The primary way of determining whether inter partes review is exceedingly harsh in its invalidation of patent claims is to compare the proceeding to other methods used for invalidating patent claims, namely inter partes reexamination, inter partes review's predecessor,[34] and district court litigation proceedings. By comparing characteristics of the three invalidation methods, including the procedural limitations of each method, the average duration of each proceeding, the average cost of each proceeding, and the average rates of claim invalidation of each proceeding, one can determine whether inter partes review is a useful and fair mechanism for challenging the validity of patent claims or whether it is unduly harsh towards the patent owner.[35] Such insight can provide a basis for determining what the future of inter partes review might be.

In actuality, the concerns over the rate of invalidation are likely unfounded and unnecessary. By comparing inter partes review to inter partes reexamination and patent litigation, the other methods have surprisingly similar invalidation rates as inter partes review. Thus, if one is going to consider the effectiveness and usefulness of inter partes review, one must look past just the rates of invalidation and consider the procedural aspects, the durational elements, and the cost considerations. By comparing the three methods, it is seen that inter partes review is a

---

[33] U.S. CONST. art. I, § 8, cl. 8.
[34] *See* Baldwin & Gin, *supra* note 9.
[35] *See id.*

fair proceeding, and is the best option for a client to use to challenge a patent in certain circumstances.

II. INTER PARTES REVIEW: THE DETAILS

The statutory requirements of inter partes review may be found in 35 U.S.C. §§ 311–319. A summary of critical components of the inter partes review procedure will be provided so that this method can be fairly compared with inter partes reexamination and district court proceedings.

A. Filing the inter partes review petition

A petition to institute an inter partes review proceeding may be filed with the Patent Office to challenge the validity of patent claims on the basis of prior art patents and printed publications.[36] Other invalidity challenges based on on-sale activities, written description or enablement issues, and issues of the patentability of the subject matter may not be raised in an inter partes review and must be reserved for a district court proceeding.[37] To date, petitions have been filed with a combination of new prior art and previously cited prior art.[38] The petitions allow for multiple prior art references to be combined.[39] In

---

[36] 35 U.S.C. § 311(b) (2012) ("A petitioner in an inter partes review may request to cancel as unpatentable 1 or more claims of a patent only on a ground that could be raised under section 102 or 103 and only on the basis of prior art consisting of patents or printed publications.").

[37] *See* Lagatta & Lewis, *supra* note 13 (noting that these defenses usually require witnesses or other evidentiary issues that a district court proceeding is well-versed at handling).

[38] *See* Siminski, et al., *supra* note 5 (noting that sixty-five percent of petitions have utilized some previously cited prior art, thirty-five percent of petitions have utilized exclusively prior art cited for the first time, and one percent of petitions have utilized only prior art previously cited before an examiner).

[39] Lisa Shuchman, *Garmin Nabs Win in First 'Inter partes Review'; The Patent Trial and Appeal Board Has Sided With Garmin International in the*

addition, the petitions can raise issues of novelty[40] and obviousness,[41] and must be limited to sixty pages in length.[42]

Strict time limits exist for when an inter partes review petition may be filed. A petition may not be filed immediately upon granting of a patent or upon the reissue of a patent, nor may a petition be filed while a post-grant review proceeding is underway.[43] However, a petition for inter partes review must be filed before filing "a civil action challenging the validity of a claim of the patent"[44] or within one year of being "served with a complaint alleging infringement of the patent" or the petition will be barred.[45]

B. Standard to institute a trial proceeding

In the petition for inter partes review, the petitioner must establish "a reasonable likelihood that the petitioner would prevail with respect to at least one claim challenged in the petition."[46] The decision,

---

First Inter partes Review Proceeding Instituted Under the America Invents Act, LAW TECH. NEWS (Nov. 18, 2013).
[40] *See* 35 U.S.C. § 102.
[41] *See Id.* § 103.
[42] 37 C.F.R. § 42.24(a)(1)(i) (2014).
[43] 35 U.S.C. § 311(c) ("A petition for inter partes review shall be filed after the later of either—(1) the date that is 9 months after the grant of a patent; or (2) if a post-grant review is instituted under chapter 32, the date of the termination of such post-grant review.").
[44] *Id.* § 315(a)(1) ("An inter partes review may not be instituted if, before the date on which the petition for such a review is filed, the petitioner or real party in interest filed a civil action challenging the validity of a claim of the patent.").
[45] *Id.* § 315(b) ("An inter partes review may not be instituted if the petition requesting the proceeding is filed more than 1 year after the date on which the petitioner, real party in interest, or privy of the petitioner is served with a complaint alleging infringement of the patent. The time limitation set forth in the preceding sentence shall not apply to a request for joinder under subsection (c).").
[46] *Id.* § 314(a) (emphasis added).

whether to institute the review proceeding or to deny the review, is not appealable.[47] The Patent Trial and Appeal Board frequently declines to review all claims and often proceeds on a subset of the grounds requested.[48]

C. Trial proceedings

Upon institution of an inter partes review trial proceeding, the review proceeds as an adversarial process between the petitioner and the patent owner.[49] Each party must be represented by a lead and back-up counsel where the lead counsel is registered to practice before the Patent Office.[50] The back-up counsel may be admitted *pro hac vice* upon proof of good cause.[51]

The inter partes review proceedings use a limited form of discovery.[52] The discovery is generally limited

---

[47] *See Id.* § 314(d); *In re* Procter & Gamble Co., 749 F.3d 1376, 1378–79 (Fed. Cir. 2014) (holding that the United States Court of Appeals for the Federal Circuit lacks authority to issue a mandamus to rescind the United States Patent & Trademark Office's decision to institute an inter partes review proceeding); St. Jude Med., Cardiology Div., Inc. v. Volcano Corp., 749 F.3d 1373, 1375 (Fed. Cir. 2014) (holding that a U.S. Patent & Trademark Office decision is not subject to appeal to the United States Court of Appeals for the Federal Circuit); Sheri Qualters, *Guidance From Federal Circuit on Inter partes Review*, NAT'L L. J. (April 29, 2014), http://www.law.com/sites/articles/2014/04/29/guidance-from-federal-circuit-on-inter-partes-review/.
[48] O'Dell & King, *supra* note 28.
[49] Christopher E. Loh & Christopher P. Hill, *How Inter Partes Review Differs from District Court Patent Litigation*, N.Y. L.J. (Dec. 9, 2013), http://www.newyorklawjournal.com/id=1202630855916/How-Inter-Partes-Review-Differs-From-District-Court--Patent-Litigation.
[50] *See id.* (citing 37 C.F.R. § 42.10(a) (2014)). Note the requirement of assigning two attorneys to a matter has the likelihood of increasing the cost to the client. The language of the Federal Regulation does not appear to have an exception that would allow a litigator with a registration number to handle the matter independently. *See id.*
[51] 37 C.F.R. § 42.10(c).
[52] *See* Sterne et al., *supra* note 24, at 40.

to depositions of witnesses who have submitted affidavits or declarations.[53] These witnesses usually take the form of experts.[54] There are three stages of discovery: mandatory initial disclosures,[55] routine disclosures,[56] and additional discovery.[57] Because mandatory initial disclosures occur only if the parties

---

[53] See id.
[54] See Prange & Morton, *supra* note 25.
[55] 37 C.F.R. § 42.51(a) ("(1) With agreement. Parties may agree to mandatory discovery requiring the initial disclosures set forth in the Office Patent Trial Practice Guide. (i) The parties must submit any agreement reached on initial disclosures by no later than the filing of the patent owner preliminary response or the expiration of the time period for filing such a response. The initial disclosures of the parties shall be filed as exhibits. (ii) Upon the institution of a trial, parties may automatically take discovery of the information identified in the initial disclosures. (2) Without agreement. Where the parties fail to agree to the mandatory discovery set forth in paragraph (a)(1), a party may seek such discovery by motion.").
[56] *Id.* § 42.51(b)(1) ("Except as the Board may otherwise order: (i) Unless previously served or otherwise by agreement of the parties, any exhibit cited in a paper or in testimony must be served with the citing paper or testimony. (ii) Cross examination of affidavit testimony is authorized within such time period as the Board may set. (iii) Unless previously served, a party must serve relevant information that is inconsistent with a position advanced by the party during the proceeding concurrent with the filing of the documents or things that contains the inconsistency. This requirement does not make discoverable anything otherwise protected by legally recognized privileges such as attorney-client or attorney work product. This requirement extends to inventors, corporate officers, and persons involved in the preparation or filing of the documents or things.").
[57] *Id.* § 42.51(b)(2) ("(i) The parties may agree to additional discovery between themselves. Where the parties fail to agree, a party may move for additional discovery. The moving party must show that such additional discovery is in the interests of justice, except in post-grant reviews where additional discovery is limited to evidence directly related to factual assertions advanced by either party in the proceeding (see § 42.224). The Board may specify conditions for such additional discovery. (ii) When appropriate, a party may obtain production of documents and things during cross examination of an opponent's witness or during authorized compelled testimony under § 42.52.").

agree,[58] mandatory initial disclosures have occurred in only a small fraction of the early proceedings.[59] Routine discovery entails taking the depositions of each side's experts.[60] Additional discovery is anything that the Board determines is necessary in the interest of justice.[61] With such a high burden, motions for additional discovery are frequently denied.[62]

An inter partes review proceeding culminates in an oral argument before a panel of Patent Trial and Appeal Board judges.[63] The proceeding utilizes the Federal Rules of Evidence.[64] The statute requires the Board to construct the claims using the *proper meaning* standard[65]

---

[58] *See* Siminski et al., *supra* note 5.
[59] *See, e.g.*, Agreement on Mandatory Discovery, paper 17, Microsoft Corp. v. SurfCast Inc., IPR2013-00292 (P.T.A.B. Aug. 26, 2013); Agreement on Mandatory Discovery, paper 12, Microsoft Corp. v. SurfCast Inc., IPR2013-00293 (P.T.A.B. Aug. 26, 2013); Agreement on Mandatory Discovery, paper 13, Microsoft Corp. v. SurfCast Inc., IPR2013-00294 (P.T.A.B. Aug. 26, 2013); Agreement on Mandatory Discovery, paper 12, Microsoft Corp. v. SurfCast Inc., IPR2013-00295 (P.T.A.B. Aug. 26, 2013); Agreement on Mandatory Discovery, paper 12, Oracle Corporation v. Click-to-Call Techs. LP, IPR2013-00312 (P.T.A.B. Aug. 23, 2013); *See also* Siminski et al., *supra* note 5.
[60] *See* Siminski et al., *supra* note 5.
[61] Decision on Motion for Additional Discovery, paper 26, Garmin Int'l, Inc. v. Cuozzo Speed Techs. LLC, IPR2012-00001 (P.T.A.B. Mar. 5, 2013) (discussing five factors to be considered when determining whether the interests of justice are met: 1) more than a possibility and mere allegation, 2) litigation positions and underlying basis, 3) ability to generate equivalent information by other means, 4) easily understandable instruction, and 5) requests not overly burdensome to answer); *see also* Loh & Hill, *supra* note 49 (noting that the "usefulness" standard discussed in *Garmin* is higher than the basic relevance standard used in litigation).
[62] *See* Loh & Hill, *supra* note 49.
[63] *See id.*
[64] *See id.*
[65] *See* 35 U.S.C. § 301(d) (2012)("A written statement submitted pursuant to subsection (a)(2), and additional information submitted pursuant to subsection (c), shall not be considered by the Office for any purpose other than *to determine the proper meaning of a patent claim*

and not use the *broadest reasonable interpretation* standard,[66] though there seems to be some inconsistency between the statute and the standard as applied.[67] Following the oral argument, the Board will issue a final written decision affirming or invalidating some or all of the patent claims.[68] This decision is then appealable to the Federal Circuit.[69] Upon a finding of validity, the petitioner is estopped from requesting or maintaining a proceeding before the Patent Office[70] or asserting in a civil action[71] on any "ground that the petitioner raised or reasonably could have raised during that inter partes review."[72]

D. Duration

A critical characteristic of the inter partes review is the defined limit on the duration of the proceedings. Following the filing of a petition to institute an inter partes review, the Board has three months after the filing of the patent owner's preliminary response to

---

in a proceeding that is ordered or instituted pursuant to section 304, 314, or 324. If any such written statement or additional information is subject to an applicable protective order, such statement or information shall be redacted to exclude information that is subject to that order.") (emphasis added).

[66] Robert M. Asher, *Claim Construction on the Verge of Transformation: The Disruptive Promise of Inter Partes Review*, SUNSTEIN KAHN MURPHY & TIMBERS (Apr. 2012), http://sunsteinlaw.com/claim-construction-on-the-verge-of-transformation-the-disruptive-promise-of-inter-partes-review/.

[67] *See id.* ("[T]he PTO has proposed that the 'broadest reasonable construction' standard be applied in inter partes reviews.").

[68] *See* 35 U.S.C. § 318(a).

[69] *Id.* § 319.

[70] *Id.* § 315(e)(1).

[71] *Id.* § 315(e)(2).

[72] *Id.*; *see also* Charles L. Gholz, Michael L. Kiklis, & Alexander B. Englehart, *Is The Estoppel Of The New AIA Proceedings Worse Than Interference Estoppel?*, INTELL. PROP. TODAY (Jan. 2013), http://www.iptoday.com/issues/2013/01/is-estoppel-new-aia-proceedings-worse-than-interference-estoppel.asp.

make a decision to grant or deny the petition.[73] Where a proceeding is instituted, the Board enters a final written decision within one year, which is extendable up to six months for good cause.[74] Thus, the entire inter partes review duration from petition to final written decision cannot be longer than eighteen to twenty-four months as defined by the statute.[75]

E. Cost

Although proportionally few inter partes reviews have reached a final written decision,[76] sources have tried to approximate the overall cost of an inter partes review.[77] For fees due to the Patent Office, an inter partes review petition costs $9,000 while the post-institution fee is $14,000.[78] If the petition challenges more than twenty claims, a $200 fee per claim in excess of twenty is applied. [79] If the review is instituted with greater than fifteen claims, a $400 fee per claim in excess of fifteen is applied.[80] Based on a median billing rate of $340 per hour and an estimated 135 attorney hours necessary to prepare an inter partes review petition, the petition is projected to cost $46,000, in

---

[73] *See* 35 U.S.C. § 314(b) ("The Director shall determine whether to institute an inter partes review under this chapter pursuant to a petition filed under section 311 within 3 months after—(1) receiving a preliminary response to the petition under section 313; or (2) if no such preliminary response is filed, the last date on which such response may be filed.").
[74] *Id.* § 316(a)(11).
[75] *See* Asher, *supra* note 66.
[76] Lagatta & Lewis, *supra* note 13.
[77] *See* 37 C.F.R. § 42.15(a) (2014); Changes to Implement Inter Partes Review Proceedings, 77 Fed. Reg. 7041 (Feb. 10, 2012) (proposed Feb. 10, 2012) (to be codified at 37 C.F.R. pt. 42); *id.*
[78] *See* 37 C.F.R. § 42.15(a).
[79] *See id.*
[80] *See id.*

addition to the filing fee.[81] A preliminary response is projected to require 100 attorney hours and cost $34,000.[82] Still, the greatest costs are expected to occur post-institution with estimated costs for expert witnesses, depositions, and trial preparation rising to an estimated $300,000 to $800,000[83] for a total estimated cost of $400,000 to $900,000 through trial.

III. INTER PARTES REEXAMINATION: THE DETAILS

The Optional Inter partes Reexamination Procedures Act of 1999 created, for the first time, a mechanism for a third party to actively participate in proceedings challenging the validity of patent claims before the Patent Office.[84] The inter partes reexamination procedure was designed to reduce the amount of patent litigation in the United States district courts.[85] Although the Patent Office enacted the ex partes reexamination procedure in 1980, the proceeding was unpopular because of a lack of third-party involvement in the process,[86] which would then be subject to estoppel measures.[87] A summary of the characteristics of inter partes reexamination will be

---

[81] Changes to Implement Inter Partes Review Proceedings, 77 Fed. Reg. at 7057–58 (proposed Feb. 10, 2012) (to be codified at 37 CFR Part 42).
[82] *Id.*
[83] Lagatta & Lewis, *supra* note 13.
[84] Kenneth L. Cage & Lawrence T. Cullen, *An Overview of* Inter partes *Reexamination Procedures*, 85 J. PAT. & TRADEMARK OFF. SOC'Y 931, 939 (2003).
[85] *Id.* at 938.
[86] 145 CONG. REC. H11,769 (daily ed. Nov. 9, 1999) ("Congress enacted legislation to authorize ex parte reexamination of patents in the USPTO in 1980, but such reexamination has been used infrequently since a third party who requests reexamination cannot participate at all after initiating the proceedings.").
[87] Stefan Blum, Note, *Ex Parte Reexamination: A Wolf in Sheep's Clothing*, 73 OHIO ST. L.J. 395, 420 (2012).

provided in order to foster comparisons with inter partes review. [88]

A. Filing the inter partes reexamination petition

The inter partes reexamination procedure was limited to patents filed on or after November 29, 1999.[89] Reexamination petitions could challenge the validity of a patent on basis of patentability over prior art patents and other printed publications.[90] Thus, while challenges based on 35 U.S.C. § 103 and some portions of § 102 were permitted, challenges based on section 112 were not permitted.[91] Unlike an ex parte reexamination, neither the patent owner[92] nor the Patent Office[93] could request or institute an inter partes reexamination.

B. Standard to institute a reexamination

An inter partes reexamination proceeding was instituted where a *substantial new question* of patentability existed.[94] Though the standard used the term *new*, this did not mean that all previously cited prior art was excluded.[95] Legislation signed on November 2, 2002,[96] clarified that the term *new* did not

---

[88] For a more thorough descriptions of the inter partes reexamination procedure see Cage & Cullen, *supra* note 84.
[89] *Id.* at 931.
[90] *Id.* at 940-41.
[91] *Id.*
[92] This is likely because no practical advantage is obtained by conducting an inter partes reexamination absent a third party compared to simply conducting an ex parte reexamination. It would just cost the petitioner significantly more money. *See id.* at 939 (noting that an inter partes reexamination fee is $8,800 and an ex parte reexamination fee is $2,520).
[93] *Id.* at 944-45 (noting that an inter partes reexamination may not be instituted solely at the Director's discretion).
[94] *Id.* at 941.
[95] *See id.* at 940-41.
[96] *See id.* (quoting 35 U.S.C. § 312(a) (2012) ("the existence of a substantial new question of patentability is not precluded by the fact

exclude previously cited art, a position that was challenged in *In re Portola Packaging, Incorporated*.[97] The determination of whether or not a substantial new question of patentability existed was not appealable.[98]

Inter partes reexamination operated from November 29, 1999,[99] until it was replaced with inter partes review on September 16, 2012.[100] Between September 16, 2011 and September 16, 2012, the AIA shifted the standard for instituting an inter partes reexamination.[101] The AIA replaced the substantial new question standard with the inter partes review reasonable likelihood standard.[102]

C. The reexamination

An inter partes reexamination was an examinational proceeding[103] similar to the application process for a patent. However, a third party was given thirty days to reply to all office actions and all responses by the patent owner.[104] Inter partes reexaminations were originally conducted by a new examiner[105] from the group of examiners responsible for examining patent applications, but in 2005, the Patent Office created the Central Reexamination Unit to centralize the reexamination

---

that a patent or printed publication was previously cited by or to the Office or considered by the Office.")).

[97] *In re* Portola Packaging, Inc., 110 F.3d 786 (Fed. Cir. 1997) (holding a substantial new question of patentability could not be found in an ex parte reexamination where the petition for reexamination relied completely on previously cited prior art).
[98] Cage & Cullen, *supra* note 84, at 941.
[99] *Id.* at 931.
[100] Baldwin & Gin, *supra* note 9; Kalinsky & Nguyen, *supra* note 10.
[101] MPEP § 2601 (9th ed., Mar. 2014).
[102] *Id.*
[103] Baldwin & Gin, *supra* note 9 (quoting H.R. REP. NO. 112-98, at 46 (2011)).
[104] *See* Cage & Cullen, *supra* note 84, at 946.
[105] *See id.* at 942.

proceedings into a single group of senior examiners responsible for handling reexaminations.[106]

During reexamination, the patent owner could amend the granted claims or substitute in new claims so long as any amendments did not expand the scope of the granted claims.[107] The submission of amendments was governed by the same rules governing amendments during patent prosecution; however, third party responses to the patent owner's amendments were required within a non-extendable thirty days.[108] During reexamination, the examiner construed the claims using the broadest reasonable interpretation standard.[109] An inter partes reexamination proceeding could maintain the broadest reasonable interpretation standard even if a district court proceeding previously rendered a claim construction using the proper meaning of a patent claim standard.[110]

Inter partes reexamination remained an "examinational" proceeding;[111] however, unlike the prosecution of a patent, neither party could request an interview with the examiner.[112] This was done so that the patent owner did not obtain an unfair advantage,[113]

---

[106] Robert C. Laurenson, *A Low-Cost Alternative to Litigation After PTO Reforms*, LAW360 (Sept. 10, 2007, 12:00 AM), http://www.law360.com/articles/34443/a-low-cost-alternative-to-litigation-after-pto-reforms.
[107] *See* Cage & Cullen, *supra* note 84, at 946.
[108] *See id.*
[109] *See* Asher, *supra* note 66.
[110] *See In re* Trans Tex. Holdings Corp., 498 F.3d 1290, 1298 (Fed. Cir. 2007).
[111] Baldwin & Gin, *supra* note 9 (quoting H.R. REP. NO. 112-98, at 46 (2011)).
[112] *See* Cage & Cullen, *supra* note 84, at 945 & n.70 (citing 37 C.F.R. § 1.955 (2000)).
[113] *See id.* at n.71 (citing Rules To Implement Optional Inter Partes Reexamination Proceedings, 65 Fed. Reg. 18154, 18161-62 (Apr. 6, 2000)).

so the proceedings could progress quickly,[114] and so the interview did not become an adversarial encounter if both parties were allowed to participate.

Following a determination of patentability and the closing of an inter partes proceeding, either the patent owner or the third party could appeal.[115] Initially, a third party was limited to appealing to the Board of Patent Appeals and Interferences; whereas the patent owner could appeal to the Board of Patent Appeals and Interferences and then to the Federal Circuit.[116] Following a November 2, 2002 legislative amendment, a third party could then also appeal the Board's decision to the Federal Circuit for inter partes reexaminations that began after the date of the amendment.[117] However, there was no mechanism to appeal decisions to the District Court for the District of Columbia.[118]

Following all appeals, the third party was estopped from further pursuing any action on issues of patentability that were resolved.[119] In other words, the third party was barred from asserting in any civil action "any ground which the third-party requester raised or could have raised during the inter partes reexamination proceedings."[120] The third party was also barred in any subsequent inter partes reexamination from challenging a "patent claim on the basis of issues which that party or its privies raised or could have raised in

---

[114] *Id.*
[115] *See id.* at 949.
[116] *See id.* at 950.
[117] *Id.*
[118] *Id.* at 950–51 ("[T]his avenue of appeal was not included in the legislation because it is rarely taken in existing ex parte reexaminations, and its elimination should prevent undue delay in the inter partes reexamination process.").
[119] *See id.* at 952.
[120] 35 U.S.C. § 315 (2006) (amended 2011).

such civil action or inter partes reexamination proceeding."[121]

D. Duration

An inter partes reexamination was still an "examinational" proceeding[122] though it was conducted with "special dispatch within the Office."[123] Despite the special dispatch, inter partes reexaminations were often regarded as "suffer[ing] from a protracted timetable."[124] The entire inter partes reexamination process took "a few years before the examiner, a couple of years before the Board of Appeals, and a year at the Federal Circuit Court of Appeals."[125] Without considering the durations of the appeals to the Board and the court of appeals, an inter partes reexamination still took approximately three years to reach a final decision.[126] The Office hoped to reduce the average time to reach a final decision to two years with the implementation of the Central Reexamination Unit, but this was not successful.[127]

E. Cost

An inter partes reexamination petition was required to be accompanied by an $8,800 fee payable to the Patent Office.[128] However, if a substantial new question

---

[121] *Id.* § 317.
[122] Baldwin & Gin, *supra* note 9 (quoting H.R. REP. NO. 112-98, at 46 (2011)).
[123] 35 U.S.C. § 305.
[124] Asher, *supra* note 66.
[125] *Id.*
[126] *See Inter partes Reexamination Filing Data*, U.S. PATENT & TRADEMARK OFFICE (Sept. 30, 2013) [hereinafter U.S. Patent & Trademark Office, *Inter Partes Data*], http://www.uspto.gov/patents/stats/inter_parte_historical_stats_roll_up_EOY2013.pdf; Baldwin & Gin, *supra* note 9.
[127] *See* Laurenson, *supra* note 106.
[128] Cage & Cullen, *supra* note 84, at 939.

of patentability was not found, the fee was returned except for an $830 filing fee.[129] In addition to the filing fee, the total cost of an inter partes reexamination was estimated to be about $280,000 inclusive of an appeal to the Federal Circuit.[130]

F. Rates of institution and claim invalidation

Inter partes reexamination was slow to be utilized having only five filings from 2000 to 2002.[131] However, the use of inter partes reexamination was statutorily limited to a patent issued from an application filed on or after November 29, 1999.[132] Thus, the use of inter partes reexamination was initially limited by the number of patents meeting the criteria that were being granted. In the final fiscal year of inter partes reexamination, 530 petitions were filed.[133] In all, 1919 inter partes reexamination petitions were filed between November 29, 1999 and September 15, 2012.[134] Of those petitions, 45% were electrical, 25% were mechanical, and 15% were chemical.[135] The majority of the petitions, roughly 76%, were involved in concurrent litigation.[136]

Once filed, approximately 93% of the reexamination petitions were granted.[137] The overwhelming majority of these petitions were granted by the examiner with a fraction granted upon petition to the Director.[138] At the conclusion of the inter partes reexamination

---

[129] *Id.* at 940.
[130] AM. INTELL. PROP. LAW ASSOC., REPORT OF THE ECONOMIC SURVEY, I-173 to I-176 (July 2011) [hereinafter AIPLA, *Survey 2011*]).
[131] U.S. Patent & Trademark Office, *Inter Partes Data, supra* note 126.
[132] *See* MPEP § 2601 (9th ed., Mar. 2014).
[133] U.S. Patent & Trademark Office, *Inter Partes Data, supra* note 126.
[134] *Id.*
[135] *Id.*
[136] *Id.*
[137] *Id.*
[138] *Id.*

proceeding, a certificate of patentability was issued.[139] Of the 696 certificates issued between 1999 and September 30, 2013, 61 percent of certificates had at least some claim changes.[140] Thirty-one percent of the issued certificates canceled all of the claims.[141] On the other hand, only 8 percent of the issued certificates affirmed all of the previously granted claims.[142]

IV. PATENT LITIGATION: THE DETAILS

The United States federal courts are the primary venue for challenging the validity of patents, usually defenses in patent infringement proceedings.[143] With more patent litigation being filed in the district courts than ever before[144] and with the cost of patent litigation continuing to rise,[145] alternative methods of challenging a patent may be necessary. However, patent litigation continues to offer types of validity challenges that are not yet available through other means.[146] Thus, it is unlikely that the rate of patent litigation will subside in the near future.

---

[139] *See* MPEP § 2688 (9th ed. Rev. 1, Mar. 2014).
[140] U.S. Patent & Trademark Office, *Inter Partes Data, supra* note 126.
[141] *Id.*
[142] *Id.*
[143] *See* ROBERT SMYTH, UNITED STATES PATENT INVALIDITY STUDY 2012 (Sept. 2012), https://www.morganlewis.com/pubs/Smyth_USPatentInvalidity_Sept 12.pdf.
[144] CHRIS BARRY ET AL., PRICEWATERHOUSECOOPERS LLP, 2012 PATENT LITIGATION STUDY: LITIGATION CONTINUES TO RISE AMID GROWING AWARENESS OF PATENT VALUE 6 (2012), *available at* http://patentlyo.com/media/docs/2013/03/2012-patent-litigation-study.pdf.
[145] *See* AIPLA, *Survey 2011, supra* note 130, at 35; AM. INTELL. PROP. LAW ASSOC., REP. OF THE ECON. SURVEY 34 (2013) [hereinafter AIPLA, *Survey 2013*].
[146] Roger A. Ford, *Patent Invalidity Versus Noninfringement*, 99 CORNELL L. REV. 71, 78–81 (2013).

A. Patent litigation defenses

When accused of patent infringement, an individual may raise defenses of invalidity and noninfringement.[147] For the defense of invalidity, an individual can challenge the validity of a patent on the basis that the inventor did not comply with the statutory rules of patentability.[148] In this way, an invalidity challenge focuses on "the state of the world when the patent was granted rather than the details of the defendant's accused product or process."[149] There are three classes of invalidity defenses.[150] The first involves issues of novelty[151] and nonobviousness.[152] The novelty requirement necessitates that the "invention not have been known, used, or described by others before the patent applicant came up with the claimed invention."[153] The nonobviousness requirement necessitates "that an invention not have been obvious to a person having ordinary skill in the art as of the time of invention."[154] The second class of invalidity defenses[155] involves the adequacy of the disclosure[156] in the patent including issues of written description, enablement, and definiteness. The third class of invalidity defenses[157] involves challenges to the patentability of the subject

---

[147] See 35 U.S.C. § 282(b) (2012).
[148] Ford, *supra* note 146, at 78.
[149] *Id.*
[150] *Id.*; see also Andres Sawicki, *Better Mistakes in Patent Law*, 39 FLA. ST. U. L. Rev. 735 (2012).
[151] 35 U.S.C. § 102.
[152] *Id.* § 103.
[153] Ford, *supra* note 146, at 79.
[154] *See id.*
[155] *Id.* at 79–80.
[156] *See id.* at 80; *see also* 35 U.S.C. § 112 (codifying the requirements of a patent applicant's specification).
[157] *See* Ford, *supra* note 146, at 80.

matter[158] such as when the invention is not useful or is overly abstract.[159]

In addition to challenging the validity of a patent, an accused infringer may raise the defense of noninfringement.[160] A noninfringement defense contends that even if the patent is valid, the patent claims do not read onto the actions or products of the accused infringer.[161] In this manner, accused infringers may either challenge the validity of the patent on many grounds or may attest that their actions or products do not fall within the claims of the patent.

B. Standards of proof

When a patent is challenged in a district court proceeding, the challenger faces an uphill battle.[162] The United States Patent Act[163] has defined what has become known as the presumption of validity. The presumption of validity mandates that a patent be held valid unless the challenger presents *clear and convincing evidence* of invalidity.[164] The clear and convincing evidence standard is a "very high evidentiary bar" for a

---

[158] *See id.* at 80-81; *see also* 35 U.S.C. § 101 (codifying the requirements for subject matter patent eligibility).
[159] MPEP § 2104 (9th ed., Rev. 1 Mar. 2014).
[160] 35 U.S.C. § 282(b)(1); *see* 6 R. CARL. MOY, MOY'S WALKER ON PATENTS § 17:14 (4th ed. 2013).
[161] Ford, *supra* note 146, at 81.
[162] *See* Doug Lichtman & Mark A. Lemley, *Rethinking Patent Law's Presumption of Validity*, 60 STAN. L. REV. 45, 51 (2007).
[163] 35 U.S.C. § 282(a) ("A patent shall be presumed valid. Each claim of a patent (whether in independent, dependent, or multiple dependent form) shall be presumed valid independently of the validity of other claims; dependent or multiple dependent claims shall be presumed valid even though dependent upon an invalid claim. The burden of establishing invalidity of a patent or any claim thereof shall rest on the party asserting such invalidity."); *see also* Lichtman & Lemley, *supra* note 162, at 51.
[164] *Id.* (internal quotation marks omitted).

challenger to overcome.[165] The standard is higher than the *mere preponderance of the evidence* standard[166] and may be more closely likened to the *beyond a reasonable doubt* standard used in criminal proceedings.[167] Though the policy considerations behind the standard are not clear, the district courts use the presumption of validity as a basis for giving deference to the Patent Office's granting of a patent.[168]

A crucial stage in patent litigation is the court's claim construction.[169] Claim construction in litigation uses the "proper meaning" standard.[170] The proper meaning of a patent claim is determined by a combination of intrinsic and extrinsic evidence with an emphasis on the intrinsic evidence.[171] Intrinsic evidence consists of the patent's specification and the prosecution history.[172] Extrinsic evidence "consists of all evidence external to the patent and prosecution history, including expert and inventor testimony, dictionaries, and learned treatises."[173]

C. Duration

---

[165] *Id.*
[166] *See* Parker v. Motorola, Inc., 524 F.2d 518, 521 (5th Cir. 1975).
[167] *See, e.g.*, Ludlow Corp. v. Textile Rubber & Chem. Co., 636 F.2d 1057, 1059 (5th Cir. 1981) ("The burden on one who would invalidate a patent is a heavy one. It has been described variously as one of proof 'beyond a reasonable doubt', and is one 'by clear and convincing evidence.'") (quoting Zachos v. Sherwin-Williams Co., 177 F.2d 762, 763 (5th Cir. 1949); Hobbs v. U.S. Atomic Energy Comm'n, 451 F.2d 849, 856 (5th Cir. 1971) ("[T]he presumption of patent validity may be rebutted only by a quantum of proof—whether it be called clear and convincing or beyond a reasonable doubt—which is greater than a mere preponderance of the evidence."); Kiva Corp. v. Baker Oil Tools, Inc., 412 F.2d 546, 551 (5th Cir. 1969)).
[168] Lichtman & Lemley, *supra* note 162, at 52.
[169] *See* Markman v. Westview Instruments, Inc., 517 U.S. 370 (1996).
[170] Asher, *supra* note 66.
[171] Phillips v. AWH Corp., 415 F.3d 1303, 1317 (Fed. Cir. 2005).
[172] *Id.*
[173] *Id.* (quoting *Markman*, 52 F.3d at 980 (en banc)).

Many factors go into determining the duration of a patent litigation proceeding.[174] The average time-to-trial from 1995 to 2011 was 2.3 years.[175] This duration only slightly increased to 2.5 years for the recent the period of 2005 to 2011.[176] This slight increase in time-to-trial may be related to the increased case volume[177] or based on other factors. Despite the national average exceeding two years, certain districts have had substantially shorter time-to-trial durations.[178] For example, the District Court of the Eastern District of Virginia had a median time-to-trial of 0.97 years over seventeen cases, and the District Court of the Western District of Wisconsin had a median time-to-trial of 1.07 years over ten cases.[179] Even the District Court of the District of Delaware had a median time-to-trial duration of 1.9 years over 105 cases.[180]

D. Cost

Patent litigation is an expensive endeavor.[181] Litigation costs include both attorneys' fees and costs related to product investigation, prior art searches, and expert testimonies.[182] As the number of patent litigation cases continues to rise,[183] so too does the cost of patent litigation.[184] In 2011, the median cost of patent litigation where less than $1,000,000 was at stake, was $350,000

---

[174] BARRY ET AL., *supra* note 144, at 22.
[175] *Id.* at 5.
[176] *Id.* at 21.
[177] *Id.*
[178] *Id.* at 22.
[179] *Id.*
[180] *Id.*
[181] *See* AIPLA, *Survey 2011, supra* note 130, at 35.
[182] *Id.*
[183] BARRY ET AL., *supra* note 144, at 6.
[184] *See* AIPLA, *Survey 2011, supra* note 130, at 35; AIPLA, *Survey 2013, supra* note 145, at 34.

through discovery and $650,000 overall.[185] When more than $25,000,000 was at stake, the median cost of litigation rose to $3,000,000 through discovery and $5,000,000 overall.[186] Contrasting the costs in 2011 with the costs in 2013, the median cost of litigation, where less than $1,000,000 was at stake, was still $350,000 through discovery but rose to $700,000 overall.[187] Similarly, the median cost of litigation, where over $25,000,000 was at stake, was still $3,000,000 though discovery but rose to $5,500,000 overall.[188] Thus, patent litigation is not cheap by any measure.[189]

E. Rates of patent litigation and patent invalidation

The rate at which patent cases are being filed in the district courts continues to rise.[190] In 2011, there were 4,015 patent cases filed.[191] This marked a 22 percent increase from 2010.[192] Thus, patent litigation is more prevalent than ever.[193]

As the volume of patent cases increases,[194] the rate that district courts are finding patents valid is decreasing.[195] From 2007 to 2011, there were 283 cases filed in a district court where a disposition on validity

---

[185] AIPLA, *Survey 2011, supra* note 130, at 35.
[186] *Id.*
[187] AIPLA, *Survey 2013, supra* note 145, at 34.
[188] *Id.*
[189] *See id.*; AIPLA, *Survey 2011, supra* note 130, at 35.
[190] BARRY ET AL., *supra* note 144, at 6.
[191] *Id.*
[192] *Id.*
[193] *See id.*
[194] *See id.*
[195] *See* SMYTH, *supra* note 143, at 2 (stating the methods utilized as follows: "Data for this article was compiled by searching for all patent cases on Westlaw and LexisNexis from 2007 to 2011 that were filed in a federal district court where a disposition on the validity of a patent was decided. Two-hundred and eighty-three cases were identified from 2007 to 2011 where the validity of a claim in a patent was challenged.").

was made.[196] Of those, only 14 percent were determined to be valid and enforceable.[197] The validity rate was 20 percent in 2007 for fifty-eight cases, but the rate decreased to only 6 percent in 2011 over forty-eight cases.[198] Interestingly, the number of cases where a decision on the validity of the patent was made stayed roughly the same over the measured period.[199] Patents related to mechanical devices and pharmaceutical drugs had the highest rates of invalidation.[200] Lastly, from 2002 to May 2012, the Federal Circuit affirmed the invalidity findings over 70 percent of the time.[201]

V. COMPARING INTER PARTES REVIEW, INTER PARTES REEXAMINATION, AND PATENT LITIGATION

Inter partes review replaced inter partes reexamination on September 16, 2012.[202] In order to determine whether inter partes review is a fair and quality mechanism to challenge patents, it can be compared to inter partes reexamination and patent litigation based on procedural aspects, duration, costs, and rates of institution and claim cancelling. More thorough procedural comparisons can be found elsewhere, but this report will focus on significant differences that might affect a client's decision to utilize inter partes review.

---

[196] *Id.*
[197] *Id.*
[198] *Id.*
[199] *Id.*
[200] *Id.* at 9.
[201] *Id.* at 4–8 ("Data for this section was compiled by searching for all patent cases on Westlaw and LexisNexis from 2002 to May 25, 2012 that were appealed to the Federal Circuit. 1,800 cases were reviewed and sorted based on whether the case was decided on patent invalidity.").
[202] Kalinsky & Nguyen, *supra* note 10.

A. Procedural comparison

Before comparing the procedural characteristics of the three methods, two critical points must be made. First, inter partes review and inter partes reexamination were designed to give third parties a fast and relatively cheap mechanism to challenge the validity of a patent on the basis of prior art patents and printed publications outside of district court proceedings.[203] Second, in both inter partes proceedings, the rules favor the third-party challenger "who enjoys an unlimited amount of time to plan a strategy to attack the patent, secure experts to support his position, and prepare written reports."[204] By contrast, the discovery stage of a trial acts as an equalizer.

1. Acceptable grounds to challenge patent's validity

The change from inter partes reexamination to inter partes review transformed the third party validity-challenging proceedings before the Patent Office "from an examinational to an adjudicative proceeding."[205] Inter partes reexamination operated as a "prosecution-like" proceeding whereas inter partes review now operates as a type of "mini-trial,"[206] utilizing some of the standards previously reserved for litigation.[207] Unlike the inter partes methods, district courts can hear validity challenges on all matters of novelty,[208]

---

[203] *See* Baldwin & Gin, *supra* note 9; Leslie A. McDonell & Robert A. Pollock, *Inter Partes Review: Tips For The Patent Holder*, FINNEGAN (May 24, 2013), http://www.finnegan.com/resources/articles/articlesdetail.aspx?news=339129db-4df9-4439-a216-91cca9ba55f3.
[204] Baldwin & Gin, *supra* note 9.
[205] *Id.* (quoting H.R. REP. NO. 112-98, at 46 (2011)).
[206] Baldwin & Gin, *supra* note 9.
[207] Asher, *supra* note 66.
[208] *See* 35 U.S.C. § 102 (2012).

obviousness,[209] written description,[210] and subject matter.[211] These additional challenges, namely written description, subject matter, and novelty challenges based on non-prior art patents and printed publications, to the validity of a patent are excluded from inter partes review because they are believed to require witnesses and other evidentiary proceedings[212] for which a district court is better situated.[213] However, when challenging solely on the basis of prior art patents and printed publications, the judges of the Patent Trial and Appeal Board may be more willing to allow for the combination of multiple prior art references relative to district courts.[214]

2. Length considerations

There were no limits to the number of grounds that challengers could raise against the validity of a claim in an inter partes reexamination.[215] Similarly, there were no limits to the number of claim amendments that a patent owner could make.[216] The inter partes review procedure does not prohibit the practice of amending claims as such amendments may be beneficial to clarify ambiguities within the claims;[217] however, the *inter partes* review only allows for "a reasonable number of substitute claims."[218] Consequently, the average number

---

[209] *See id.* at § 103.
[210] *See id.* at § 112.
[211] *See id.* at § 101.
[212] *See* FED. R. CIV. P. 26–36.
[213] Lagatta & Lewis, *supra* note 13.
[214] *See* Shuchman, *supra* note 39.
[215] Davis, *Tips for Killing Patents, supra* note 11.
[216] The number of amendments proposed by the patent owner could range from a few dozen to hundreds. Siminski, et al., *supra* note 5.
[217] *See* 4 LESTER HORWITZ & ETHAN HORWITZ, PATENT OFFICE RULES & PRACTICE § 42.12 (Matthew Bender 2014) (citing the USPTO's response to comment 30 made in regards to 37 CFR Part 42 [Docket No. PTO-P-2011-0083]).
[218] 35 U.S.C. § 316(a)(9) (2012).

of proposed amended claims in an inter partes review proceeding is only six with even fewer being admitted.[219] As a result, the average length of an inter partes reexamination petition was 246 pages.[220] An inter partes review petition, by contrast, is limited to sixty pages[221] and many district courts impose brief limits, which vary from ten to twenty-five pages.[222]

3. Oral arguments

The shift "from an examinational to an adjudicative proceeding"[223] was designed to make the validity-challenging proceeding before the Patent Office truly adversarial.[224] Whereas declarations supporting one's position could be filed in an inter partes reexamination proceeding, parties could never challenge the declarations through depositions.[225] The shift to allow expert depositions is a critical part of a party's inter partes review case.[226] An oral argument, which was previously limited on appeal to the Board of Patent Appeals and Interferences, is now a part of the inter partes review proceedings.[227] While these litigation-like components of discovery and oral arguments may make a client feel like they are more effectively challenging the validity of the patent claims before the

---

[219] *See* Siminski et al., *supra* note 5.
[220] As measured from October 1, 2010, to June 30, 2011. PATENT OFFICE RULES & PRACTICE, *supra* note 217, at 12-778 (stating the USPTO's consideration of the economic impact of the final rules on small entities).
[221] Davis, *Tips for Killing Patents*, *supra* note 11.
[222] HORWITZ & HORWITZ, *supra* note 217, at 12-778.
[223] *See* Baldwin & Gin, *supra* note 9 (quoting H.R. REP. NO. 112-98, pt.1, at 46 (2011)).
[224] *Id.*
[225] *Id.*
[226] *See id.*; Prange & Morton, *supra* note 25.
[227] *See* Baldwin & Gin, *supra* note 9.

Patent Office, these changes bring with it litigators and litigation-like costs.[228]

4. Institution standards

There is a statutory procedural change to go from the petition stage to the institution of the inter partes proceedings. In inter partes reexamination, a proceeding was instituted if a "substantial new question of patentability" was raised in the petition.[229] In inter partes review, a proceeding is instituted if "a reasonable likelihood that the petitioner would prevail with respect to at least one challenged claim."[230] On the surface, it appears that inter partes review has a heightened institution standard.[231] However, September 16, 2011 to September 15, 2012 provided a case study as to whether the implementation of the two standards is in fact different.[232] During this period, inter partes reexaminations utilized the reasonable likelihood standard for institution.[233] In 2011, 342 of 366 requests for inter partes reexamination were granted under the substantial new question standard for a granting rate of 93 percent.[234] Of the initial forty-two reexamination orders issued under the reasonable likelihood standard, thirty-eight were granted for a granting rate of 90 percent.[235] Thus, despite the statutory definitions of the standards, there does not appear to be an as-applied difference between the standards.[236]

---

[228] *See* Loh & Hill, *supra* note 49.
[229] Cage & Cullen, *supra* note 84, at 941.
[230] 35 U.S.C. § 314(a) (2012).
[231] HORWITZ & HORWITZ § 42.108, *supra* note 217.
[232] *See* MPEP § 2601 (9th ed. Rev. 1, Mar. 2014).
[233] *Id.*
[234] Smyth, *supra* note 143, at 14.
[235] *Id.*
[236] *See id.*

5. Claim construction standards

Across the three proceedings, there is a sharp contrast among the claim construction standards. Inter partes reexamination used the broadest reasonable interpretation standard.[237] This interpretation standard coincided with an ability to freely amend the claims so as to resolve ambiguities because of the broad interpretation standard.[238] By contrast, district court proceedings utilize the proper meaning standard[239] paired with a presumption of validity.[240] In inter partes review, the statute requires the Board to construct the claims using the "proper meaning of a patent claim."[241] This shift in claim construction standard means that inter partes review proceedings do not require as extensive of claim amendment procedures.[242] Despite the statutory language stating that the proper meaning standard is to be used before the Patent Office, there is doubt as to whether the proper meaning standard or the broadest reasonable interpretation standard is being used in inter partes reviews.[243] The fact that inter partes review does not contain a presumption of patent validity is consistent with the notion that the *broadest possible interpretation* standard is being used.[244] Thus, if

---

[237] *See* In re Hyatt, Rambus, Inc., 753 F.3d 1253, 1255 (Fed. Cir. 2014); Asher, *supra* note 66.
[238] PATENT OFFICE RULES & PRACTICE, *supra* note 217.
[239] Asher, *supra* note 66.
[240] 35 U.S.C. § 282(a) (2012); Microsoft Corp. v. i4i Ltd. P'ship, 131 S. Ct. 2238, 2242 (2011).
[241] 35 U.S.C. § 301(d) (2012).
[242] *See id.* at § 316(a)(9); PATENT OFFICE RULES & PRACTICE, *supra* note 217, at 12-880 (2014)(citing the USPTO's response to comment 35 regarding 37 CFR Part 42).
[243] *See* Asher, *supra* note 66 ("What does the AIA mean by the 'Proper Meaning' of a Patent Claim?").
[244] During examinational proceedings, the patent or putative-patent is given the broadest possible interpretation because the claims have not been finalized or are in the process of being reexamined. Conversely, adjudicative proceedings are working with finalized patent claims.

the Patent Office is using the broadest reasonable interpretation standard, the claim construction standard used for inter partes review favors the challenger because there is no presumption of validity.[245]

6. Standards of proof

The second legal standard that separates patent litigation from the inter partes methods is the standard of proof required to invalidate a patent.[246] Given the presumption of validity that exists in district court proceedings,[247] a patent may be invalidated in a district court proceeding only if the challenger presents clear and convincing evidence of invalidity.[248] Conversely, a challenger in an inter partes review need only establish invalidity by a preponderance of the evidence.[249] This was the same standard used for an inter partes reexamination.[250] This lower standard in the inter partes methods favors the challenger.[251]

7. Estoppel effects

The shift to inter partes review brought about a major shift in estoppel effects on inter partes methods. Both proceedings require the petitioner to identify a real party in interest to be bound by the decision.[252]

The claims no longer get the broadest possible interpretation but are given the presumption of validity. To have both a broadest possible interpretation and a presumption of validity would be inconsistent with the prior uses of the standards. Furthermore, the absence of both standards places the patent owner at a disadvantage on both fronts. *Id.*; Lagatta & Lewis, *supra* note 13.
[245] Lagatta & Lewis, *supra* note 13.
[246] *See* Asher, *supra* note 66.
[247] 35 U.S.C. § 282(a).
[248] Microsoft Corp. v. i4i Ltd. P'ship, 131 S. Ct. 2238, 2242 (2011).
[249] 37 C.F.R. § 42.1(d) (2014).
[250] In re Swanson, 540 F.3d 1368, 1377 (Fed. Cir. 2008).
[251] *See* Shah, *supra* note 12; Asher, *supra* note 66.
[252] *See* Cage & Cullen, *supra* note 84, at 952–53; Gholz, Kiklis, & Englehart, *supra* note 72, at 1.

However, two important differences exist.[253] First, inter partes reexamination utilizes the "raised or could have raised" standard;[254] whereas, inter partes review utilizes the "raised or reasonably could have raised" standard.[255] By statutory construction, the inter partes review estoppel standard is more narrow than the inter partes reexamination estoppel standard.[256] However, in inter partes review, estoppel is effective upon a final written decision; whereas, estoppel in inter partes reexamination is only effective after all appeals have been exhausted.[257] This different temporal estoppel effect may impact whether a judge would be willing to grant a discretionary stay in concurrent litigation pending the completion of the proceeding before the Patent Office.[258] Thus, the estoppel standard in inter partes review may be less harsh, but its immediate effect makes estoppel in inter partes review more potent.

8. Summation of procedural differences

Collectively, in comparing the two inter partes methods, inter partes review appears to have harsher procedural rules than inter partes reexamination. These harsher elements include limitations to length of the petition, the institution standard, the statutory claim construction standard, the immediacy of estoppel and

---

[253] See Lagatta & Lewis, supra note 13.
[254] 35 U.S.C. § 315(c) (2006) (amended 2011).
[255] Id. § 315(e).
[256] See Gholz, Kiklis, & Englehart, supra note 72 (discussing Congress' deliberate intention of relaxing the estoppel standard in the new inter partes review).
[257] See Asher, supra note 66.
[258] See Siminski et al., supra note 5 (discussing Kyocera Corp. v. Softview, LLC, IPR2013-00004 (P.T.A.B. Dec. 21, 2012), where the court denied a motion to stay after a petition for an inter partes reexamination was filed, but later granted a motion to stay after a petition for inter partes review was filed).

the appellate rights. Though these changes are limiting, they allow inter partes review to be concluded faster than inter partes reexamination proceedings, which has secondary effects such as increasing the likelihood that a concurrent district court proceeding will be stayed pending the decision from the Patent Trial and Appeal Board.

In comparing inter partes review to patent litigation, the limited scope and limited discovery rules may favor a patent owner more in an inter partes review than district court litigation. However, the claim construction standard likely being used and the standard of proof required to invalidate a patent clearly favor the challenger in the inter partes review. Thus, from a procedural perspective, it seems that inter partes review may be an adequate substitute for patent litigation with respect to what may be challenged in an inter partes review.

B. Durational comparison

The three patent-challenging methods are not exceptionally fast. Inter partes review has a statutory limit of eighteen to twenty-four months.[259] This inter partes review duration reduces the maximum duration by one-third relative to the average duration of an inter partes reexamination.[260] An inter partes review's statutory limit is not substantially faster than the

---

[259] Asher, *supra* note 66; *see* 35 U.S.C. § 316(a)(11) (2012) (stating that a final determination shall be made no later than one-year from institution, to be extendable for up to six months); 35 U.S.C. § 314(b) (stating that a decision on institution shall occur within three-months after receiving a patent owner's preliminary response); 37 C.F.R. § 42.107(b)(2014) ("The preliminary response must be filed no later than three months after the date of a notice indicating that the request to institute an inter partes review has been granted a filing date.").

[260] *See* U.S. Patent & Trademark Office, *Inter Partes Data*, *supra* note 126, at 1.

median time-to-trial of 2.5 years.[261] Additionally, some district courts have time-to-trial durations substantially shorter[262] than the inter partes review proceeding. Thus, it may not be temporally efficient to file an inter partes review in all cases. While an inter partes review may be faster than patent litigation as a stand-alone process, it has the potential to greatly elongate the litigation process when a stay is granted. However, given the claim invalidation rates to date,[263] it is more likely to shorten the litigation proceedings.

C. Cost comparison

The transition from "an examinational to an adjudicative proceeding"[264] has resulted in substantial cost differences at the Patent Office between the methods. For inter partes reexamination, the Patent Office required an $8,800 fee[265] but returned all but about $830 if a substantial new question of patentability was not found.[266] When filing an inter partes review a minimum fee of $23,000 is required, though this amount continues to rise as additional claims are challenged.[267] If the Board denies the petition to institute the inter partes review, then the post-institution fee of at least $14,000 is returned.[268] Therefore, even if an inter partes review is not instituted, the fee payable to the Patent Office for an

---

[261] BARRY ET AL., *supra* note 144, at 21.
[262] *Id.* at 22.
[263] *See* Prange & Cyrus, *supra* note 25 ("[T]he survival rate of claims is about 9.1%).
[264] Baldwin & Gin, *supra* note 9 (quoting H.R. Rep. No. 112-98, at 46 (2011)).
[265] Cage & Cullen, *supra* note 84, at 939.
[266] *Id.* at 940.
[267] *See* 37 C.F.R. § 42.15(a) (2014).
[268] Setting and Adjusting Patent Fees, 78 Fed. Reg. 4212, 4233 (Jan. 18, 2013) (to be codified at 37 C.F.R. pts. 1, 41, 42).

inter partes review is still greater than the fee payable for the institution of an inter partes reexamination.

Additionally, the transition from "an examinational to an adjudicative proceeding"[269] has resulted in substantial overall cost differences between the methods. An inter partes reexamination was estimated to cost $280,000.[270] That amount constitutes the low-end of the approximated cost of an inter partes review.[271] Overall, an inter partes review is projected to cost $300,000 to $800,000.[272] This substantial increase is most directly tied to the litigation-like expenses of discovery, depositions, and use of experts.[273] Thus, the expediency and the litigation-like aspects of inter partes review make it considerably more expensive both in the initial petition to the Patent Office and in overall costs of the proceedings.

As patent litigation has become more popular,[274] patent litigation costs have risen.[275] Though many factors can go into determining the overall cost of litigation, namely the amount of damages at stake, the cost of litigation on average can range from almost one million to six million dollars.[276] While the cost of an inter partes review is considerably less than the cost of patent litigation, this is not entirely a fair comparison. Of the early inter partes review filers, roughly 90 percent were involved in concurrent litigation.[277] Thus,

---

[269] *See* Baldwin & Gin, *supra* note 9 (quoting H.R. Rep. No. 112-98, at 46 (2011)).
[270] Wu & Maebius, *supra* note 1 (citing AIPLA *Survey 2011*, *supra* note 130, at I-173 to I-176).
[271] *See* Lagatta & Lewis, *supra* note 13.
[272] *Id.*
[273] *See id.*
[274] BARRY ET AL., *supra* note 144, at 6.
[275] *See* AIPLA, *Survey 2011*, *supra* note 130, at 35.
[276] AIPLA, *Survey 2013*, *supra* note 145, at 34.
[277] Kalinsky & Nguyen, *supra* note 10.

inter partes review is an intermediate proceeding of the overall litigation. If a defendant can get a stay of litigation[278] and is successful in invalidating all of the challenged patent claims, then the inter partes review costs were well spent. If the challenger is unsuccessful at invalidating all of the patent claims, then inter partes review costs plus the litigation costs may be greater than just the litigation costs, even though the inter partes review decision will have an estoppel effect on the litigation.[279] Thus, filing an inter partes review is a calculated financial risk which may result in savings or in additional costs for both parties, but given the claim invalidation rates to date,[280] it seems to be a worthwhile risk for most defendants.

D. Rates of institution and claim cancelling

In comparing the utility of each method for a patent challenger, one must consider what types of patents the methods are challenging; the rate of institution of the proceeding; and subsequently, the rate at which patent claims are canceled. The inter partes review and inter partes reexamination are used primarily for challenging electrical and mechanical patents, though inter partes review is more skewed towards challenging electrical patents. [281] Next, inter partes reexaminations were

---

[278] *See Id.*; 35 U.S.C. § 315(2); Siminski et al., *supra* note 5; Ryan Davis, *Judges At Odds Over Staying Cases for 3rd-Party Review*, Law360 (June 17, 2014, 8:42 PM), http://www.law360.com/articles/547846/judges-at-odds-over-staying-cases-for-3rd-party-aia-review.
[279] 35 U.S.C. § 315(e)(1) (2012).
[280] *See Experts Rule, supra* note 25.
[281] *See* U.S. Patent & Trademark Office, *Inter Partes Data, supra* note 126 (noting forty-five percent of filings were directed at electrical patents and twenty-five percent of filings were directed at mechanical patents); AIA STATISTICS, *supra* note 19 (noting 71.9% of filings have been directed at electrical patents and 15.3% of filings have been directed at mechanical patents).

instituted in 93 percent of the 2005 decisions from November 29, 1999, to September 30, 2013.[282] Comparatively, inter partes reviews were initially instituted at a rate of 96 percent[283] but have subsequently subsided to approximately 78 percent.[284] It is unclear whether this decrease is due to a refinement of the Patent Office's use of the reasonable likelihood standard or is a result of an increased number of marginal inter partes review applications. Recall, that as of this writing, there were 1,310 inter partes review petitions filed in 2014;[285] whereas, there were only 530 inter partes reexamination petitions filed in the last year it was available.[286] Overall, it seems that inter partes reviews and inter partes reexaminations are instituted at roughly the same rate depending on when in time one looks.

The two inter partes methods were designed to challenge the validity of patent claims on the basis of prior art patents and printed publications.[287] Surprisingly, despite the procedural differences noted above, the two methods have approximately the same rate of patent invalidation. In inter partes reexamination, only 8 percent of the issued certificates affirmed all of the previously patented claims.[288] As of June 18, 2014, roughly 17 percent of inter partes review decisions have affirmed all previously patented

---

[282] See U.S. Patent & Trademark Office, *Inter Partes Data, supra* note 126.
[283] O'Dell & King, *supra* note 28.
[284] See AIA STATISTICS, *supra* note 19.
[285] *Id.*
[286] See U.S. Patent & Trademark Office, *Inter Partes Data, supra* note 126.
[287] See Lagatta & Lewis, *supra* note 13; Laurenson, *supra* note 106.
[288] See U.S. Patent & Trademark Office, *Inter Partes Data, supra* note 126.

claims;[289] however, as of July 2014, only 9 percent of claims were held valid overall.[290] When district court invalidation rates are considered, the results are not that different. From 2007 to 2011, only 14 percent of patents were held valid where a disposition on validity was rendered in a district court proceeding.[291] This is near identical to the 17 percent of inter partes reviews which have been held valid from September 16, 2012, to June 18, 2014.[292] Recall, patent litigation includes all types of validity challenges. Thus, despite the concern for the cancellation rates of claims in inter partes review and the characterization of Patent Trial and Appeal Board judges as "death squads," the invalidation rates in inter partes review are no worse than in inter partes reexamination or patent litigation.[293] If anything, the invalidation rates for the inter partes review may be more favorable to the patent owner than in the previously available inter partes reexamination.

While the rates of affirming patents are similar between the two inter partes methods, the levels of invalidation diverge. In inter partes reexaminations, 31 percent of certificates cancelled all of the claims while 61 percent of the issued certificates resulted in some claim changes (e.g. claims were amended, canceled, or invalidated).[294] In inter partes review, 70 percent of the final decisions cancelled all of the claims while only 13 percent of the final decisions left some claims intact.[295] Thus, the two mechanisms may have similar rates for

---

[289] CHRISTOPHER DAVIS & LINHDA NGUYEN, IPR FINAL DECISION STATISTICS (June 28, 2014) (on file with author).
[290] See Experts Rule, supra note 25.
[291] See Smyth, supra note 143.
[292] DAVIS & NGUYEN, supra note 289.
[293] See Experts Rule, supra note 25.
[294] See U.S. Patent & Trademark Office, Inter Partes Data, supra note 126.
[295] DAVIS & NGUYEN, supra note 290.

affirming an entire patent, but they vary on whether some claims may survive the proceeding; as is evidenced by 40 percent fewer patents having survivable claims in inter partes reexamination relative to inter partes review.[296]

E. Conclusions of method comparison

In deciding whether inter partes review is a useful and fair mechanism for challenging the validity of patents, the institution and patent invalidation rates provide valuable insight. Because the institution rates are actually lower for inter partes review than inter partes reexamination and the patent invalidation rates are the lowest among the three methods, it is possible that the inter partes review is a more advantageous process for patent owners compared to the inter partes reexamination. Perhaps the concern about the inter partes review institution and invalidation rates has developed because of the sheer volume of inter partes review petitions being filed.

If the inter partes review proceeding seems "fair" from a statistical standpoint, many of the other characteristics are left to the personal preference of the client. In deciding whether a client prefers inter partes reexamination, patent litigation, or the new inter partes review, the client must decide how he or she wants to challenge the validity of the given claims and how quickly he or she wants the process done. Clients satisfied with an examinational proceeding lacking discovery, depositions, and experts were probably happier with the cheaper inter partes reexamination process and are sad to see it go. Doubling or tripling the cost of the validity challenge before the Patent Office may discourage use. However, if clients are convinced

---

[296] *See* U.S. Patent & Trademark Office, *Inter Partes Data, supra* note 126; DAVIS & NGUYEN, *supra* note 290.

they are getting a better challenge, then the cost may be worth it. Additionally, a shortened may encourage a stay of litigation proceedings, and may save the client money, as approximately 90 percent of early inter partes review petitions were filed when the patent was involved in concurrent litigation.[297]

VI. CONCLUSIONS

An early concern regarding inter partes review has been the rate at which patents are being invalidated.[298] However, when compared to other patent-invalidating methods, namely inter partes reexamination[299] and patent litigation,[300] the rate of patent invalidation is not alarming. In fact, the rates of the three methods are surprisingly similar, finding only 8 to 17 percent of challenged patents valid.[301] It should be noted that while early inter partes reviews may have had a higher invalidation rate, the most recent statistics indicate that it has the lowest invalidation rate of the three proceedings.[302]

A. If patents are going to be invalidated, what is the best method to use?

The preceding research and analysis show that patents are being invalidated at high rates regardless of the mechanism used.[303] Multiple factors may contribute to why patents are found invalid at such a high

---

[297] Kalinsky & Nguyen, *supra* note 10.
[298] See *Experts Rule*, *supra* note 25.
[299] See U.S. Patent & Trademark Office, *Inter Partes Data*, *supra* note 126.
[300] See Smyth, *supra* note 143.
[301] See *id.*; DAVIS & NGUYEN, *supra* note 289; U.S. Patent & Trademark Office, *Inter Partes Data*, supra note 126.
[302] See Smyth, *supra* note 143; DAVIS & NGUYEN, *supra* note 289; U.S. Patent & Trademark Office, Inter partes *Data*, *supra* note 126.
[303] See Smyth, *supra* note 143; DAVIS & NGUYEN, *supra* note 289; U.S. Patent & Trademark Office, *Inter Partes Data*, *supra* note 126.

frequency. Some part of it may be a result of changes in interpreting of obviousness[304] or subject-matter patentability[305] because of United States Supreme Court rulings.[306] For instance, patents granted under a prior interpretation of obviousness or subject-matter patentability may now be especially susceptible to being challenged. Others argue that patent examiners do not do their jobs well.[307] However, when clients can pay lawyers and technical experts seemingly endless amounts of money to challenge what a patent examiner does in roughly eighteen hours, the rate of invalidation is not the result of poor examinations.[308] In fact, the high invalidation rates do not acknowledge the fact that most patents are never litigated or even licensed.[309] Thus, if the few patents challenged, relative to the total number granted, are going to be invalidated at a high rate, it is important that clients choose the best method available to them.

Though no longer available,[310] inter partes reexamination was a slow,[311] limited[312] method of challenging patents. However, inter partes reexamination was the cheapest method because it was an examinational proceeding with no discovery procedures.[313] While it was effective at invalidating

---

[304] KSR Int'l Co. v. Teleflex Inc., 550 U.S. 398 (2007).
[305] *See* Alice Corp. Pty. v. CLS Bank Int'l, 134 S. Ct. 2347 (2014); Bilski v. Kappos,
561 U.S. 593 (2010).
[306] Wu & Maebius, *supra* note 1.
[307] Ford, *supra* note 146, at 87–88.
[308] Mark A. Lemley, *Rational Ignorance at the Patent Office*, 95 NW. U. L. REV. 1495, 1502 (2001).
[309] *Id.* at 1497.
[310] Kalinsky & Nguyen, *supra* note 10.
[311] *See* U.S. Patent & Trademark Office, *Inter Partes Data*, *supra* note 126.
[312] *See* Cage & Cullen, *supra* note 84, at 941 & n. 50.
[313] *See* Baldwin & Gin, *supra* note 9.

patents,[314] its prolonged duration[315] made it ineffective to use as part of a litigation strategy because judges were unwilling to grant stays in the litigation pending the inter partes reexamination.[316] Though it comes with an added financial burden, inter partes review is an overall better method of challenging the validity of patents because, in contrast to inter partes reexamination, judges seem to be willing to grant stays in litigation.[317] Since most inter partes reviews are filed where there is concurrent litigation,[318] the ability to obtain a stay can save challengers litigation costs because the Patent Trial and Appeal Board will likely simplify the issues at trial. Thus, inter partes review is favorable to inter partes reexamination.

In considering whether inter partes review should be utilized in favor of patent litigation, one must consider the location and complexity of the litigation. Some districts have time-to-trial durations substantially shorter[319] than the eighteen to twenty-four months that an inter partes review takes. In these situations, use of an inter partes review would prolong the overall proceedings and should be very carefully considered before being used. Additionally, if the litigation is particularly complex with many invalidity defenses, beyond prior art patents and publications and noninfringement defenses, the fraction of issues simplified in an inter partes review may make the inter

---

[314] *See* U.S. Patent & Trademark Office, *Inter Partes Data*, supra note 126.
[315] *See id.*
[316] *See* Siminski et al., *supra* note 5 (discussing *Softview LLC v. Kyocera* where the court denied a motion to stay after a petition for a inter partes reexamination was filed but later granted a motion to stay after a petition for inter partes review was filed).
[317] *Id.*
[318] *See* Kalinsky & Nguyen, *supra* note 10.
[319] BARRY ET AL., *supra* note 144, at 22.

partes review less useful than in other litigation situations. Thus, parties need to determine whether an inter partes review is actually useful to their situation.

B. *The future of* inter partes *review*

Inter partes review is already more popular than many believed it would be.[320] However, if it continues to grow in popularity, it may outpace its usefulness. Less than two years in, more than twice as many inter partes reviews are being filed compared to the last year of inter partes reexaminations.[321] If this rate continues, the Director will likely be forced to impose a cap on the number of inter partes reviews that can be filed each year.[322] The determining factor will be whether the Patent Office can hire and retain enough Patent Trial and Appeal Board judges to maintain the rate of inter partes reviews.[323]

In the not too distant future, inter partes review may become less popular through no fault of its own. On the same day that inter partes review replaced inter partes reexamination, the Patent Office also introduced a second patent-challenging proceeding, the post-grant review.[324] However, unlike inter partes review which could immediately be initiated on patents over nine months old, post-grant review required challenged patents to have an effective filing date of March 16, 2013, which coincides with the shift to first-to-file

---

[320] *See* Lagatta & Lewis, *supra* note 13; Siminski et al., *supra* note 5.

[321] *See* AIA STATISTICS, *supra* note 19; U.S. Patent & Trademark Office, *Inter Partes Data, supra* note 126.

[322] Siminski et al., *supra* note 5; *see* 37 C.F.R. § 42.102(b) (2014).

[323] Siminski et al., *supra* note 5.

[324] Kevin B. Laurence & Matthew C. Phillips, *Post-Grant Review Proceedings Compared with EPO Opposition*, INTELL. PROP. TODAY (Dec. 2011), *available at* http://www.iptoday.com/issues/2011/12/post-grant-review-proceedings-compared-with-epo-oppositions.asp.

priority.[325] As a result, post-grant review may not be feasible in a widespread manner until 2016 or 2017.[326]

Post-grant review has the potential to supersede inter partes review for two reasons. First, post-grant review allows a patent to be challenged on all types of invalidity including usefulness, subject-matter, novelty, obviousness, and written description.[327] Thus, post-grant review may be more useful as a pre-litigation proceeding. Additionally, whereas an inter partes review cannot be filed until nine months after a patent has been granted,[328] a post-grant review must be filed prior to nine months after a patent has been granted.[329] In this way, the use of inter partes reviews may become less common if clients decide to challenge the validity of a patent immediately upon the granting of their competitor's patent instead of waiting until litigation proceedings begin. It is hard to know whether inter partes review will continue to be popular once a critical mass of first-to-file patents exists, but there is no question that given the right circumstances, it is currently the best mode of challenging the validity of patents on prior art issues.

---

[325] *Id.*
[326] Sterne et al., *supra* note 24.
[327] 35 U.S.C. § 321(b) (2012) ("A petitioner in a post-grant review may request to cancel as unpatentable 1 or more claims of a patent on any ground that could be raised under paragraph (2) or (3) of section 282(b) (relating to invalidity of the patent or any claim).").
[328] *Id.* § 311(c).
[329] *Id.* § 321(c).

A SHORT HISTORY OF PATENT REMEDIES
JAMES RYAN[†]

I. Introduction 167
II. Patents in Early English Law 168
III. Early Patent Remedies 171
    A. Damage Provisions 1790–1800 171
    B. The Early History of Equity in
    Patent Remedies 174
    C. Award of Damages in Early Patent Cases 180
    D. Analysis of Damages and Equity 1790–1836 186

IV. The Development of Patent Remedies
After 1836 187
    A. Remedies Available at Law 188
    B. Equity in Patent Law 201
    C. Analysis of Damages and Equity after 1836 210

V. Reasonable Royalties and Ongoing Royalties 212
    A. The History of Reasonable Royalties 212
    B. The (Short) History of Ongoing Royalties 216

VI. Conclusion 219

[†] William Mitchell College of Law, *Juris Doctor* Candidate, May 2015. I would like to thank Professor Carl Moy and the students in the William Mitchell Intellectual Property Institute for their contribution to this paper. Thank you also to the staff and editors of Cybaris, and Professor Tom Cotter at the University of Minnesota for their edits and comments.

I. INTRODUCTION

Judge Kathleen O'Malley of the United States Court of Appeals for the Federal Circuit has recently called for reconsideration of when a patentee can recover enhanced damages from a willful infringer.[1] This is in light of two unanimous Supreme Court decisions, both issued on April 29, 2014, which overturned the Federal Circuit's handling of attorney fees in patent cases.[2] These decisions call into question the Federal Circuit's understanding of Supreme Court precedent[3] that has been the basis for attorney fees and enhanced damages.[4] This paper provides guidance on how enhanced damages and the entire subject of patent remedies (in both law and equity) should be reassessed. History shows that that there is an interdependent and intricate relationship of law and equity in patent remedies that has been missing in most of the current literature. This paper argues that the current applications of reasonable royalties, lost profits, enhanced damages, injunctions, and ongoing royalties should all be reevaluated in light of this history.

The first part of this article is a brief history of patents and their remedies in English law. The second part of this article reviews the early patent statutes with a focus on treble damages and their relationship with equity. The third part of the article discusses the evolution of various remedies prevalent in the 19th century, both at law and in equity. Finally, this article

---

[1] Halo Elecs., Inc. v. Pulse Elecs., Inc., 769 F.3d 1371, 1385 (Fed. Cir. 2014) (O'Malley, J., concurring).
[2] See Octane Fitness, L.L.C., v. Icon Health & Fitness, Inc., 134 S. Ct. 1749, 1752–53 (2014); Highmark, Inc. v. Allcare Health Mgmt. Sys., Inc., 134 S. Ct. 1744, 1747–48 (2014).
[3] See Octane Fitness, L.L.C., 134 S. Ct. at 1752–53, 1757 (overturning the "objective baselessness" standard for attorney fees); Highmark, Inc., 134 S. Ct. at 1747 (holding that an appellate court should review the award of attorney fees in patent cases for abuse of discretion).
[4] See Halo Elecs., Inc., 769 F.3d at 1385.

reviews reasonable royalties and ongoing royalties.

II. Patents in Early English Law

English history shows the politics of patents and the distinction between law and equity. In the 14th century, England granted "Letters Patent" to those who brought new industry to England.[5] These were not monopolies, but rather a license to foreign businessmen to come to England and practice their trade.[6] It was not until the 15th century that the grantees of these patents began to use the power of the Crown to develop monopolies.[7] Later, these monopolies were granted to basic items of commerce.[8] From the Crown's perspective, granting these monopolies was an easy way to gain favor with patent holders and was also a means to increase the Crown's treasury by way of fees.[9] Patentees often used equity courts (the English Court of Chancery, which has historically had a close relationship to the Crown[10]) and sometimes coercion to enforce their monopolies.[11]

---

[5] *See* Ramon A. Klitzke, *Historical Background of the English Patent Law*, 41 J. Pat. Off. Soc'y 615, 623 (1959).

[6] *Id.* at 623 ("The Letters Patent of protection granted . . . at this time were like passports which allowed [foreigners] to come to England and practice their trade."); Edward C. Walterscheid, *The Early Evolution of the United States Patent Law: Antecedents (Part 2)*, 76 J. Pat. & Trademark Off. Soc'y 849, 850 (1994).

[7] *See* 1 R. Carl Moy, Moy's Walker on Patents § 1:4 (4th ed. 2013).

[8] *Id.*

[9] *Id.* The word "patent" was not used until later. Edward C. Waltershield, *The Early Evolution of the United States Patent Law: Antecedents (Part 1)*, 76 J. Pat. & Trademark Off. Soc'y 697, 700 (1994).

[10] The Court of Chancery was derived from the King's Courts. D. M. Kerly, An Historical Sketch of the Equitable Jurisdiction of the Court of Chancery 7–9 (Fred B. Rothman & Co. 1986) (1890).

[11] *See* 4 David Hume, The History of England 345 (1778), *available at* http://oll.libertyfund.org/titles/hume-the-history-of-england-vol-4 ("Such high profits naturally begat intruders upon their commerce; and in order to secure themselves against encroachments, the patentees were armed with high and arbitrary powers from the council, by which they were enabled to oppress the people at pleasure, and to exact money from such as they thought proper to accuse of interfering with their patent.").

Because the Letters Patent covered basic commodities that the public had no choice but to buy, the prevention of continued infringement by way of an injunction (an equitable remedy) to preserve the monopoly was the relief sought. Rarely did patentees use common law courts, as these courts shared the public's disdain for the monopolization of basic commodities; therefore, patentees could not hope to find relief in common law courts.[12]

The recognition of social harm placed on the English citizens resulted in the passage of the Statute of Monopolies in 1623, which voided all patents.[13] However, the statute allowed the grant of new patents to those who created new inventions.[14] Though patents for inventions fared better in common law courts than those patents that monopolized basic commodities, patents and their enforcement by the Court of Chancery were still treated with distrust. James I, who sought to limit patents early in his reign[15] (20 years before the Statute of Monopolies was passed[16]) had confided jurisdiction to the courts of common law and excluded chancery jurisdiction from determining a patent's force or validity.[17] This would delay any equitable relief to patentees until, and only if, the validity of the patent was confirmed and legal relief was

---

[12] MOY, *supra* note 7, § 1.5; Klitzke, *supra* note 5, at 645. An excellent example is the case of Edward Darcy's license for making and importing playing cards. E. Wyndham Hulme, *The History of the Patent System Under the Prerogative and at Common Law*, 16 L.Q. REV. 44, at 51 (1900) *reviewed in* Klitzke, *supra* note 5, at 645. Darcy's decision to bring an infringement action is described as a "disastrous mistake" because challenges to the validity of his license were prohibited, that is until he brought the case in front of the common law court. Klitzke, *supra* note 5, at 645.
[13] *See* Statute of Monopolies, 21 Jac. 1, c. 3, § I (1623) (Eng.).
[14] *See id.* § VI.
[15] MOY, *supra* note 7, § 1:4.
[16] Klitzke, *supra* note 5, at 647–48.
[17] *See* 3 WILLIAM C. ROBINSON, THE LAW OF PATENTS FOR USEFUL INVENTIONS §§ 932, 1081 (1890).

inadequate.[18] Though the validity and enforcement of a patent resided in courts of law in theory,[19] eventually this divide was eroded when chancellors granted preliminary injunctions to accompany the suits at law.[20] This was but one example of the Court of Chancery resisting any interference of the Crown's prerogative (the grant of patents) from common law courts.[21]

There are important points to be made from this early history that contextualize the rest of this paper: First, it was understood early on that the value of the patent is the monopoly pricing.[22] Second, there is a social cost to monopoly pricing, which leads to resistance of granting equity to patentees.[23] Third, the dual system of courts of law and courts of equity, and the rivalry between those courts, which was influential in early United States politics. Finally, notice the theoretical divide between law and equity, and the tendency to ignore it. These points are all relevant to understanding patent remedies in the United States.

---

[18] *Id.* § 1081.
[19] *Id.*
[20] *Id.*
[21] *See* ROBINSON, *supra* note 21, § 932 n.3 (citing Wilson v. Tindal, (1841), 1 Web. P.C. 730 (Eng.) (noting where the judge treated the trial at law as within the chancery court). Eventually, Parliament conferred all equity powers to the courts of law in patent cases in 1854.
[22] ROBINSON, *supra* note 17, § 932 ("The redress afforded by an action at law consisting simply in an award of damages for past infringements was early found to be inadequate for the protection of the patentee."). It is important to note that this article does not assert that a patent and a monopoly are synonymous, as doing so is highly controversial. *See* ALBERT WALKER, TREATISE ON LAW AND INVENTIONS § 12 (6th ed. 1929). The assertion is that a patentee has exclusive control of pricing, which is not necessarily a monopoly "in the old sense of the word." *Id.* § 12, p. 17.
[23] Critiques of the monopoly system surfaced in English Parliament as early as 1571. Klitzke, *supra* note 5, at 644.

III. Early Patent Remedies

Modern scholarship treats early patent remedies as an artifact not deserving much attention. But if we listen to Judge O'Malley's call to reassess enhanced damages, then the history of early statutes should be given more attention. First, a discussion of the early U.S. patent statutes with a focus on mandatory treble damages and inadequate explanations of its origin from contemporary analysis. Second, equity will be discussed, which explains the origin of the mandatory treble damages. Third, a discussion of the manner in which damages were awarded before 1836, which would go on to influence the law of patent damages for the rest of the 19th century.

A.   Damage Provisions 1790-1800

Article I, Section 8 of the U.S. Constitution confers to Congress the power to grant patents in order to promote the useful arts.[24] It took just one year for Congress to exercise that power with the 1790 Patent Act.[25] The 1790 statute allowed the plaintiff to recover damages (determined by a jury) and possession of the infringing device.[26] While this provision might seem to be the default award, comparatively it was weak because the copyright statute of the same year[27] allowed a penalty of fifty cents per copied sheet in addition to damages and possession of the copied material.[28] The lack of a punitive remedy illustrates an overall distrust of patents.

The 1790 Patent Act had several problems and was not controlling for long. One issue was that an

---

[24] U.S. CONST. art. I, § 8, cl. 8.
[25] *See* 1 Stat. 109 (1790).
[26] *Id.* § 4.
[27] *See generally* Copyright Act of 1790, 1 Stat. 124.

[28] *See* 1 Stat. 109 (1790).

application for a patent had to be approved by a panel consisting of the Secretary of State, Secretary of War, and Attorney General.[29] Presumably these esteemed men had much to do, and the 1793 patent statute released these officers of their patent obligations.[30] This is the most well known change, but not the only one, as the damages provision was also amended.[31] The 1793 act mandated that infringers pay at least three times the amount the patentee usually received for either selling the patented invention or licensing the invention.[32] The purpose of this change must be made by inference because there is no record of who recommended this change or why it was done.[33]

The change in remedies in 1793 is often attributed to Joseph Barnes, who published a pamphlet criticizing the 1790 statute and the proposed H.R. 166, both of which provided that the damages allowed would be determined by juries.[34] Barnes distrusted juries, whom he felt would refuse to award damages to monopolists.[35] However, these facts only answer why Barnes wanted the change; why Congress made the change is still not answered. It is unlikely that Congress simply read Barnes's pamphlet and voted accordingly without question. Thomas Jefferson, who held juries in high

---

[29] *Id.* § 1.
[30] Patent Act of 1793, 1 Stat. 318 (1793), *reprinted in* EDWARD C. WALTERSCHEID, TO PROMOTE THE PROGRESS OF USEFUL ARTS: AMERICAN PATENT LAW AND ADMINISTRATION 1787-1836, at 479 app. VIII (1998).
[31] Patent Act of 1793, 1 Stat. 318 § 5 (1793), *reprinted in* WALTERSCHEID, *supra* note 30, at 481 app. VII.
[32] *Id.*
[33] H.R. 121, 1st Cong. (1791) (enacted) *reprinted in* WALTERSCHEID, *supra* note 34, at 109 app. VI; H.R. 166, 1st Cong. (1792).
[34] WALTERSCHEID, *supra* note 30, at 209–10.
[35] *Id.* at 109 (citing J. BARNES, TREATISE ON THE JUSTICE, POLICY, AND UTILITY OF ESTABLISHING AN EFFECTUAL SYSTEM OF PROMOTING THE PROGRESS OF USEFUL ARTS, BY ASSURING PROPERTY IN THE PRODUCTS OF GENIUS, 4-5 (1972)).

regard,[36] would not agree with Barnes's distrust of juries. Yet, it is widely held that Jefferson was influential in the passage of the 1793 statute.[37] Furthermore, patent monopolies were a "bugaboo" for Jefferson and his Republicans who would have welcomed jury interference.[38] Unless we are to believe that Congress ignored Jefferson's view of patents but listened attentively to Barnes, Barnes cannot be the sole explanation of the treble damages provision.[39]

Subsequent amendments to the 1793 statute demonstrate that juries were not the motivation for the treble damages provision. The 1800 amendment to the patent statute provided that an infringer should pay "a sum equal to three times the actual damage sustained."[40] The jury, then, would determine the actual damage. If there was a distrust of juries to handle patent cases, that distrust was soon forgotten. Still, the courts were obligated to treble the amount found by the jury.[41]

---

[36] Thomas Jefferson wrote, "I consider trial by jury as the only anchor ever yet imagined by man, by which a government can be held to the principles of its constitution." THOMAS JEFFERSON ON POLITICS & GOVERNMENT, http://famguardian.org/subjects/politics/thomasjefferson/jeff1520.htm (last visited Mar. 1, 2015).

[37] Some, including the Supreme Court, even believe that Thomas Jefferson wrote the statute himself, though this belief is likely mistaken. *See* Edward C. Walterscheid, *The Use and Abuse of History: The Supreme Court's Interpretation of Thomas Jefferson's Influence on Patent Law*, 39 IDEA 195, 209–10 (1999); Diamond v. Chakrabarty, 447 U.S. 303, 308–09 (1980); Graham v. John Deere Co., 383 U.S. 1, 7 (1966); Gen. Talking Pictures Corp. v. W. Elec. Co., 305 U.S. 124, 128 n.1 (1938) (Black, J., dissenting).

[38] *See* WALTERSCHEID, *supra* note 30, at 430.

[39] It is also unlikely a court decision at that time influenced Congress. *See* WALTERSCHEID, *supra* note 30, at 157 (citing P.J. Federico, *The Patent Trials of Oliver Evans*, 27 J. PAT. OFF. SOC'Y 586, 603 (1945)).

[40] Patent Act of April 17, 1800, 2 Stat. 37 § 3 (1800) *reprinted in* WALTERSHIED, *supra* note 30, at 490–91 app. XI).

[41] WILLARD PHILLIPS, THE LAW OF PATENTS FOR INVENTIONS; INCLUDING THE REMEDIES AND LEGAL PROCEEDINGS IN RELATION TO PATENT RIGHTS, at 435 (1837), *available at*

It is unlikely that the treble damages provision was instituted with juries in mind because the treble provision did not rise and fall with the proposed "distrust of juries" sentiment. The more likely reason is clear when one recalls the significant division between law and equity during that time.

B. *The Early History of Equity in Patent Remedies*

1. *The Relationship Between Treble Damages and Equity*

Treble damages were in place in 1793 not to punish the infringer but to adequately compensate the patentee because equity jurisdiction was almost non-existent at the time. This becomes apparent when one considers the history of equity in the United States.

The passage of the Federal Judiciary Act in 1789 created the federal courts, but the federal judicial power was still limited to only those cases in which the parties were of diverse citizenship.[42] The early patent statutes of 1790 and 1793 allowed federal courts jurisdiction only over actions at law.[43] Congress deliberately excluded equitable jurisdiction in federal courts prior to the passage of the 1790 statute.[44] Federal courts were

---

https://ia902508.us.archive.org/28/items/lawofpatentsfori00phil/lawofpatentsfori00phil.pdf.

[42] An Act to Establish the Judicial Courts of the United States, 1 Stat. 73, § 9; ROBINSON, *supra* note 18, § 1083.

[43] *Compare* Patent Act of 1793, 1 Stat. 318 § 5 (actions on the case are available to courts that have *competent* jurisdiction) *with* Patent Act of 1800 § 3 (courts have *original* jurisdiction) (emphasis added). Competent jurisdiction, apparently, means the persons were of diverse citizenship in the context of 1793. ROBINSON, *supra* note 17, § 1083.

[44] Three weeks before passage of the 1790 act, a bill proposed that a patentee could seek remedies by, "action of debt, *bill*, plaint or information." Patents Bill, H.R. 41, 1st Cong. § 4 (1790) (emphasis added) (reproduced in WALTERSCHEID, *supra* note 30, at 445 app. III). "Bill" would indicate "equity" at the time. BLACK'S LAW DICTIONARY 194 (10th ed. 2014).

therefore limited to what remedies they could offer patentees.

Recalling that the true value of the patent was (and still is) the exclusivity of the market that the new invention creates, the inability to issue injunctions against patent infringers (save for cases of diverse citizenship) was a sharp limitation for federal courts in enforcing the patent statute.[45] The reason for this limitation is that many feared that courts sitting in equity would become as powerful as the English Court of Chancery. Congress debated the extent to which equitable remedies were available in federal courts during the passage of the Federal Judiciary Act.[46] Jefferson remarked that equity was not to be overused:

> If the legislature means to enact an injustice, however palpable, the court of Chancery is not the body with whom a correcting power is lodged. That it shall not interpose in any case which does not come within a general description and admit of redress by a general and practicable rule . . .[47]

This important issue in early American politics was not limited to just patent law. The same Congress that passed the 1793 Patent Act also passed the Anti-

---

[45] *See* Seymour v. McCormick, 57 U.S. (16 How.) 480, 488 (1853) ("[E]xperience began to show that some inventions or discoveries had their chief value in a monopoly of use by the inventor, and not in a sale of licenses, the value of a license could not be made a universal rule, as a measure of damages.").
[46] MOY, *supra* note 7, § 23:4 (citing Charles Warren, *New Light on the History of the Federal Judiciary Act of 1789*, 37 HARV. L. REV. 49 (1923); Moschzisker, *Equity Jurisdiction in the Federal Courts*, 75 U. PA. L. REV. 287 (1927)); *see generally* An Act to Establish the Judicial Courts of the United States, 1 Stat. 73 (1789).
[47] Letter from Thomas Jefferson to Phillip Mazzei (Nov. 1785), http://founders.archives.gov/documents/Jefferson/01-09-02-0056.

injunction Act that prevented federal courts from meddling with state courts by way of equity.[48]

With prospective damages[49] and injunctions available only in rare circumstances, a patentee would have to continually sue for actual damages against infringers to stop continued infringement. Therefore, it was necessary that the legal damages be trebled to prevent duplicative cases.

2. Application of Equity in Early American Law

The nature of intellectual property rights was too tempting for judges to refuse equity altogether, to the point that courts may have exercised equity *ultra vires*.[50] The fluidity of equitable jurisdiction is apparent in two relevant cases. In *Morse v. Reid*, a copyright case,[51] equity was granted in the form of an injunction and payment of all the profits made by the defendant.[52] The judge might have awarded these equitable remedies based on diversity of citizenship—the only correct legal ground to do so.[53] Even still, equity should have been reserved until statutory remedies had been applied. Inexplicably, judges ignored the 1790 statute altogether before administering equity[54] and failed to reserve equitable jurisdiction until remedies at law were exhausted.

---

[48] *See* Anti-Injunction Act, 1 Stat. 333 (1793).
[49] *See* ROBINSON, *supra* note 18, § 1089.
[50] Ultra Vires is defined as "Unauthorized; beyond the scope of power allowed or granted by a corporate charter or by law." BLACK'S LAW DICTIONARY 1755 (10th ed. 2014).
[51] The Federal Register mistakenly asserts *Morse* is a patent case, as well as incorrectly stating the caption, date, and relief sought. John D. Gordan III, *Morse v. Reid: The First Reported Federal Copyright Case*, 11 LAW & HIST. REV. 21 (1993); *see* Morse v. Reed, 17 F. Cas. 873 (C.C.D.N.Y. 1796) (No. 9,860).
[52] *See* Gordan, *supra* note 51, at 33.
[53] Root v. Ry. Co., 105 U.S. 189, 192 (1881) ("Of course, in those cases the jurisdiction of the court depended on the citizenship of the parties.").
[54] *See* Copyright Act of 1790, 1 Stat. 124, §§ 2, 5.

In *Livingston v. Van Ingen*, the proposition that equity applies only in cases where damages at law are inadequate was directly challenged. After a long discussion of English cases, the court wrote:

> An injunction is an appropriate remedy for a violation of all statute rights. They are granted of course. The numerous cases decided before the revolution are conclusive on this point, and binding on this court. The remedy is contemporaneous and concurrent with the grant itself, and cannot be separated from it. The right and the remedy passed to the appellants at the same time. The remedy is a part of the grant and cannot be taken away.[55]

This case was overruled by *North River Steamboat Co. v. Livingston* over a decade later, but on the grounds that the monopoly granted by the State of New York was unconstitutional according to the landmark case *Gibbons v. Ogden*.[56] The question of when equity is appropriate was not resolved.

In those instances where federal courts were allowed equity, Congress had assumed that the courts would award damages or equity according to the tradition of the respective courts.[57] As *Morse* and *Livingston* illustrate, however, the tradition of these courts was not agreed upon.[58] In context of patent law, it is likely that equity

---

[55] Livingston v. Van Ingen, 9 Johns. 507, 536 (N.Y. 1812), *overruled by* N. River Steamboat Co. v. Livingston, Lock. Rev. Cas. 104, 726 (N.Y. 1825).
[56] *N. River Steamboat Co.*, Lock. Rev. Cas. 104, 726; Gibbons v. Ogden, 22 U.S. (9 Wheat.) 1 (1824).
[57] *See* MOY, *supra* note 7, § 23:4 (citing An Act to establish the Judicial Courts of the United States, 1 Stat. 73 (1789)); An Act to Regulate the Processes in the Courts of the United States, 1 Stat. 93 (1789).
[58] *Compare* Letter from Thomas Jefferson to Phillip Mazzei, (Nov. 1785), http://founders.archives.gov/documents/Jefferson/01-09-02-

was available to only some patentees but not others, and the basis for that determination was inconsistent.

This inconsistency might have led to Congress to allow Federal courts equitable jurisdiction in all patent cases in 1819.[59] As a result of this new jurisdiction, a patentee now had available to him or her equitable remedies in federal court. This included injunctions and equitable accounting, but courts sitting in equity could not award damages since that power belonged exclusively to courts sitting at law. Though courts sitting in equity could not award damages (until 1870),[60] the patentee now was able to obtain injunctions and a monetary award through accounting. Both remedies are discussed in more detail later.[61] Briefly, an injunction preserves the exclusivity of the market for the plaintiff by prohibiting the infringer from using the invention in the future, while accounting awards the defendant's profits "wrongfully obtained from use of the plaintiff's property."[62] Both are powerful remedies.

Why then were the treble damages kept in 1819 if equity was now available? Perhaps because these remedies were still *practically* unavailable, as only the jurisdictional obstacle for patentees was removed. The difficult procedural rules that accompanied bills in

---

0056 ("But this court whilst developing and systematising it's [sic] powers, has found, in the jealousy of the nation and it's [sic] attachment to certain and impartial law, an obstacle insuperable beyond that line [that limits the applicability of equity].") *with* THE FEDERALIST NO. 80 (Alexander Hamilton) ("There is hardly a subject of litigation between individuals, which may not involve those ingredients of *fraud, accident, trust, or hardship,* which would render the matter an object of equitable rather than of legal jurisdiction.").

[59] 3 Stat. 481, *reprinted in* WALTERSCHEID, *supra* note 30, at 491 app. XII.
[60] *See, e.g.*, Birdsall v. Coolidge, 93 U.S. 64, 68–69 (1876).
[61] *See infra* Part IV.B.
[62] Joel Eichengrun, *Remedying the Remedy of Accounting*, 60 IND. L.J. 463, 463 (1985).

equity were still in place,[63] leaving these remedies difficult to obtain. This led some in Congress in the early 1820s to attempt to amend the damages provision, for example, by making it easier to recover court costs.[64] These amendments failed because, while some may have still struggled to recover compensation, it became apparent that the remedies favored patentees too much at the time.[65] The difficulties associated with obtaining equity would have to wait for several decades.[66]

Difficulty in obtaining equity, no matter how necessary to compensate patentees, does not mean that the divide between law and equity should be ignored.[67] The 1819 act did not make legal and equitable jurisdiction concurrent, nor did any subsequent patent act.[68] The divide between law and equity remained,[69] as well as the long-tested analysis of when to grant equity, such as whether the injured party had gained adequate remedies at law.[70] The 1836 patent act preserved this divide. Section 14 of the 1836 act allowed "actions on the case" to recover actual damages[71] while Section 17

---

[63] *See* DONALD S. CHISUM, 7 CHISUM ON PATENTS § 20.02[1][b] n.20, § 20.02[1][c] (2014).

[64] *See* WALTERSCHEID, *supra* note 30, at 341 ("[Treble damages] did not allow him to recover costs in the case, so that, though gaining his cause, the patentee might in reality be a loser in the end." (quoting Representative John Taylor of New York)).

[65] *See, e.g.*, Grant v. Raymond, 31 U.S. (6 Pet.) 218, 230 (1832) (syllabus of the court) ("Under the direction of the court he has recovered a verdict for three thousand two hundred and sixty-six dollars; and is entitled, of course, to have this *trebled*, and the defendants are ruined. *Is this legal?* A bill in equity is pending also, to stop the defendants' factory.").

[66] *See infra* Part IV.B.

[67] This point is particularly important when considering the future of ongoing royalties, which is discussed in Part IV.B.

[68] *See* ROBINSON, *supra* note 17, § 1084.

[69] *Id.*

[70] *Id.*

[71] Patent Act of 1836, 5 Stat. 117 § 14 (1836).

allowed for suits in equity, "according to the course and principles of courts of equity."[72] The point is worth emphasizing, as the Supreme Court addressed this issue at length in *Root v. Lake Shore & M.S. Ry. Co.* in 1881[73] and 125 years later in *eBay v. MercExchange.*[74]

C.   *Award of Damages in Early Patent Cases*

The absence of equity to most patentees explains the mandatory treble provision from 1790 to 1836. The treble provision had perhaps an unexpected influence on how damages were assessed during that time, and (as the common law system often goes) would influence later decisions after the statute was amended.

Take, for example, Justice Joseph Story's influential jurisprudence. In *Whittemore v. Cutter*, Justice Story rejected any argument that a small infringement is no infringement at all: "For where the law has given a right, and a remedy for the violation of it, such violation of itself imports damage."[75] However, in such cases where

---

[72] *Id.* § 17; *see* CHISUM, *supra* note 6e, § 20.02[1][d] ("[The 1836 Act] fostered a cleavage as to monetary recovery which a patent owner could obtain from an infringer . . . "). Note that Chisum uses the word "foster" rather than "create."

[73] 105 U.S. 189 (1881). After much discussion of the past law, the Court concluded, "[i]t does not appear from the allegations of the bill in the present case that there are any circumstances which would render an action at law for the recovery of damages an inadequate remedy for the wrongs complained of; and, as no ground for equitable relief is presented, we are of opinion that the Circuit Court did not err in sustaining the demurrer and dismissing the bill." *Id.* at 216–17.

[74] 547 U.S. 388, 394 (2006) ("We hold only that the decision whether to grant or deny injunctive relief rests within the equitable discretion of the district courts, and that such discretion must be exercised consistent with traditional principles of equity, in patent disputes no less than in other cases governed by such standards."). The Court overruled MercExchange v. eBay, 401 F.3d 1323 (Fed. Cir. 2005), which held that injunctions are granted in patent cases absent exceptional circumstances.

[75] Whittemore v. Cutter, 29 F. Cas. 1123, 1125 (C.C.D. Mass. 1813) (No. 17,601). However, Justice Story said that mere making for experimental or philosophical use is not an infringement, but

infringement was minimal, the patentee would receive little money for compensation. Story continues, "and in the absence of all other evidence, the law presumes a nominal damage to the party."[76] Therefore, the patentee was entitled to some sort damage if the defendant infringed the patent. The important determination is what type of damages should be awarded.

Justice Story did not hesitate to award mere nominal damages, even if the infringement was blatant. Story was adamant that actual damages be only what the plaintiff suffered and could prove. In *Whittemore*, Story dismissed the plaintiff's request that damages be the estimated cost for the making of the infringing machine, or the price of the machine, reasoning that both are costs suffered only by the defendant and would compound the value of the materials and workmanship.[77] Therefore, only nominal damages (most likely less than a dollar) were awarded in the case.

Justice Story explained his reasoning as to why nominal damages could only be given in those instances that the plaintiff was unable to prove his damages.

> By the term "actual damages," in the statute, are meant such damages as the plaintiffs can actually prove, and have, in fact, sustained, as contradistinguished to mere imaginary or exemplary damages, which, in personal torts, are sometimes given. The statute is *highly penal,* and the legislature meant to limit the single damages to the real injury done, as in

---

required the making it for sale, use or profit. Making it for use or sale, without actually making a sale or use, is still an infringement, but only a nominal damage is awarded. *Id.*
[76] *Id.*
[77] PHILLIPS, *supra* note 41, at 439. *Whittemore,* 29 F. Cas. at 1125.

other cases of violation of personal property, or of incorporeal rights.[78]

Therefore, calculation of actual damages needed to be precise because the damages would be trebled. The passage continues, (the following being used by many courts and commentators that damages cannot be speculated or expanded):[79]

> In mere personal torts, as assaults and batteries, defamation of character, etc., the law has, in proper cases, allowed the party to recover not merely for any actual injury, but for the mental anxiety, the public degradation and wounded sensibility, which honorable men feel at violations of the sacredness of their persons or characters. But the reason of the law does not apply to the mere infringement of an incorporeal right, such as a patent, and the legislature meant to confine the damages to such a sum that would compensate the party for his actual loss.[80]

The early reason for treble damages (to adequately compensate patentees in lieu of equity) and the effect on patent remedies (confining damages to what could be proven) has been almost entirely lost in scholarly work. For example, Robinson, a late 19th-century patent expert, noted, "vindictive damages are not permitted, power being conferred upon the court to increase the amount fixed by the jury in cases of malicious or persistent injury."[81] Robinson errs on this point insofar as he discusses patent law before 1836 because trebling

---

[78] *Whittemore*, 29 F. Cas. at 1125 (emphasis added).
[79] *See, e.g.*, ROBINSON, *supra* note 18, § 1053 n.6.
[80] *Whittemore*, 29 F. Cas. at 1125.
[81] ROBINSON, *supra* note 18, § 1053.

the damages was mandatory, no matter whether infringement was malicious or unintentional.[82]

Without the treble provision, courts might have allowed more than just the damages that were proven. Story suggests that he might have approached damages differently, and might have included "exemplary or imaginary damages" if not for the "highly penal" nature of the statute.[83] Before his decision in *Whittemore*, he opined, "damages [should] be estimated as high, as they can be, consistently with the rule of law on this subject, if the plaintiff's patent has been violated; that wrong doers may not reap the fruits of the labor and genius of other men."[84] Justice Story admitted that the entire question should be left to the jury, rather than impose special rules:

> I rather incline to believe [leaving the jury to estimate the actual damages] to be the true course . . . The price of machine, the nature, actual state and extent of the use of the plaintiff's invention, and the particular losses to which he may have been subjected by the piracy, are all proper ingredients to be weighed by the jury in estimating the damages, *valere quantum valeant*.[85]

This included considering (but not necessarily awarding) the profits received by the defendant.[86]

---

[82] *See* Seymour v. McCormick, 57 U.S. (16 How.) 480, 488–89 (1853) (describing the mandatory treble damages "manifestly unjust").
[83] *See Whittemore*, 29 F. Cas. at 1125.
[84] Lowell v. Lewis, 15 F. Cas. 1018, 1018 (C.C.D. Mass. 1817) (No. 8568); PHILLIPS, *supra* note 41, at 440.
[85] Earle v. Sawyer, 8 F. Cas. 254, 258 (C.C.D. Mass. 1825) (No. 4247); PHILLIPS, *supra* note 41, at 443–44.
[86] PHILLIPS, *supra* note 41, at 444.

However, determining actual damages by the indirect evidence of the defendant's profits was not preferred because of the penal nature of the statute. Instead, an established license fee by the plaintiff was favored. This was for two reasons. First, the computation was easier and therefore more reliable and second, it was assumed that the license rate would still compensate the patentee because damages would be trebled.[87] It can be concluded that the emphasis on determining and proving the actual damage was out of concern of the highly penal nature of the statute and to avoid subjugating unintentional infringers to an overly-harsh penalty—the penalty mandated by the statute was enough.[88]

Even with the careful calculation of damages and hesitation to estimate damages, the law in many minds was too favorable to patentees. On a bill that would have made it easier for plaintiffs to win attorney fees, Representative Robert Vance of North Carolina said the bill would encourage fraudulent patentees to threaten litigation, and the user of the invention, "dreading a suit, prefers to pay the unjust demand of a mere adventurer."[89] A similar bill that would have awarded court costs was challenged in the House on the same grounds.[90] A Congressman attempted to compromise with repealing the treble damages provision and instead allowed costs in all cases.[91] The bill was returned to committee to discuss repealing the treble damages and instead awarding double costs.[92] The bill was defeated,

---

[87] *Id.* at 444–45.
[88] *See* Seymour v. McCormick, 57 U.S. (16 How.) 480, 488–89 (1853) (stating the 1836 Patent Act confined actual damages to limit the court's power to treble the damages).
[89] WALTERSCHEID, *supra* note 30, at 342 (citing 18 ANNALS OF CONG. 808–09 (1823)).
[90] WALTERSCHEID, *supra* note 30, at 342.
[91] *Id.* at 343.
[92] *Id.*; 18 ANNALS OF CONG. 932–37 (1823).

and despite rampant fraud (there was no real examination of applications in the patent system, but mere a registration system)[93] and predatory litigation, nothing was done on the matter until the entire system was revised in 1836.[94]

The treble damages provision was amended in 1836. The statute provided:

> [T]hat whenever, in any action for damages for using or selling the thing whereof the exclusive right is secured by any patent heretofore granted, or which shall hereafter be granted, a verdict shall be rendered to a plaintiff in such action, it shall be in the power of the court to render judgment for any sum above the amount by such judgment as the actual damages sustained by the plaintiff, not exceeding three times the amount thereof, according to the circumstances of the case.[95]

The treble provision was no longer the floor, but the ceiling. In such an environment where patent abuse was rampant,[96] it was not surprising to see the mandatory nature of the treble damages revoked. Still, the treble damages remained, even after equity was available,

---

[93] See MOY, *supra* note 7, § 1:18.
[94] See WALTERSCHEID, *supra* note 30, at 343–44.
[95] Patent Act of 1836, ch. 357, 5 Stat. 117 § 13, *reprinted in* WALTERSCHEID, *supra* note 30, at 497 app. XV; *see also* PHILLIPS, *supra* note 41, at 435–36.
[96] *See, e.g.*, Evans v. Jordan, 13 U.S. (9 Cranch) 199 (1815) (allowing an extension of a patent that had already expired); *see also* McGaw v. Bryan, 16 F. Cas. 96, 102 (S.D.N.Y. 1821) (No. 8793). In *McGaw*, Judge Van Ness, frustrated that he could not void an obviously illegal patent because he was not empowered by the statute, wrote an opinion containing an extraordinary amount of sarcasm (the first paragraph is illustrative). *Id.*

which invites the question as to why it was kept. The reason for this is discussed in a subsequent section.[97]

To summarize thus far, the first patent act contemplated that juries would determine actual damage. In 1793, the damage awarded to a patentee was now a mandatory trebling of the price of the invention or the license fee to use the invention. The treble provision, as such, was added because of the uncertainty surrounding a patentee's access to equity in federal court. In 1800, the patent act was amended to mandate trebling of actual damages, which in turn meant courts awarded damages according to contract principles rather than tort principles.[98] In 1836, treble damages were no longer mandatory, but within the discretion of the district court.[99]

D.   *Analysis of Damages and Equity 1790–1836*

The true value of the patent is the exclusive control over the market. With equity only available on an unequal basis (as the *Morse* and *Livingston* cases illustrate), a patentee must continually sue for actual damages against infringers if they hope to stop infringement. Mandatory treble damages were necessary in these circumstances.[100] Even after equity became available in 1819, the treble damages provision remained to provide an adequate remedy for those patentees who chose to bring actions at law.[101] To avoid

---

[97] *See infra* Part IV.A.3.
[98] *See* Whittemore v. Cutter, 29 F. Cas. 1123, 1125 (C.C.D. Mass. 1813) (No. 17,601).
[99] How the courts handled this new discretion is discussed in Part IV.A.3.
[100] Sen. John Ruggles, S. Report Accompanying Senate Bill No. 239, at 6 (Apr. 28, 1836) (explaining that pre-1836 patent law "offer[ed] an inadequate remedy for the [infringement] injury, by giving an action of damages.").
[101] One judge, noting that treble damages are present only at law and not in equity, recognized that the reason for the treble damages provision is that law is, by its nature, inadequate to compensate the

over-penalizing infringers, judges required that the patentee to prove damages as precisely as possible or be awarded nominal damages.

In 1819, equity jurisdiction was available to patentees in federal court. However, the procedural difficulties in obtaining equitable remedies remained, which explains why the treble damages provision was kept and why some in Congress wished to allow plaintiffs to recover costs as part, or in replacement, of damage awards.

IV. THE DEVELOPMENT OF PATENT REMEDIES AFTER 1836

Determining the precise actual damage to the plaintiff was still an emphasis after 1836,[102] even after treble damages were no longer mandatory. This is because, first, some habits are hard to break, and second, damages were still calculated from a contracts perspective. Damages were limited to the direct and immediate harm to the plaintiff from the date of the infringement to the institution of the suit.[103] This had a profound influence on patent remedies, both at law and equity.

First, the three available damages at law will be discussed. Then, how treble damages were used in conjunction with these remedies will be reviewed. Finally, equity during this period will be discussed.

---

patentee. Motte v. Bennett, 17 F. Cas. 909, 910 (C.C.D. S.C. 1849) (No. 9884) ("Indeed, if any one thing could show more plainly than another, that a trial by a jury in a patent cause was not thought the best way to compensate a patentee for an infringement of his patent, it is this legislative authority given to the court to give three-fold amount over the sum found by the verdict of a jury.").
[102] *See, e.g.*, Seymour v. McCormick, 57 U.S. (16 How.) 480, 489 (1853).
[103] ROBINSON, *supra* note 18, § 1053.

A. Remedies Available at Law

1. Established Royalty

As mentioned before, the preferred measurement of damages by a court sitting at law is the established royalty for which the patentee had licensed his patent.[104] This is the probable reason why the 1793 patent act expressly stated that such would be the actual damage.[105] The form of the license can come in any manner, so long as it shows that the owner "has put his own price upon the exercise of the right, and offered it to all who are disposed to pay the price for its enjoyment."[106] However, the royalty is rarely established.[107] The Supreme Court laid out five criteria in *Rude v. Wescott* to determine if the patent owner had fixed the value of the patent. The royalty must be 1) paid or secured before the infringement; 2) paid by such a number of persons as to indicate a general acquiescence in its reasonableness; 3) uniform at the place where the licenses are issued; 4) not paid under threat of suit or in settlement of litigation; and 5) for comparable rights or activity under the patent.[108] There are numerous defenses that both parties could invoke.[109]

The infringer could challenge that too few persons had paid a royalty before the infringement.[110] The

---

[104] *See, e.g.*, WALKER, *supra* note 23, §§ 599, 601 ("The primary method [of finding damages] consists in using the plaintiff's established royalty as a the measure of those damages."); CHISUM, *supra* note 64, § 20.02[2] (citing Clark v. Wooster, 119 U.S. 322, 326 (1886) ("It is a general rule in patent causes, that established license fees are the best measure of damages that can be used.")).
[105] Patent Act of 1793, ch. 11, 1 Stat. 318 § 5 (1793), *reprinted in* WALTERSCHEID, *supra* note 31, at 481 app. VIII.
[106] ROBINSON, *supra* note 18, § 1056.
[107] CHISUM, *supra* note 64, § 20.06[2].
[108] Rude v. Westcott, 130 U.S. 152 (1889).
[109] WALKER, *supra* note 23, §§ 601–06.
[110] *Id.* § 601.

royalty must have been paid by sufficient persons to demonstrate that the royalty was uniform. One expert explains:

> The unanimous opinion of twelve average men is thought to be most reliable criterion of guilt or innocence; but no reasonable person [say the same] of the opinion of any one of the twelve. In like manner, the unanimous acquiescence of a considerable number of men in a particular royalty, is evidence of substantial justice, while the acquiescence of one only of the same men would have no convincing force.[111]

Additionally, the patentee could not establish a royalty by threatening litigation against a large number of persons because such practice artificially raised the price.[112] The royalty must have been actually paid to prevent collusion between patentees and licensees against third parties.[113] Furthermore, there must have been a uniform royalty in the same geographical area.[114]

The plaintiff has available many defenses, as well, if he thought a royalty would be too low. He, too, could argue that established royalties in other geographic areas were inapplicable, with the difference being that the defendant was infringing in a market that the patentee intended to keep for himself.[115] He might also argue that the patent had increased in value since the royalty was established, and that the patent was valued

---

[111] *Id.*
[112] *Id.*
[113] *Id.* The requirement of actually paid is of evidentiary importance. An oath from licensees works for this requirement. *See id.*
[114] *Id.*
[115] *Id.* § 602.

low because of inability to produce or lack of commercial value.[116]

Both plaintiff and defendant have several common defenses to the established royalty. An important consideration (especially in context of reasonable royalties that are given today)[117] is that a settlement agreement for past infringement "[did] not establish *nor tend to establish* a royalty."[118] The other defenses to be made against an established royalty are: a royalty for purchase price of the patented invention may be too high or low for use of the device,[119] a royalty to make and use cannot be used to establish the royalty to make and sell,[120] and the extent the patented invention is used in the other royalties must be factored in.[121] These defenses, collectively, are all grounds that will, inarguably and absolutely, undermine the major premise of using established royalties in the first place—that the established royalty was the value that the patentee has fixed for all to enjoy.

It is not difficult to believe, then, that the standard set by *Rude* is rarely met.[122] The reason that established royalties are not often the measure of damages is not because of *Rude* or because of the numerous defenses, but rather because of the truth and persuasiveness of the reasons behind the defenses. If it is important that damages be calculated precisely, established royalties should not be the measure of damages when the plaintiff has not set the value of the patent in that

---

[116] *Id.*
[117] *See infra* Part V.A.
[118] WALKER, *supra* note 23, § 603 (emphasis added); *see* Rude v. Westcott, 130 U.S. 152, 164 (1889).
[119] WALKER, *supra* note 23, § 604.
[120] *Id.* § 605.
[121] *Id.* § 606.
[122] CHISUM, *supra* note 64, § 20.06[2]; Rude v. Westcott, 130 U.S. 152 (1889). The *Rude* Court remanded the case for nominal damages rather than an established royalty. *Rude*, 130 U.S. at 167.

manner. The value of the patented invention is its market exclusivity. When a patentee chooses to take advantage of the market by making the invention, the value of the patent cannot be realized in licenses. Accordingly, licensees do not to want to pay a uniform patent rate because each granted license has diminishing returns to the licensee as the exclusivity of the market share is eroded. Therefore, the established royalty rarely exists, not because of a difficult Supreme Court rule or the numerous defenses against such a rule, but because the patent's value is most often its exclusive nature, which is not realized in the grant of non-exclusive licenses.[123]

2. Lost Profits

Lost profits are the best monetary compensation at law for the lost value of the patent due to infringement. Such compensation is aimed to remedy the harm to the patentee when the patentee:

> Is able to supply the whole demand for the article it covers, and where the whole demand would go to him, in the absence of infringement; the losses inflicted upon him by an infringer, may consist in reducing his sales, or in reducing his prices, or in both those injurious ways.[124]

In the 19th century, there were several different manners in which a defendant could prove lost profits, either directly or indirectly.[125] A plaintiff could directly show the sales and prices before the injury and the resulting effect done by the defendant.[126] In such cases,

---

[123] In fact, an established royalty would preclude the patentee from claiming lost profits. *See* Yale Lock Co. v. Sargent, 117 U.S. 536, 552 (1885).
[124] WALKER, *supra* note 23, § 607.
[125] *See* ROBINSON, *supra* note 18, §§ 1061–1064.
[126] *Id.* § 1061.

it did not matter exactly how infringement eroded the plaintiff's profits, only that the harm came by way of the infringement.[127] Additionally, price erosion, a decrease in demand and resulting sale of the product, or harm to reputation of the patentee or the patentee products, would all constitute direct evidence of lost profits.[128] Though defendant's profits could not be considered *direct* evidence of the plaintiff's harm, it could be used *indirectly*.[129]

However, *Seymour v. McCormick*[130] curbed the use of that indirect evidence. Cyrus McCormick invented a reaping machine used to harvest wheat.[131] Having patented a first version in 1834, he sought a new patent in 1845 for relatively small improvements.[132] The improvements in the latter patent were a seat and an improved reel, both of which were relatively inexpensive to make.[133] The district court judge instructed that the profit for the old machine disclosed in the then-expired 1834 patent could be recovered, and thus the jury awarded both the profit of the use of the old machines and the price of the improvement.[134]

Without doubt the trial court instructed the jury incorrectly, as the effect of his instructions amounted to

---

[127] *See id.*
[128] *Id.*
[129] *Id.* § 1062 ("There is no presumption, either of law or fact, that the plaintiff has lost all that the defendant has gained, or that the defendant's advantage is equal to the plaintiff's loss. But the pecuniary benefit which the defendant has derived from the unlawful use of the invention . . . the jury may infer the amount by which the plaintiff's sales and prices have been reduced through the infringement."); *see also* Philp et. al. v. Nock 84 U.S. (17 Wall.) 460, 462 (1873). Routinely the jury instructions highlighted the difference. *See, e.g.*, McComb v. Brodie, 15 F. Cas. 1290, 1294–95 (C.C.D. La. 1872).
[130] 57 U.S. (16 How.) 480 (1853).
[131] *Id.* at 480.
[132] *Id.*
[133] *Id.* at 480–81.
[134] *Id.* at 481.

a renewal of the 1834 patent.[135] The Court's dicta, however, is riddled with unfortunate errors that would do great harm to the future of patent remedies. First, the Court incorrectly stated that the jury could increase damages if the infringement was "wanton or malicious" to punish the defendant, when that power had only, and ever, resided with the Court.[136] Pursuant to that, the categorical dismissal of treble damages pre-1836 influenced how enhanced damages would be applied in the future.[137] Second, the Court suggested established royalties were favorable,[138] even though the reasons for favoring established royalties were outdated with the passage of the 1836 statute.[139] As a result, lost profits were confined to instances when the patent covered a new machine and therefore infringement "would destroy the whole value of the monopoly,"[140] setting a legal standard that must be met before a jury could award lost profits.

Again, the holding in *Seymour* was not controversial, as it cannot be said that small improvements in a train engine would entitle "whole profits arising from skill, labor, and capital" of the entire railroad industry.[141] But the Court, while noting that in some instances the jury could award a fraction of the profits based on the fraction of the improvement, only allowed this when

---

[135] *Id.* at 482.
[136] *Id.* at 489; *see* ROBINSON, *supra* note 18, § 1069 ("[Increasing the damage award] is distinctively the province of the court, and confers no authority upon the jury, on any ground, to transcend the limits of the actual damages which have been established by the evidence."); Whittemore v. Cutter, 29 F. Cas. 1123, 1125 (C.C.D. Mass. 1813) (No. 17,601).
[137] *See Seymour*, 57 U.S. at 488; *infra* Part IV.A.3.
[138] *See Seymour*, 57 U.S. at 490 ("It is only where, from the peculiar circumstances of the case, no other rule can be found, that the defendant's profits become the criterion of the plaintiff's loss.").
[139] *See* text accompanying notes 85–88 (established royalties preferred because of the mandatory treble damages).
[140] *Seymour*, 57 U.S. at 489.
[141] *Id.* at 490.

there was evidence for such a fraction.[142] Otherwise, a patent for an improvement in an old machine was confined to an established royalty.

Seymour's detrimental effect on lost profits was evident in the several cases that involved William Burdell and Augustus Denig.[143] The case began in 1865 when the plaintiff, Burdell, assignee of a patent for a sewing machine, sued Denig and Wiliam Lee for damages at law for patent infringement.[144] Burdell argued for lost profits because the defendants infringed his close monopoly in the county of his residence.[145] Burdell further proved that his patent mentioned a particular sewing machine, the Singer model, which the defendants had used to make their profits.[146] Burdell's patent covered a feeding machine to be used with the Singer model.[147] These facts convinced the jury to award him the profits it thought the plaintiff *might have gained* if not for infringement, but the circuit court overturned the jury verdict because the Singer sewing machine "had nothing whatever to do" with the damages that the plaintiff suffered.[148] The Court cited *Seymour*, noting the small improvement in the railroad engine does not unfairly entitle the patentee to the "entire amount of profits made by the railroad."[149] Thus the effect of *Seymour*: the jury's conclusion that the patented mechanism was not a mere small improvement (akin to the facts in *Seymour*) but one of a substantial nature, was thrown out because the court concluded that the defendant's profits could not be used as indirect

---

[142] *Id.*; *cf.* text accompanying notes 78–81 (damages must be actually proved because of the *mandatory* treble damages).
[143] Burdell v. Denig, 4 F. Cas. 695 (S.D. Ohio 1865) (No. 2142), *vacated*, Burdell v. Denig, 92 U.S. 716 (1875).
[144] Burdell v. Denig, 4 F. Cas. at 697.
[145] *Id.*
[146] *Id.*
[147] *Id.*; Burdell v. Denig, 92 U.S. 716, 722 (1875).
[148] *Burdell*, 4 F. Cas. at 698.
[149] *Id.* at 699.

evidence of the plaintiff's lost profits. Burdell would plead the same question in subsequent proceedings, but to no avail.[150]

Seymour's dicta eroded lost profits, a plaintiff's most valuable remedy in a court of law. Ironically, *Seymour*'s dicta did not stop the nightmare scenario of a patentee gaining entire profits of a business for small improvements. It only prevented that nightmare scenario in actions at law, not bills of equity.[151]

Today, the use of indirect evidence to prove lost profits was reinstated with the *Panduit* case and later *Rite-Hite*.[152] A plaintiff must prove that all the infringing sales would have been made by the plaintiff if not for infringement, quantify the profits displaced, and demonstrate that the plaintiff was able to make those sales.[153] Though it may now be proved indirectly, such indirect evidence is controversial.[154] Additionally, lost profits are sometimes considered in calculation of a reasonable royalty, which is also controversial.[155] It is this indeterminate calculation that is at the heart of the controversy, both past and present.

---

[150] Burdell v. Denig, 92 U.S. at 722.
[151] Westinghouse Elec. & Mfg. Co. v. Wagner Elec. & Mfg. Co., 225 U.S. 604, 620 (1912) ("On established principles of equity, and on the plainest principles of justice, the guilty trustee cannot take advantage of his own wrong. The fact that he may lose something of his own is a misfortune which he has brought upon himself . . . .").
[152] Rite-Hite Corp. v. Kelley Co., 56 F.3d 1538 (Fed. Cir. 1995); Panduit Corp. v. Stahlin Bros. Fibre Works, Inc, 575 F.2d 1152, 1156 (6th Cir. 1978).
[153] *Panduit*, 575 F.2d at 1156.
[154] *See* Amy L. Landers, *Liquid Patents*, 84 DENV. U. L. REV. 199, 256 (2006).
[155] *See* Mark A. Lemley, *Distinguishing Lost Profits from Reasonable Royalties*, 51 WM. & MARY L. REV. 655, 667–68 (2009).

3. *Application of Treble Damages after 1836*

When discussing treble damages, this article has thus far focused on the mandatory nature of damages from 1793 to 1836.[156] To reiterate, the treble damages were placed so as to ensure adequate compensation to patentees,[157] many of whom did not have access to equity.[158] The 1836 statute no longer mandated treble provisions,[159] as patentees had more than enough access to remedies after the 1819 act allowed patentees access to equitable remedies in federal court regardless of the citizenship of the parties.[160] The statutory language, which remains fundamentally the same today, gives district courts sole discretion to enhance damages.[161] The application of enhanced damages after 1836 will be the focus of this section.

Courts were quick to limit enhanced damages to particular facts that focused on the infringer's conduct. This was a natural reaction to the principle critique of mandatory treble damages—that it was unjust to penalize an "innocent" infringer.[162] Courts, however, struggled to determine which particular facts warrant enhanced damages.

One court contemplated that many conditions must be met: that the invention had to be valuable, the infringement wanton, the litigation expensive, and the

---

[156] *Supra* Part III.A, B.1.
[157] *See supra* note 106.
[158] *Supra* Part III.B.1.
[159] Patent Act of 1836, 5 Stat. 117 § 14, *reprinted in* WALTERSCHEID, *supra* note note 31, at 505 app. XV.
[160] Patent Act of 1819 Act, 3 Stat. 481, *reprinted in* WALTERSCHEID, *supra* note note 35, at 491 app. XII.
[161] *See* 35 U.S.C. § 284 (2012).
[162] Seymour v. McCormick, 57 U.S. (16 How.) 480, 488 (1853) ("Experience had shown the very great injustice of a horizontal rule equally affecting all cases without regard to their particular merits.").

verdict wholly inadequate.[163] Some judges required that only the infringement be wanton.[164] These courts err to the extent that these cases interpreted *Seymour v. McCormick* as requiring willful or wanton infringement rather than the four-element test.[165] The passage often cited states:

> Experience had shown the very great injustice of a horizontal rule equally affecting all cases, without regard to their peculiar merits. The defendant, who acted in ignorance or good faith, claiming under a junior patent, was made liable to the same penalty with the wanton and malicious pirate. This rule was manifestly unjust. For there is no good reason why taking a man's property in an invention should be trebly punished, while the measure of damages as to other property is single and actual damages.[166]

This passage says nothing of infringers squarely in the middle of innocent infringers and wanton pirates. The Supreme Court addressed this question in later cases and did not limit the power of the district courts to use their discretion. In *Clark v. Wooster* (1886), the Court suggested that enhanced damages could be used for compensatory purposes.[167] Again, in *Topliff v. Topliff*, the

---

[163] Schwarzel v. Holenshade, 21 F. Cas. 772, 773 (D.C.S.D. Ohio 1866) (No. 12,506).
[164] *See* Brodie v. Ophir Silver Min. Co., 4 F. Cas. 202, 204 (C.C.D. Cal. 1867) (No. 1919) (citing *Seymour*, 57 U.S. at 488).
[165] *See, e.g.*, In re Seagate, 497 F.3d 1360, 1368 (Fed. Cir. 2007). *In re Seagate* also cited a Supreme Court case which asserted that the treble damages provision was linked to willful infringement, but that assertion was mere dicta and did not cite any support. *See* Aro Mfg. Co. v. Convertible Top Replacement Co., 377 U.S. 476, 508 (1964).
[166] *Seymour*, 57 U.S. at 488–89.
[167] Clark v. Wooster, 119 U.S. (16 How.) 322, 326 (1886) ("There may be damages beyond this . . . but these are more properly the subjects of

Court seemed to suggest it would not disagree with the district court, one way or another, in the district court's use of enhanced damages.[168]

Indeed, in the 19th century there were at least two such cases that made considerations other than willfulness of the infringer. In *Russell v. Place*, the court thought it was proper to enhance damages if the jury did not compensate the plaintiff enough against any willful infringer.[169] The court suggested that willful infringers are not limited to "wanton or malicious pirate[s]",[170] but those who made an "erroneous estimate of the plaintiff's rights."[171] In *Peek v. Frame*, the court considered price erosion and the approximated lost profits in a decision to increase damages.[172]

Willfulness became an important consideration only when district courts balanced the behavior of the parties. A patentee who did not practice his invention was not allowed enhanced damages.[173] Good faith was enough to avoid enhanced damages, and in one case lowered the singular damage proven by the plaintiff.[174] These considerations are indicative of law on damages in general. As one judge recognized, when charging the jury to determine damages:

> [T]he question of damages being one of compensation, of which it is always, in such cases, difficult to fix a standard, much must depend upon the discretion

---

allowance by the court under the authority given to it to increase damages."); CHISUM, *supra* note 64, § 20.03[4][b][ii].

[168] *See* 145 U.S. 156, 174 (1892); CHISUM, *supra* note 64, § 20.03[4][b][ii].

[169] 21 F. Cas. 57, 58 (C.C.N.D.N.Y. 1871) (No. 12,161); *see also* ROBINSON, *supra* note 21, §1069 n. 3.

[170] *See Seymour*, 57 U.S. at 489.

[171] *Russell*, 21 F. Cas. at 58.

[172] 19 F. Cas. 97, 98 (C.C.S.D.N.Y. 1871) (No. 10,903).

[173] ROBINSON, *supra* note 23, § 1069.

[174] Hogg v. Emerson, 52 U.S. (11 How.) 587, 607 (1850).

of the jury, who may sometimes properly take the conduct and motives of a defendant into consideration.[175]

Just as the jury might take into account the parties' behavior, judges will do the same when charged with a power to increase damages.

There are two problems, however, with balancing party equities, both made apparent by the current state of the law today. First, the original purpose of the treble provision, which was to provide adequate remedy for those who try their case at law rather than equity, is lost when behavior is the sole criteria.[176] As of this publication, courts may no longer use enhanced damages to better compensate patentees,[177] and therefore must rely on equity in some way to be fully compensated. Willful infringement is required even though it has never been a statutory requirement for enhanced damages.[178]

The second problem is that the Court of Appeals for the Federal Circuit, which has appellate jurisdiction over all patent cases,[179] has struggled to create standards that allow district courts to apply enhanced damages consistently. *In re Seagate* articulates the current standard, which is "objective recklessness."[180] This standard brings with it a certain consistency (in a way) but has effectively discouraged the exercise of the court's discretion in awarding enhanced damages. The

---

[175] Parker v. Hulme, 18 F. Cas. 1138, 1144 (C.C.E.D. Pa. 1849) (No. 10,740).
[176] *See* In re Seagate Tech., 497 F.3d 1360, 1378–80 (Fed. Cir. 2007) (Gajarsa, J., concurring) (describing when a district court might use enhanced damages for remedial purposes).
[177] Jurgens v. CBK, Ltd., 80 F.3d 1566, 1570 (Fed. Cir. 1996).
[178] *See Seagate*, 497 F.3d at 1377 (Gajarsa, J., concurring).
[179] 28 U.S.C. § 1295(a)(4)(A) (2012).
[180] *See Seagate*, 497 F.3d at 1371 (opinion of the court) (raising the threshold for enhanced damages from what was "akin to negligence" to a heightened "objective recklessness" standard).

Federal Circuit was persuaded by Supreme Court precedent unrelated to patent law,[181] without accounting for the history of the patent statute.[182]

The current test for enhanced damages cannot be correct when one considers how attorney fees are awarded. Attorney fees in patent suits may be granted in "exceptional cases," language that is not present in the damages provision.[183] Despite the differences in language, the Federal Circuit has required essentially the same test.[184] However, two Supreme Court decisions in 2014 have made it easier to win attorney fees.[185] If "objective recklessness" is a harsh standard for attorney fees, then it is a necessary conclusion that it is too harsh a standard for enhanced damages. It is on this matter that Judge O'Malley of the Federal Circuit has called for

---

[181] *Id.* at 1370 (citing Safeco Ins. Co. of Am. v. Burr, 551 U.S. 47 (2007) (interpreting the Fair Credit Reporting Act)).

[182] *Id.* at 1377–78 (Gajarsa, J., concurring) (recounting the history of the treble damages provision and noting that "actual damages provable at law—though not 'inadequate' in the equitable sense—could nevertheless be less than sufficient to compensate the patentee. In such a case, a discretionary enhancement of damages would be appropriate for entirely remedial reasons, irrespective of the defendant's state of mind."); WALKER, *supra* note 23, § 613 ("Increased damages may properly be awarded by a Court, where it necessary . . . to prevent a defendant infringer from profiting from his own wrong, whether that wrong was intentional or was unwitting.").

[183] 35 U.S.C. § 285 (2012) (attorney fees); *cf. id.* § 284 (damages).

[184] *See* iLOR, LLC. v. Google, Inc., 631 F.3d 1372, 1376–77 (Fed. Cir. 2011) (noting that the objective recklessness standard applied for both § 284 and § 285, once again only allowing an award of attorney fees "when there has been some material inappropriate conduct related to the matter in litigation").

[185] Octane Fitness, LLC v. Icon Health & Fitness, 134 S. Ct. 1749, 1758 (2014) (objective recklessness standard rejected as it "would appear to render § 285 largely superfluous"); Highmark, Inc. v. Allcare Health Mgmt. Sys., Inc., 134 S. Ct. 1744, 1749 (2014) (award of attorney fees should be reviewed for abuse of discretion). Both of these decisions were issued on April 29, 2014. *See Octane Fitness*, 134 S. Ct. 1749; *Highmark*, 134 S. Ct. 1744.

reconsideration of the standard for enhanced damages in light of recent Supreme Court decisions.[186]

B. *Equity in Patent Law*

There were two forms of equitable remedies available to patentees in the 19th century: injunction and accounting of profits. The substantive[187] and procedural[188] rules of equitable remedies are not from any statute, patent or otherwise. Rather, they hail from the traditions of the English Court of Chancery, which were incorporated in the United States by way of the Federal Judiciary Act of 1789.[189] These procedural rules were largely discarded with the merger of law and equity in the 1938 Federal Rules of Civil Procedure,[190] but the substantive rules have remained unaffected by a recent reorganization of the Judiciary Act.[191] This section will first discuss the history and application of injunctions, followed by the grant of profits by equitable accounting.

---

[186] Halo Elecs., Inc. v. Pulse Elecs., Inc., 769 F.3d 1371,1384–85 (Fed. Cir. 2014).
[187] Robinson v. Campbell, 16 U.S. (3 Wheat.) 212, 221–22 (1818) (substantive equitable rules inherited from England).
[188] Hayburn's Case, 2 U.S. (2 Dall.) 409, 413-14 (1792) ("The Court considers the practice of the Courts of King's Bench and Chancery in England as affording outlines for the practice of this Court, and that it will from time to time make such alterations therein as circumstances may render necessary."), *available at* https://supreme.justia.com/cases/federal/us/2/409/case.html.
[189] H. Tomás Gómez-Arostegui, *Prospective Compensation in Lieu of a Final Injunction in Patent and Copyright Cases*, 78 FORDHAM L. REV. 1661, 1691 (2010).
[190] *Id.* at 1692; Stainback v. Mo Hock Ke Lok Po, 336 U.S. 368, 382 n.26 (1949) ("Notwithstanding the fusion of law and equity by the Rules of Civil Procedure, the substantive principles of Courts of Chancery remain unaffected.").
[191] *See* Gómez-Arostegui, *supra* note 194, at 1692.

1. Injunctions

A patentee's best remedy for infringement is an injunction, as this preserves market exclusivity.[192] Conceptually, instituting preliminary injunctions is very different than permanent injunctions because the preliminary injunction is granted without full knowledge of the merits of the controversy, whereas the permanent injunction is meant to stop activity that is decidedly illegal.[193] However, the evolution of preliminary and permanent injunctions has been identical, albeit not contemporaneous.

The English practice of instituting a preliminary injunction to accompany the suit at law[194] was inherited in kind by the United States.[195] In the early 19th century, the preliminary injunction was granted on the same conditions as in England—that is, if the patentee signed an affidavit[196] and there were no "glaring defects" to the patent.[197] The only apparent difference between the applications of these injunctions was the frequency of the applications filed by patentees.[198] Phillips, in his 1830 treatise on patent law, theorized that patentees were satisfied with remedies at law (apparently impressed with the treble damages provision),[199] but

---

[192] ROBINSON, *supra* note 23, § 1168 ("The exercise of its preventive jurisdiction . . . is the most potent and most valuable of all methods provided by the law for the protection of the owner of a patent.").
[193] *Id.* § 1169.
[194] *See supra* text accompanying note 26.
[195] PHILLIPS, *supra* note 42, at 453-54 (citing, as examples, Justice Washington's opinions in Ogle v. Ege, 18 F. Cas. 619 (C.C.D. Pa.1826) (No. 10,462), Isaacs v. Cooper, 13 F. Cas. 153 (C.C.D. Pa. 1821) (No. 7,096)).
[196] PHILLIPS, *supra* note 42, at 454.
[197] Isaacs, 13 F. Cas. At 154. As to defects to the patent, the older the patent, the more it was presumed valid. *See* Sullivan v. Redfield, 23 F. Cas. 357 (C.C.D.N.Y. 1825) (No. 13,597).
[198] PHILLIPS, *supra* note 42, at 454.
[199] *Id.*; *see* Patent Act of 1800, 2 Stat. 37, § 3, *reprinted in* WALTERSCHEID, *supra* note 35, at 489 app. XI.

one contemporary treatise points out that equity was not readily available.[200] The latter should be more convincing, considering that the "most potent" remedy for a patentee is an injunction[201] and that damage awards were often never proved.[202]

As preliminary injunctions became more accessible after 1819,[203] the requirements to obtain them became more stringent. Validity of the patent was no longer the sole consideration.[204] A preliminary injunction was granted only after considering the traditional considerations of the balance of harms to the plaintiff,[205] the behavior of the parties,[206] and the public interest.[207] In one case, there was no harm to a plaintiff's exclusive market because the invention was only for a small improvement.[208] In *Bliss v. City of Brooklyn*, an injunction was denied because the invention was necessary for public use in case of fires; this was despite certainty of validity and infringement.[209] Still, Robinson in his 1890 treatise found the principal question to be the validity of the patent when granting injunctions:

> Though it may work hardship to the defendant or other parties, and though

---

[200] CHISUM, *supra* note 67, § 20.04[1][a][i].
[201] *See* ROBINSON, *supra* note 23, §1168.
[202] *See supra* Part III.A.
[203] Patent Act of 1819, 3 Stat. 481, *reprinted in* WALTERSCHEID, *supra* note 35, at 491 app. XII.
[204] Although, it is still a prominent consideration. As an illustrative example, Robinson's treatise spends seventeen sections discussing the different types of evidence that would show a patent valid. *See* ROBINSON *supra* note 21, § 1173–90.
[205] *Id.* § 1193.
[206] *Id.* § 1194–97 (preliminary injunctions not granted in cases of estoppel, laches, improper purpose, or the defendant's good faith).
[207] *Id.* § 1200.
[208] Batten v. Silliman, 2 F. Cas. 1028, 1030 (C.C.E.D. Pa. 1855) (No. 1106).
[209] Bliss v. City of Brooklyn, 3 F. Cas. 706, 707 (C.C.E.D.N.Y. 1871) (No. 1544).

> the defendant offers such security against future losses as the plaintiff may require it, the infringement will not be permitted to continue to the manifest and injurious violation of the patent . . . . [The other considerations] may avail the [defendant] where principal questions are in doubt . . . but where the plaintiff's case is clear, and his injury imminent, the court will never hesitate to grant the desired relief.[210]

Yet, before this soliloquy, Robinson acknowledges the importance of other equitable considerations.[211] Preliminary injunctions in all areas of the law, generally, have been granted inconsistently.[212] But this is a necessary evil, because preliminary injunctions are of such importance that certainty on the merits is not the only consideration. The interests of justice and fairness are also considered, and therefore should be within the discretion of the district court when considering equitable remedies.[213]

The evolution of permanent injunctions to consider "outside" factors in patent remedies mirrors that of preliminary injunctions, but at a substantially slower rate. As courts slowed the pace of granting preliminary injunctions out of caution,[214] there was no reason for hesitation in the case of permanent injunctions. When a

---

[210] ROBINSON, *supra* note 18, § 1201 (internal citations omitted).
[211] *See id.*
[212] *See generally* John Leubsdorf, *The Standard for Preliminary Injunctions*, 91 HARV. L. REV. 525 (1978).
[213] *See* Rice & Adams Corp v. Lathrop, 278 U.S. 509, 514 (1929) (the district court decision to grant or deny the injunction was in its discretion); Mayview Corp. v. Rodstein, 480 F.2d 714, 715 (9th Cir. 1973) ("[O]nce validity is established . . . and infringement shown, general equitable principles apply to the remaining prerequisites to an injunction.").
[214] *See* CHISUM, *supra* note 64, § 20.04[1][a][iii] (contemporary rule is that preliminary injunctions should only be issued on strong evidence of both validity and infringement).

patentee petitioned the court for a permanent injunction, validity and infringement were already established. It was presumed that injunctions should be granted as a matter of course.[215] Other than inequitable conduct or perhaps a substantial social harm, no equitable principles were weighed against granting the injunction.[216] Whether these injunctions were granted with no consideration made of the remedy available at law,[217] or granted because monetary remedies were inherently inadequate,[218] it was clear that district courts almost always granted the patentee a permanent injunction.[219] In 2006, the Supreme Court unanimously held that traditional equitable principles should be considered when granting an injunction,[220] thus the substantive rules for granting permanent injunctions are now substantially the same as for preliminary injunctions.[221]

---

[215] ROBINSON, *supra* note 18, § 1170.
[216] Gómez-Arostegui, *supra* note 189, at 1665–66.
[217] *See* Livingston v. Van Ingen, 9 Johns. 507, 536 (N.Y. 1812) (No. 8420) *overruled on unrelated grounds by* N. River Steamboat Co. v. Livingston, 1825 WL 1859 (N.Y. 1825) ("An injunction is an appropriate remedy for a violation of all statute rights. They are granted of course."); ROBINSON, *supra* note 17, § 1220 ("[Injunctions are] granted irrespective of his right to profits or damages or any other form of relief...."); Gómez-Arostegui, *supra* note 190, at 1665.
[218] *See* eBay v. MercExchange, L.L.C., 547 U.S. 388, 395 (2006) (Roberts, C.J., concurring) ("From at least the early 19th century, courts have granted injunctive relief upon a finding of infringement in the vast majority of patent cases. This 'long tradition of equity practice' is not surprising, given the difficulty of protecting a right to *exclude* through monetary remedies that allow an infringer to *use* an invention against the patentee's wishes—a difficulty that often implicates the first two factors of the traditional four-factor test."); *see also* DAN B. DOBBS, 1 LAW OF REMEDIES 58 (2d ed. 1993) (asserting that legal rights have traditionally taken into account remedies available at law).
[219] Gómez-Arostegui, *supra* note 190, at 1665.
[220] *eBay*, 547 U.S. at 391 (opinion of the Court).
[221] *See* Gómez-Arostegui, *supra* note 190, at 1665.

2. Accounting

Accounting is an equitable remedy in which the defendant pays the plaintiff for profits that the defendant had unlawfully acquired.[222] The remedy is available when the defendant had legal rights of something that should have belonged to the plaintiff,[223] and therefore the defendant is made to pay whatever gains it made through use of the plaintiff's property back to the plaintiff. Accounting is, essentially, a disgorgement of the defendant's profits.

Before accounting was precluded by a statute change in 1948, it was the most potent remedy for monetary awards, either in law or in equity. The remedy became unacceptable in patent law as it became procedurally untenable.

For example, a farmer harvests crops with a machine, but the machine was invented and patented by another. The farmer used this machine without permission of the inventor, and therefore infringed.[224] Although the farmer, who read about the patent and made the machine based on that knowledge, has legal title to the machine itself, the concept of the machine belongs to the inventor. Therefore, the title to the machine should have belonged to the inventor, and the farmer used the invention in a "constructive trust."[225] The profits or income from use of the machine therefore belong to the inventor.[226] Unlike lost profits,

---

[222] *See* DOBBS, *supra* note 219, at 588.
[223] *Id.* at 587.
[224] *See* 35 U.S.C. § 271(a) (use of a patented machine constitutes infringement).
[225] *See* DOBBS, *supra* note 218, at 587.
[226] *Id.* at 588.

the inventor is entitled to the profits even if he could not possibly exploit the market himself.[227]

The Patent Act of 1819 conferred jurisdiction to federal courts sitting in equity to exercise the remedy of accounting in all patent cases.[228] There were three obstacles the plaintiff had to overcome to receive an accounting. First, because courts of equity did not traditionally decide questions of fact, accounting required complex procedural maneuvers.[229] The equity court sometimes acted as a court of law and paneled a jury,[230] or it would require the plaintiff to file a complaint in law as well as equity.[231] The second obstacle was that, in situations where the infringer made no profits from the infringement, the patentee had no remedy available.[232] Finally, a bill for accounting required the patentee to file for an injunction as well,[233] because the infringer was not literally a trustee.[234] If an injunction was not available, say, because the patent had expired,[235] then equitable accounting was closed off to the patentee—otherwise plaintiffs needed only make a general prayer of relief in equity.[236]

---

[227] ROBINSON, *supra* note 18, § 1136 ("[Accounting includes] all the benefits which the defendant has derived from the invention, without reference to the amount which the plaintiff might otherwise have received.").
[228] Patent Act of 1819, 3 Stat. 481, *reprinted in* WALTERSCHEID, *supra* note 30, at 491 app. XII.
[229] *See, e.g.*, Van Hook v. Pendleton, 28 F. Cas. 998, 999–1000 (C.C.S.D. N.Y. 1848) (discussing the equitable rules in creating a factual record).
[230] This is the "feigned issue." *See* CHISUM, *supra* note 63, § 20.02[1][c].
[231] *Id.*
[232] City of Elizabeth v. Am. Nicholson Pavement Co., 97 U.S. 126, 139 (1877) ("[T]hough the defendant's general business be ever so profitable, if the use of the invention has not contributed to the profits, none can be recovered.").
[233] Root v. Lake Shore & M.S. Ry. Co., 105 U.S. 189, 194, 215–216 (1881).
[234] *Id.* at 214.
[235] *See, e.g.*, Parks v. Booth, 102 U.S. 96, 107 (1880) (denying injunction because patent had expired).
[236] Stevens v. Gladding, 58 U.S. (17 How.) 447, 453 (1854).

These limitations, however, were minor compared to the requirements to receive damages at law[237] for two reasons: first, the obstacles to equitable remedies were applied inconsistently;[238] second, the complex procedural maneuvers were substantially reduced in the 1875 patent act when courts in equity were expressly empowered to empanel a jury in patent cases,[239] and they were fully relieved when law and equity merged in 1938.[240] Additionally, the 1870 patent act allowed a patentee to recover legal damages (royalties or lost profits) if equitable accounting proved insufficient.[241] Finally, the requirement that an accounting action be accompanied by an infringement action was relaxed.[242]

Still, there were several problems with accounting. The process was—and still is—excruciatingly slow,[243] taking years to determine damages.[244] Depending on which party could benefit from dragging out the

---

[237] For the difficulties of winning an award for legal damage, see *supra* Part III.A.

[238] The *Root* opinion presents indirect evidence that the case law was inconsistent. See *Root*, 105 U.S. at 191 ("An examination of the practice and opinions of the Circuit Courts undoubtedly shows much diversity, incapable of reconciliation . . . .").

[239] Act of Feb. 16, 1875, ch. 77, § 2, 18 Stat. 315, 316.

[240] *See* Ross v. Bernhard, 396 U.S. 531, 539–540 (1970) ("Purely procedural impediments to the presentation of any issue by any party, based on the difference between law and equity, was destroyed.").

[241] Act of July 8, 1870, Ch. 230, § 55, 16 Stat. 198, 206 (1870); Birdsall v. Coolidge, 93 U.S. 64, 69 (1876) ("Gains and profits are still the proper measure of damages in equity suits, except in cases where the injury sustained by the infringement is plainly greater . . . ."). Note, however, that the inverse was not true—an action of law could not recover the infringer's profits by way of accounting. *E.g.*, Coupe v. Royer, 155 U.S. 565, 582 (1895).

[242] *See* Clark v. Wooster, 119 U.S. 322, 323–25 (1886) (noting equity jurisdiction established though the patent expired just 15 days before the complaint was filed); CHISUM, *supra* note 63, § 20.02[1][e].

[243] Eichengrun, *supra* note 63, at 471.

[244] *See* Vincent P. Tassinari, *Compiled Legislative History of 35 U.S.C. § 284: The Patent Compensation Statute*, 31 UWLA L. REV. 45, 70 (2000).

proceeding, a plaintiff or defendant could use the delay as leverage for a settlement.[245] There were substantial questions of proof and apportionment. Courts struggled to determine who had the burden of proof, and how to correctly apportion the profits.[246] Such problems occurred because the infringer was not, in the tradition of accounting, a trustee for an account, and therefore accounting was an imperfect test for patent remedies.[247] Collectively, these problems too often resulted in a "denial of justice because of delay of justice."[248]

Courts today interpret the passage of the 1946 act as disallowing accounting procedures, and therefore, a plaintiff cannot recover the profits made by the infringers by accounting.[249] However, whether this was Congress's intent is debatable: Congress may have simply put it in the Court's power to award the infringer's profits immediately with a reasonable royalty.[250] It was the Supreme Court in *Aro Manufacturing Co. v. Convertible Top Replacement Co.*,

---

[245] *See id.* at 69-70 (discussing testimony reporting to Congress a case that took twenty years for awards to be granted). Notice that the "delay of justice" does not indicate it favors plaintiffs or defendants. *Id.* at 70.
[246] *See generally* CHISUM, *supra* note 64, § 20.02[3] (describing the "intricacies" of determining the account).
[247] *Cf.* Eichengrun, *supra* note 63, at 477–81 (offering clarity on the burden of proof in traditional accounting when the defendant is a trustee).
[248] Tassinari, *supra* note 245, at 70.
[249] Eric E. Bensen, *Apportionment of Lost Profits in Contemporary Patent Damages Cases*, 10 VA. J. L. & TECH. 8, 27 (2005).
[250] Georgia-Pacific Corp. v. United States Plywood Corp., 243 F. Supp. 500, 521–22 (S.D.N.Y. 1965); *see also*, Tassinari, *supra* note 245, at 81 ("Although the bill would not preclude the recovery of profits as an element of general damages, yet by making it unnecessary to have proceedings before masters and empowering equity courts to assess general damages irrespective of profits, the measure represents proposed legislation which in the judgment of the committee is long overdue."). Notice that the report fails to distinguish recovery of lost profits from the infringer's profits.

(1964)[251] that eliminated the use of accounting.[252] However, this particular holding should carry little precedential value. The issue of damages was not before the Court, and the part of the opinion discussing accounting was not part of the majority opinion.[253] Yet, even if *Aro* is unpersuasive, lower courts are likely to avoid accounting when other remedies are available because the accounting would still substantially delay justice.

C. Analysis of Damages and Equity after 1836

Prior to 1836, legal damages were automatically trebled so as to provide adequate compensation because equity was largely unavailable. Courts found it necessary to calculate the damages award precisely because any mistake in the calculation would be trebled. The assumption was that the treble provision was enough to provide adequate compensation without the need to estimate damages.

However, if damages could not be proved by either an established royalty or lost profits, then the plaintiff could only recover nominal damages. Royalties were rarely established because royalties did not realize a patent's true value. Lost profits were unavailable to most patentees unless they created and fostered a new market with their invention. As a result, nominal damages were the singular damages, and trebled nominal damages were still nominal.

The Patent Act of 1836 amended the treble provision from a mandatory calculation to place it within the discretion of the court. Rather than allowing damages to be estimated by the jury, it still required that the singular damages be calculated precisely as

---

[251] 377 U.S. 476, 506-07 (1964) (plurality opinion).
[252] Benson, *supra* note 250, at 28.
[253] *Id.*

before. The lack of compensation at law for many patentees continued after 1836—that is until the advent of the reasonable royalty, discussed in the section below.

While patentees at law were undercompensated, they could find more fertile ground in courts of equity. For established patents, preliminary injunctions were increasingly granted, which placed the patentee in an excellent position for settlement negotiation. Likewise, permanent injunctions were granted as a matter of course. Because equity did not demand the sort of precision in calculation of damages, patentees could even recover substantial monetary damages by way of accounting, such as the entire profit made by the infringer for use of the product. In stark contrast with *Seymour*, a patentee could recover the profits of a defendant even if the defendant's infringement constituted a small improvement for a machine or product. As a result of substantially better remedies, patentees were eager to bring actions in equity.[254]

But even if the possible award was substantial, receiving a monetary award in equity was impracticable. Accounting was extremely time consuming and often contentious, resulting in litigation for damages long after the initial suit—a substantial delay of justice. In 1946, accounting procedures were scratched, but patentees are now offered reasonable royalties as the measure of minimum recovery.

---

[254] Hilton Davis Chem. Co. v. Warner-Jenkinson Co., 62 F.3d 1512, 1567 (Fed. Cir. 1995), *rev'd*, 520 U.S. 17 (1997) (Nies, J., dissenting) (noting that there were virtually no jury cases in patent law after the 1870 amendment).

V. Reasonable Royalties and Ongoing Royalties
A. The History of Reasonable Royalties

Courts increasingly tried to avoid awarding nominal damages in patent suits and instead began to award a reasonable royalty for the past use of the patented invention. The reasonable royalty is markedly different from other legal remedies in that precision is no longer required for this damage to be awarded. It is by far the most prevalent award today.[255]

Perhaps the first use of the reasonable royalty was in the case of *Hayden v. Suffolk Mfg. Co.*[256] The district court instructed that the jury could consider an amount based on a license to a third party and the value that the defendant had derived from use of the invention.[257] The Supreme Court affirmed, stating, "There being no established patent or license fee in the case, in order to get at a fair measure of damages, or even an approximation to it, general evidence must necessarily be resorted to."[258]

Coupe v. Royer went in a different direction.[259] While recognizing that district courts have been inconsistent in the application of damage rules, the Supreme Court held that damage calculations could not be guesswork.[260] The case involved a machine that supposedly improved the quality of leather.[261] The

---

[255] *See* Chris Barry et. al. *2011 Patent Litigation Study: Patent Litigation Trends As The "America Invents Act" Becomes Law*, PRICEWATERHOUSECOOPERS, at 14 (2011), available at http://www.aipla.org/resources2/intlip/Documents/Other-International-Events/US-Bar-JPO-Liaison-Council-2012/2011-patent-litigation-study.pdf.
[256] 11 F. Cas. 900 (C.C.D. Mass. 1862).
[257] *Id.* at 907.
[258] Suffolk Mfg. Co. v. Hayden, 70 U.S. (3 Wall.) 315, 319 (1866).
[259] 155 U.S. 565 (1895).
[260] *Id.* at 581–83.
[261] Royer v. Coupe, 29 F. 358, 368 (C.C.D. Mass. 1886), *rev'd*, Coupe v. Royer, 155 U.S. 565 (1895).

defendants argued that the machine was useless.[262] While the plaintiff testified that the invention increased the price of the hide by three or four dollars, he conceded that the jury should only award one dollar per hide.[263] The jury agreed and accepted the estimation by the plaintiff of the cost.[264] The Supreme Court reversed, suggesting that the plaintiff must show what the defendant had gained before it could be used as indirect evidence.[265]

Courts would later distinguish these two cases. While it is true that the plaintiff in *Hayden*, unlike the plaintiff in *Coupe*, had more proof of the actual value of the patented invention, recall that a single license "does not tend to establish"[266] the value of a patent; the rule set by *Rude v. Wescott* in 1889[267] should have effectively overturned *Hayden*.

However, the law has moved away from *Rude* and *Coupe*. The Supreme Court in the 1915 decision *Dowagiac Mfg. Co. v. Minn. Moline Plow Co.*[268] changed the momentum, permanently, in favor of a reasonable royalty. The Court changed its approach, treating infringement as a tort on property interests[269] rather than a breach of contract, therefore allowing more flexibility.[270] Likewise, two preceding cases from the

---

[262] *Id.* at 372.
[263] *Id.* at 371.
[264] *Id.* at 360 (syllabus of the court).
[265] Coupe v. Royer, 155 U.S. 565, 583 (1895).
[266] *See* text accompanying note 123.
[267] 130 U.S. 152, 167 (1889) (damages must be shown by "clear and definitive proof.").
[268] 235 U.S. 641 (1915).
[269] *Id.* at 648.
[270] *See* RESTATEMENT (SECOND) OF TORTS § 912 cmt. c (1979) (noting that expert estimations on the value of land can be "far from certain"); *see also* John C. Jarosz & Michael J. Chapman, *The Hypothetical Negotiation and Reasonable Royalty Damages: The Tail Wagging the Dog*, 16 STAN. TECH. L. REV. 769, 786 (2013) ("[R]easonable royalty damages are a form of *general damages* intended to compensate for the *tort* of

circuit courts, both cited in *Dowagiac*,[271] characterized infringement as tortious conduct.[272] Despite *Dowagiac*'s attempt to say that reasonable royalties were consistent with precedent,[273] this case marked a fundamental shift from how patent damages were approached just twenty years earlier.[274]

Congress tried to codify this change in 1922, amending the statute to provide that "reasonable compensation" would be awarded, with the assistance of experts, in cases where damages could not be determined with "reasonable certainty."[275] The major issue with the 1922 act is that reasonable royalties were available only in actions of equity, not law, which meant that accounting was still necessary.[276] The error was reversed in 1946, when the patent statute was amended to state that patentees were entitled "at least to a reasonable royalty," eliminating nominal damages.[277] Reasonable royalties are still the floor today.[278]

The modern application of reasonable royalties is a hotly debated topic.[279] To review briefly, a court uses a

---

patent infringement. They are not, and were not intended to be, a form of contract damages, retroactive or otherwise.").
[271] *Dowagiac*, 235 U.S. at 650.
[272] Bemis Car Box Co. v. J G Brill Co, 200 F. 749, 754 (3d Cir. 1912); U.S. Frumentum Co. v. Lauhoff, 216 F. 610, 615 (1914).
[273] *See Dowagiac*, 235 U.S. at 648.
[274] Recall that Justice Story explicitly stated that infringement was not a tort. Whittemore v. Cutter, 29 F. Cas. 1123, 1125 (C.C.D. Mass. 1813) (No. 17,601).
[275] Act of February 18, 1922, Pub. L. No. 147, ch. 58, 42 Stat. 389, 393 § 8.
[276] *Id.*; *see* Tassinari, *supra* note 245, at 57 ("When the court enters a decree finding infringement, the practice is to . . . take an accounting . . . .").
[277] Act of August 1, 1946, 79 Pub. L. 587, ch. 726, 60 Stat. 778.
[278] 35 U.S.C. § 284 (2012).
[279] *See, e.g.*, Mark. A. Glick, *The Law and Economics of Patent Infringement Damages*, 10 UTAH B.J. 11, 15 (1997) ("One of the most confusing areas of patent damage law is the calculation of a reasonable royalty."); Jarosz & Chapman, *supra* note 270; Layne S. Keele, *"ResQ"ing Patent*

legal fiction. To determine the reasonable royalty, the court must imagine the parties are willing partners negotiating a royalty.[280] Expert testimony is accepted, concentrating on the so-called *Georgia-Pacific* factors.[281] The fifteen factors were not meant to be an exhaustive list,[282] but nevertheless, many courts have used them to determine the royalty.[283] The factors are a mix of the same considerations that are used to determine established royalties, lost profits, and accounting.[284] The method has been sharply criticized, with critics mostly agreeing that royalties have been estimated too high in light of the entire market value rule, which states that a patentee is entitled to the entire profit of an infringing product if the patented improvement drove the market of the product.[285]

It is important to note, however, the nature and rationale of reasonable royalty. Precision was the controlling concern in the 19th century. Reasonableness, not precision, is the controlling concern today. Despite valiant efforts in economic models to bring precision to the calculation of

---

Infringement Damages after ResQNet: The Dangers of Litigation Licenses as Evidence of a Reasonable Royalty, 20 TEX. INTELL. PROP. L.J. 181 (2012).
[280] CHISUM, *supra* note 64, § 20.07[1].
[281] *See* Georgia-Pacific Corp. v. U.S. Plywood Corp., 318 F. Supp. 1116, 1120 (S.D.N.Y. 1970).
[282] *Id.*
[283] CHISUM, *supra* note 64, § 20.07[1][d].
[284] For example, royalties received by the patentees (the first factor) are viewed much like established royalties, except established royalties would not consider license agreements settled under threat of litigation. *Georgia-Pacific*, 318 F. Supp. at 1120; *see generally* Keele, *supra* note 279 (discussing the dangers of using settlements in calculation of a reasonable royalty). The attempt by the patentee to keep a close monopoly (factor three) is considered just as in lost profits. *Georgia-Pacific*, 318 F. Supp. at 1120.
[285] *See, e.g.*, Lemley, *supra* note 156, at 659.

reasonable royalties,[286] there is no reconciliation between the principles of reasonableness and precision.

B. The (Short) History of Ongoing Royalties

In 2006, *eBay v. MercExchange*,[287] overturned the old rule of granting permanent injunctions as a matter of course. Naturally, some successful patent litigants will find it more difficult to obtain injunctions. In those situations, what remedies are available if an injunction is denied?

The Federal Circuit has held that a district court may award ongoing royalties.[288] The court defined ongoing royalties as, "a reasonable royalty in light of the ongoing infringement."[289] For authority, the court relied on a previous 1985 Federal Circuit case[290] and a 1973 Supreme Court case that stated ongoing royalties are "well-established forms of relief when necessary to an effective remedy, particularly where patents have provided the leverage for . . . antitrust violation adjudication."[291] This is thin support, especially the use of the Supreme Court case, because there the United States had express statutory authority for an ongoing royalty.[292]

---

[286] *See, e.g.*, Thomas F. Cotter, *Four Principles for Calculating Reasonable Royalties in Patent Infringement Litigation*, 27 SANTA CLARA COMPUTER & HIGH TECH. L.J. 725 (2011).
[287] 547 U.S. 388, 390 (2006).
[288] Paice L.L.C. v. Toyota Motor Corp., 504 F.3d 1293, 1314–15 (Fed. Cir. 2014).
[289] *Id.* at 1315.
[290] Shatterproof Glass Corp. v. Libbey-Owens Ford. Co., 758 F.2d 613, 628 (Fed. Cir. 1985).
[291] United States v. Glaxo Group Ltd., 410 U.S. 52, 93 (1973).
[292] *See* 15 U.S.C. § 4 (2012) (United States attorneys have duty to institute proceedings in equity antitrust cases, and may "bring forth the case and praying the case and praying that such violation shall be enjoined *or otherwise prohibited*") (emphasis added).

Ongoing royalties are a form of equitable relief, as legal damages are confined to harm actually inflicted.[293] Because the award of ongoing royalties was not practiced in England before 1789,[294] Congress must either expressly or implicitly allow courts to award ongoing royalties.[295] Scholarly articles have debated whether courts have the authority to issue ongoing royalties.[296] On one hand, the sections for remedies in preceding patent statutes have increasingly allowed legal damages during equitable proceedings,[297] which might indicate that all equitable remedies should be available to fully compensate the patentee.[298] However, it is arguable that subsequent changes to the statute purposely avoided compulsory licenses (that is, government-forced ongoing royalties).[299] It is a question that the Supreme Court may need to answer in the near future, though some justices on the Court have hinted at rejecting a court's ability to issue ongoing royalties.[300]

---

[293] *See Paice*, 504 F.3d at 1313 n.13, 1314; Bos. Sci. Corp. v. Johnson & Johnson, No. C 02-0790 SI, 2009 WL 975424, at *5 (N.D. Cal. April 9, 2009); Whittemore v. Cutter, 29 F. Cas. 1123, 1125 (C.C.D. Mass. 1813) (No. 17,601) (damages are what the plaintiff had in fact sustained, that is, no prospective damages); ROBINSON, *supra* note 17, § 1088.

[294] *See* Gómez-Arostegui, *supra* note 190, at 1699–1708 (concluding there was no such equity practice in England).

[295] *Id.* at 1685.

[296] *See, e.g., id.* at 1661 (arguing courts lack authority). *Contra* Mark A. Lemley, *The Ongoing Confusion Over Ongoing Royalties*, 76 MO. L. REV. 695, 697 (2011) (arguing courts have authority).

[297] *See* Patent Act of 1870, ch. 230, 16 Stat. 198-217, § 55; Act of February 18, 1922, Pub. L. No. 147, ch. 58, 42 Stat. 389, 393 § 8.

[298] *See* 35 U.S.C. § 284 (2012).

[299] *See* Gómez-Arostegui, *supra* note 190, at 1724 ("[I]t is impossible to argue that Congress contemplated and incorporated a judicially imposed compulsory license....").

[300] *See* eBay Inc. v. MercExchange, L.L.C., 547 U.S. 388, 396 (2006) (Kennedy, J., concurring) ("When the patented invention is but a small component of the product the companies seek to produce and the threat of an injunction is employed simply for undue leverage in

Assuming, *arguendo*, that courts have the power to issue ongoing royalties under the theory of equity, the question of how to determine that royalty remains.[301] In light of the history of preliminary and permanent injunctions, it is important to remember that ongoing royalties serve an equitable purpose. Therefore, the four-factor test historically employed by courts of equity should be applied to ongoing royalties,[302] and courts should refrain from considering the same factors that were used to determine past damages.[303]

If courts do not have the power to issue ongoing royalties, courts may still compensate patentees by enhancing damages by way of the treble provision.[304] The purpose of the treble damages provision was to provide adequate remedies to those who do not have access to equity.[305] District courts could simply use this provision to compensate patentees if district courts were given more discretion to access treble damages than is currently permitted by the Federal Circuit.

But is also important to remember why plaintiffs are seeking ongoing royalties in the first place. It is because

---

negotiations, legal damages may well be sufficient to compensate for the infringement . . . .").

[301] The Federal Circuit currently holds that there is no right to jury for this equitable remedy. Paice L.L.C. v. Toyota Motor Corp., 504 F.3d 1293, 1315-16 (Fed. Cir. 2007).

[302] *See* eBay v. MercExchange, L.L.C., 547 U.S. 388, 391 (2006).

[303] *Contra* Lemley, *supra* note 156, at 702-3 (arguing that reasonable royalties should be used to determine ongoing royalties, and stating, "[c]uriously . . . Federal Circuit panels addressing the issue seem to believe that the question is entirely different from the issue of past damages."). *But see* ROBINSON, *supra* note 18, § 1050 ("The principles adopted in the courts of equity cannot be imported into the courts of law, or those into equity, without *serious confusion and inevitable mistake* . . . . It is . . . of primary importance that in discussing damages at law, or profits and damages in equity, each topic should be kept free form the special doctrines appertaining to the other . . . .") (emphasis added).

[304] 35 U.S.C. § 284 (2012).

[305] *Supra* Part III.B.1.

the patentee was denied a permanent injunction. Since *eBay*, permanent injunctions have usually been denied to non-practicing entities ("NPEs").[306] NPEs are extremely controversial. Much debate has surrounded reforming the patent code to prevent some of the entities, derisively called "patent trolls," from coercing license agreements by threatening litigation.[307] In light of the history recounted in this article, the solution to these NPEs might be found without reform.

Before 1946, NPEs could not recover enhanced damages.[308] Furthermore, these speculators were not likely to prove actual harm during litigation because they did not choose to enjoy the monopoly.[309] Courts simply award the statutory minimum and refuse to grant enhanced damages (which is consistent with history) and refuse ongoing royalties (because those who do not act equitably receive none) if the district court feels that the NPE has acted contrary to the purpose of the patent system. With only a reasonable royalty available, bad-behaving NPEs ("trolls") could not use litigation to coerce licenses.

VI. CONCLUSION

Calculation of damages and equity are persistently difficult in every area of the law.[310] Accordingly, the history presented here shows that remedies have been inconsistent. This inconsistency in patent remedies reflects competing policy interests. For example, businesses that have worked, developed, and depended

---

[306] Andrew Beckerman-Rodau, *The Aftermath of eBay v. MercExchange*, 89 J. PAT. & TRADEMARK OFF. SOC'Y, 631, 632-33 (2007).
[307] *See generally* Colleen V. Chien, *Of Trolls, Davids, Goliaths, and Kings*, 87 N.C. L. REV. 1571 (2009).
[308] ROBINSON, *supra* note 18, § 1069.
[309] *See id.* § 1062.
[310] 11-55 CORBIN ON CONTRACTS § 55.1 ("The law of remedies has probably always involved a greater degree of uncertainty than has the system of rules by which rights and duties are determined.").

on their patents deserve protection. However, speculators do not invoke sympathy when they indiscriminately threaten infringement suits. Granting both the same royalty does little to advance policy goals.

History may be an invaluable guide on how to effectuate desired policy goals. Juries should determine the award that it believes would fully compensate the patentee. If such award is too small given the facts of the case, district courts should use their discretion to increase damages pursuant to the patent statute. Equity (injunctions and ongoing royalties) should be granted to those who practice their patents equitably. Such practices would be consistent with history and provide much needed flexibility in patent enforcement.

ADAPTING ALICE: HOW TO FORMULATE A REPEATABLE TEST BASED ON *ALICE V. CLS BANK*

KELLY FERMOYLE[†]

I. Introduction 223

Ii. Historical development..225

   A. *In re Abrams*: point of novelty 225

   B. Strengths and weaknesses of the point-of-novelty test..227

   C. *Parker v. Flook* 228

   D. *Diamond v. Diehr* 231

Iii. Current state of the law: *Mayo* and *Alice* 234

   A. *Mayo v. Prometheus* 234

   B. *Alice v. Cls bank*..237

Iv. How the federal circuit can adapt the *Alice* test.....242

   A. Objective of the *Alice* test 243

   B. How to square *Diehr* with *Alice* 246

   C. Why the *Alice* test is flexible...................................248

   D. Proposed adaption of *Alice*..................................... 250

V. Analysis of adapted test... 257

   A. *In re Abrams*...258

[†] Kelly Fermoyle, J.D. Candidate 2016, William Mitchell College of Law.

    B. *Parker v. Flook* 258
    C. *Diamond v. Diehr* 259
    D. *Mayo v. Prometheus* 259
    E. *Alice v. Cls bank* 260
Vi. Conclusion 261

I. INTRODUCTION

The Supreme Court's recent decision in *Alice Corp. v. CLS Bank International*[1] has received significant criticism.[2] Though the outcome the Court reached may be reasonable, the "framework" that the Court uses fails to guide future inquiries of fringe patents such as the claim in *Alice*. The test, originally created in *Mayo Collaborative Services v. Prometheus Laboratories, Inc.*,[3] essentially determines subject matter eligibility by first determining whether a claim is not subject-matter eligible, and, if it is not, then by determining if it actually is eligible.[4] That description may be a slight embellishment, but nevertheless, the guidance the test gives for future disputes is minimal.

Subject matter eligibility is broadly defined in 35 U.S.C. § 101 as "any new or useful process, machine,

---

[1] 134 S. Ct. 2347 (2014).
[2] *See, e.g.*, McRO, Inc. v. Valve Corp., No. SACV 13-1874-GW(FFMx), 2014 WL 4772200, at *5 (C.D. Cal. Sept. 22, 2014) (comparing the *Alice* test to Justice Stewart's infamous phrase: "I know it when I see it"); Eclipse IP, LLC v. McKinley Equip. Corp., No. SACV 14-742-GW(AJWx), 2014 WL 4407592, at *3 (C.D. Cal. Sep. 4, 2014); Richard Lloyd, *Alice Decision Makes Software Innovation Landscape Bleaker, Rader Claims*, IAM Blog (Sep. 01, 2014), http://www.iam-magazine.com/Blog/Detail.aspx?g=32997d05-6cd8-49d9-af8d-4a4888a4fcf2 (quoting former Federal Circuit chief judge Rader, referring to *Mayo* and its application to *Alice*: "It causes me great pain to recognise the worst case in patent law history doesn't come out of India or Pakistan or Vietnam or China even, it comes from the United States as recently as a few years ago.").
[3] 132 S. Ct. 1289 (2012).
[4] *Alice*, 134 S. Ct. at 2355 (quoting *Mayo*, 132 S. Ct. at 1294) ("First, we determine whether the claims at issue are directed to one of those patent-ineligible concepts . . . . [S]tep two of this analysis [is] a search for an 'inventive concept'—*i.e.*, an element or combination of elements that is 'sufficient to ensure that the patent in practice amounts to significantly more than a patent upon the [ineligible concept] itself.'").

manufacture, or composition of matter, or any new and useful improvement thereof."[5] The Court has created implicit exceptions, found nowhere in the statute, for "laws of nature, natural phenomena, and abstract ideas."[6] Since patent claims are composed of elements,[7] some of which may fall within the implicit exceptions while others may not, a claim that is part statutory and part non-statutory can be difficult to characterize. These claims are a hybrid mixture of statutory and non-statutory elements.[8] Much of the recent debate about the scope of § 101 involves these hybrid claims.[9] This article proposes a test to procedurally determine the patentability of a hybrid claim.

This article proceeds as follows. Part II describes the historical development of the law handling hybrid patent claims. Part III explains the current test as created in *Mayo* and *Alice*. Part IV argues that the current test is ambiguous, but also flexible and amenable to a proposed adapted test. In Part V, this article concludes that courts could use the proposed test in determining patentability of difficult hybrid patent claims.

---

[5] 35 U.S.C. § 101 (2012).

[6] *Mayo*, 132 S. Ct. at 1293 (quoting Diamond v. Diehr, 450 U.S. 175, 185 (1981)).

[7] *See generally* MICHAEL D. SCOTT, SCOTT ON MULTIMEDIA LAW § 8.03 (3d ed. 2014).

[8] *See Ex parte* Lyell, No. 89-0461, 1990 WL 354583, at *3 (B.P.A.I. Apr. 9, 1990) ("We however do recognize that certain types of claims which appear to be 'hybrid' are permitted in U.S. patent practice."). For a detailed discussion of hybrid claims, see 1 R. CARL MOY, MOY'S WALKER ON PATENTS §§ 5:65–85 (4th ed. 2013).

[9] *See, e.g.*, *Alice*, 134 S. Ct. at 2354; *Mayo*, 132 S. Ct. at 1293; Bilski v. Kappos, 561 U.S. 593, 597–99 (2010); Jacob S. Sherkow, *The Natural Complexity of Patent Eligibility*, 99 IOWA L. REV. 1137, 1139 (2014).

II. HISTORICAL DEVELOPMENT

Since "[a]t some level, 'all inventions . . . embody, use, reflect, rest upon, or apply laws of nature, natural phenomena, or abstract ideas,'"[10] examples of hybrid claims that consist of both statutory and non-statutory elements could likely be found throughout the patent system's history.[11] Formal discussion on this topic began in the early 1950s with the judiciary responding to these types of claims by creating the "point-of-novelty" test.[12] This section will explain this test and then examine the later cases of *Parker v. Flook* and *Diamond v. Diehr* and the conflict of law that began to build.[13]

A. In re Abrams: Point of Novelty

The United States Court of Customs and Patent Appeals (CCPA), the predecessor to the Federal Circuit, issued the clearest opinion articulating the point-of-novelty test. *In re Abrams*[14] involved claims "for Petroleum Prospecting Method."[15] In this case, the non-statutory elements of the claim were objected to as "purely mental in character."[16] The illustrative claim four recites "a method of prospecting for petroliferous deposits" with six steps; the court determined the last three were "mental steps."[17] The first three steps were determined to be statutory elements: "*sinking* a number of boreholes," "*sealing* off each said boreholes from the

---

[10] *Alice*, 134 S. Ct. at 2354 (2014) (quoting *Mayo*, 132 S. Ct. at 1289 (2012)).
[11] *See* MOY, *supra* note 8, § 5:65.
[12] *See infra* Parts II.A–B.
[13] *See infra* Parts II.C–D.
[14] 188 F.2d 165 (C.C.P.A. 1951).
[15] *Id.* at 165.
[16] *Id.*
[17] *See id.*

atmosphere," and *"reducing* the pressure."[18] The three mental steps involved *"measuring* the rate of pressure rise," *"determining* the rate . . . at a standard reference," and *"comparing* the rates . . . to detect anomalies."[19]

Abrams asserted that analyzing mental-step claims such as this needed a logical rule to follow.[20] Abrams's brief proposed a rule, which the court appeared to adopt implicitly, that determines patentability by sorting claims into one of three categories.[21] The first category is where all method steps "are purely mental in character,"[22] which would clearly not be patentable. The second and third are the difficult ones. The second category is where "a method claim embodies both positive and physical steps as well as so-called mental steps," but the novelty is in the mental steps; "then the claim is considered unpatentable for the same reason that it would be if all the steps were purely mental in character."[23] The last category is where the novelty "resides in one or more of the positive and physical steps," and contains patentable subject matter.[24]

Though the court did not disagree with Abrams's proposed rule in *Abrams*, it nevertheless found that the claim fell within the second category of claims.[25] The court found steps "involving therein such purely mental terms as 'determining', 'registering', 'counting',

---

[18] *Id.* (emphasis added).
[19] *Id.* (emphasis added).
[20] *Id.* at 166.
[21] *See id.* The court does not expressly state its approval of the test, but the court simply applies the test in making its determination. *See id.* at 167.
[22] *Id.* at 166.
[23] *Id.*
[24] *Id.*
[25] *Id.* at 170 ("[I]t seems to us that they are eliminated from the applicability of appellant's proposed rule 3, and fall within No. 2.").

'observing', 'measuring', 'comparing', 'recording', and 'computing'" to be non-statutory.[26] Since the first two steps were determined to be "old for the purposes of the present application," the novelty was in the final three steps, which involved measuring, determining, and comparing respectively.[27] Since the court determined that these terms were non-statutory, the claim failed the test.[28]

B. Strengths and Weaknesses of the Point-of-Novelty Test

The point-of-novelty test articulated in *In re Abrams* was prominent in the U.S. Patent and Trademark Office for about two decades before it began to fall out of favor from the courts.[29] The strengths of the point-of-novelty test are that it is based on articulated rules and that the required novelty had to be in "both positive and physical steps."[30] But the test suffers from some significant weaknesses. First, it does not evaluate the claim as a whole.[31] Second, there is some ambiguity about how to handle a claim when there is more than one single point of novelty.[32] Third, when "the novelty does rest in the physical steps, the invention can properly be claimed by truncating the claim language to

---

[26] *Id.* at 167.
[27] *Id.* at 168.
[28] *Id.*
[29] *See* Application of Musgrave, 431 F.2d 882, 889 (C.C.P.A. 1970) ("It remains our view that we need not be encumbered in our reasoning by the 'Rules' of Abrams for the reason that they have never enjoyed the approval of this court."); MOY, *supra* note 8, § 5:66.
[30] *In re Abrams*, 188 F.2d at 166.
[31] *See, e.g.*, Diamond v. Diehr, 450 U.S. 175, 188 (1981) (holding that the claim should be viewed as a whole to determine patentability).
[32] Clearly if there is no novelty, the claim should not be considered valid, but it is unclear how the claim should be rejected. Alternatively, if there is more than one point of novelty, the test does not indicate how it should be handled.

recite only the physical steps."[33] Largely in response to these shortcomings, the point-of-novelty test gradually fell out of favor.[34]

In 1972, the Supreme Court decided *Gottschalk v. Benson*, one of its first decisions to establish guidelines for patentability of computer programs.[35] The patent at issue was a method for "converting binary-coded decimal numerals into pure binary numerals."[36] The Court found the claims far too broad to be eligible for patent protection.[37] The Court declined to use the point-of-novelty test,[38] though it could be argued that the claim falls within the first category of *In re Abrams* because all the steps are "purely mental in character."[39] The Court left open the question of patentability of computer programs in general, but said the debate "indicate[s] to [the Court] that considered action by the Congress is needed."[40]

C. Parker v. Flook

The Supreme Court's next computer program case came six years later in *Parker v. Flook*.[41] Flook applied for a patent for a method of updating alarm limits during catalytic conversion.[42] According to the majority

---

[33] 1 DONALD S. CHISUM, CHISUM ON PATENTS § 1.03 (2014).
[34] *See* Application of Musgrave, 431 F.2d 882, 889–92 (C.C.P.A. 1970).
[35] Gottschalk v. Benson, 409 U.S. 63 (1972).
[36] *Id.* at 64.
[37] *Id.* at 68.
[38] *See* CHISUM, *supra* note 33, § 1.03.
[39] *In re Abrams*, 188 F.2d 165, 166 (C.C.P.A. 1951). The steps are not purely mental in the sense that they are performed on a computer, but "[t]he mathematical formula involved here has no substantial practical application except in connection with a digital computer." *Benson*, 409 U.S. at 71.
[40] *Benson*, 409 U.S. at 73.
[41] 437 U.S. 584 (1978).
[42] *See id.* at 585.

opinion, "[t]he only novel feature of the method is a mathematical formula," which is used to calculate the alarm limit that signals the "presence of an abnormal condition indicating either inefficiency or perhaps danger."[43]

The examiner rejected Flook's application because "a patent on this method 'would in practical effect be a patent on the formula or mathematics itself.'"[44] The examiner concluded that it was not eligible subject matter.[45] On appeal, the Board of Appeals of the Patent and Trademark Office (PTAB) determined the application failed the point-of-novelty test[46] because the novelty was in the non-statutory portion, specifically the algorithm.[47] The Court of Customs and Patent Appeals (CCPA) reversed, deciding that the claim's limitation to use only in catalytic conversion would not allow the patent to preempt all uses of the formula.[48] Parker, the Acting Commissioner of Patents and Trademarks filed a petition for writ of certiorari.[49] Parker expressed concern about the number of additional applications that would be filed because of the explosion of the software industry.[50]

---

[43] *Id.*
[44] *Id.* at 587.
[45] *See id.*
[46] *See supra* Part A.
[47] *See Flook*, 437 U.S. at 587 ("[T]he 'point of novelty in [respondent's] claimed method' lay in the formula or algorithm described in the claims.").
[48] *See* Application of Flook, 559 F.2d 21, 23 (C.C.P.A. 1977), *rev'd sub nom. Flook*, 437 U.S. 584 ("The present claims do not preempt the formula or algorithm contained therein, because solution of the algorithm, per se, would not infringe the claims.").
[49] *Flook*, 437 U.S. at 587.
[50] *See id.* at 587–88.

The Supreme Court explicitly said that the case turned on subject matter eligibility, and "[did] not involve the familiar issues of novelty and obviousness that routinely arise under §§ 102 and 103."[51] The Court even assumed that Flook's formula was "novel and useful and that he discovered it."[52] Though the method was clearly a process in the ordinary meaning of the word, the concern was that "[t]he line between a patentable 'process' and an unpatentable 'principle' is not always clear."[53] Flook argued that the presence of a "post-solution activity" distinguished his case from cases in which only the algorithm is patented.[54] In particular, the post-solution activity was the "adjustment of the alarm limit to the figure computed according to the formula."[55] The Court rejected the notion that post-solution activity alone could distinguish this case from previous decisions.[56] The problem, said the majority, was that allowing post-solution activity to establish patentability creates an incentive to append the broadest limitation after the formula.[57]

In a six-to-three decision, the majority opinion held that "it is absolutely clear that respondent's application contains no claim of patentable invention."[58] The majority determined that every element of the claim besides the formula was well-known in the art, and therefore "the claimed method [was] nonstatutory."[59]

---

[51] *Id.* at 588.
[52] *Id.*
[53] *Id.* at 589.
[54] *Id.* at 589–90.
[55] *Id.* at 590.
[56] *See id.*
[57] *See id.*
[58] *Id.* at 594.
[59] *Id.* at 595 (quoting *In re Richman*, 563 F.2d 1026, 1030 (C.C.P.A. 1977)).

The opinion rejected the argument that the determination could be made under §§ 102 and 103, stating that these were not "the kind of 'discoveries' that the statute was enacted to protect."[60] Though the Court said the conclusion was "based on reasoning derived from opinions written before the modern business of developing programs for computers was conceived,"[61] it appears they felt compelled to prevent this type of claim from entering the patent system.

The dissent acknowledged that although "it may well be that under the criteria of §§ 102 and 103 no patent should issue on the process claimed in this case," the method did fit under the process requirement of § 101.[62] According to the dissent, the problem with the majority's formulation was that "it strikes what seems to me an equally damaging blow at basic principles of patent law by importing into its inquiry under 35 U.S.C. § 101 the criteria of novelty and inventiveness."[63] The dissent was referring to the concept that determining whether the claim is novel must wait until later consideration under § 102.[64]

D. *Diamond v. Diehr*

Less than three years after *Flook*, the Supreme Court addressed subject matter eligibility again in *Diamond v.*

---

[60] *Id.* at 593.
[61] *Id.* at 595.
[62] *Id.* at 600 (Stewart, J., dissenting).
[63] *Id.*
[64] Jeffrey A. Simenauer, Note, *Patentability of Computer-Related Inventions: A Criticism of the PTO's View on Algorithms*, 54 GEO. WASH. L. REV. 871, 902 (1986).

Diehr.[65] The Court, in a five-to-four decision, seemingly reached the opposite outcome as *Flook*.[66]

Diehr addressed subject matter eligibility for "a process for curing synthetic rubber which includes in several of its steps the use of a mathematical formula and a programmed digital computer."[67] Rather than updating an alarm limit as in *Flook*,[68] the formula in Diehr's method was used to calculate the appropriate cure time for the rubber.[69] Also unlike *Flook*, the formula was well-known in the art.[70] The procedural posture in *Diehr* was almost identical to *Flook*.[71] The patent examiner rejected the claims on the grounds they were drawn to nonstatutory subject matter.[72] The PTAB, relying on *Flook*, affirmed the examiner's

---

[65] Diamond v. Diehr, 450 U.S. 175 (1981).
[66] *Compare Diehr*, 450 U.S. at 190 ("The question therefore of whether a particular invention is novel is 'wholly apart from whether the invention falls into a category of statutory subject matter.'" (quoting *In re* Bergy, 596 F.2d 952, 961 (C.C.P.A. 1979))), *with Flook*, 437 U.S. at 594 ("Here it is absolutely clear that respondent's application contains no claim of patentable invention. The chemical processes involved in catalytic conversion of hydrocarbons are well known, as are the practice of monitoring the chemical process variables, the use of alarm limits to trigger alarms, the notion that alarm limit values must be recomputed and readjusted, and the use of computers for automatic monitoring-alarming.'").
[67] *Diehr*, 450 U.S. at 177.
[68] *Flook*, 437 U.S. at 587.
[69] *Diehr*, 450 U.S. at 177.
[70] *Id* at 177 n.2. The method used the Arrhenius' equation expresses the dependence of the rate constant of a reaction on temperature. JULIA BURDGE & JASON OVERBY, CHEMISTRY: ATOMS FIRST 576 (2nd ed., 2011).
[71] In both cases, the patent examiner rejected the application, which was affirmed by the PTAB and later reversed by the CCPA. This was followed by a petition for certiorari from the commissioner of Patents and Trademarks. *Compare Diehr*, 450 U.S. at 180, *with Flook*, 437 U.S. at 587.
[72] Application of Diehr, 602 F.2d 982, 984 (C.C.P.A. 1979) *aff'd sub nom.* Diamond v. Diehr, 450 U.S. 175 (1981).

decision.[73] Noting that "[n]ovelty considerations have no bearing on whether claims define statutory subject matter under § 101," the CCPA reversed.[74] Diamond, the Commissioner of Patents and Trademarks, sought certiorari from the Supreme Court.[75]

Despite the glaring similarities, the majority opinion explained that the difference between this case and *Flook* was that the Court did not view the claims "as an attempt to patent a mathematical formula, but rather to be drawn to an industrial process for the molding of rubber products."[76] The limitations in the claim other than the formula (e.g., "installing rubber in a press," "closing the mold," and "automatically opening the press at the appropriate time") were significant enough to compel the majority that the patent was for the entire process, not just the formula.[77]

In dissent, Justice Stevens, author of the majority opinion in *Flook*,[78] believed the patent was truly for an "improved method of calculating the time that the mold should remain closed during the curing process."[79] As such, he believed that it was non-statutory

---

[73] *Id.* ("It is our view that the only difference between the conventional methods of operating a molding press and that claimed in appellants' application rests in those steps of the claims which related to the calculation incident to the solution of the mathematical problem or formula used to control the mold heater and the automatic opening of the press.").
[74] *Id.* at 989.
[75] *Diehr*, 450 U.S. at 181.
[76] *Id.* at 192.
[77] *See id.* at 191-92.
[78] *Flook*, 437 U.S. at 585. The four dissenters, Stevens, J., Brennan, J., Marshall, J., Blackmun, J. were all in the majority opinion of *Flook*. Compare *id.* at 585, 598 (dissenting opinion), *with Diehr*, 450 U.S. at 193 (dissenting opinion).
[79] *Diehr*, 450 U.S. at 206-07 (Stevens, J., dissenting).

for the same reasons as *Flook*.[80] In dissent, Stevens went even further by proposing "an unequivocal holding that no program-related invention is a patentable process under § 101 unless it makes a contribution to the art that is not dependent entirely on the utilization of a computer."[81]

III. CURRENT STATE OF THE LAW: MAYO AND ALICE

Though *Mayo*[82] did not involve a computer-related invention, a discussion of the framework used by the Court in *Mayo* is necessary because this framework was explicitly adopted in *Alice*.[83] It appears that the Supreme Court has chosen to use the following test in *Mayo* for all inventions involving "laws of nature, natural phenomena, and abstract idea[s]."[84]

A. Mayo v. Prometheus

The patent at issue in *Mayo* claimed a process for determining whether a given dosage level of thiopurine drugs is too low or too high for patients with autoimmune diseases.[85] The representative patent claim consists of steps of (1) "administering" the drug, (2) "determining" the level of the drug present in the patient's body, and then using the level to "indicate" if it is too low or too high.[86] Prometheus Laboratories was

---

[80] *See id.* at 219.
[81] *Id.*
[82] Mayo Collaborative Services v. Prometheus Laboratories, Inc., 132 S. Ct. 1289 (2012).
[83] Alice Corp. v. CLS Bank Int'l, 134 S. Ct. 2347, 2355 (2014) ("In [*Mayo*] we set forth a framework for distinguishing patents that claim laws of nature, natural phenomena, and abstract ideas from those that claim patent-eligible applications of those concepts.").
[84] *Compare Mayo*, 132 S. Ct. 1289 *with Alice*, 134 S. Ct. 2347.
[85] *Mayo*, 132 S. Ct. at 1294.
[86] The Federal Circuit and the Supreme Court took claim 1 as representative. U.S. Patent No. 6,355,623 (filed Apr. 8, 1999) ("A

the sole and exclusive licensee of the patent.[87] Prometheus sold diagnostic tests utilizing the patented claim to Mayo, but Mayo stopped purchasing from Prometheus and decided to make its own tests.[88]

In a unanimous opinion, the Court reiterated a concern about "upholding patents that claim processes that too broadly preempt the use of a natural law."[89] Rather, the Court would only uphold those patents that have "transformed these unpatentable natural laws into patent-eligible applications of those laws."[90] The Court first determined that the patent describes a law of nature, specifically the relationship between the concentration of the drug and the likelihood that the drug administration is appropriate.[91] The Court then asked, do the "claims add *enough* to their statements of the correlations to allow the processes they describe to qualify as patent-eligible processes that *apply* natural laws?"[92]

---

method of optimizing therapeutic efficacy for treatment of an immune-mediated gastrointestinal disorder, comprising: (a) administering a drug providing 6-thioguanine to a subject having said immune-mediated gastrointestinal disorder; and (b) determining the level of 6-thioguanine in said subject having said immune-mediated gastrointestinal disorder, wherein the level of 6-thioguanine less than about 230 pmol per 8×10^8 red blood cells indicates a need to increase the amount of said drug subsequently administered to said subject and wherein the level of 6-thioguanine greater than about 400 pmol per 8×10^8 red blood cells indicates a need to decrease the amount of said drug subsequently administered to said subject.").

[87] *Mayo*, 132 S. Ct. at 1295.
[88] *Id.* at 1295–96.
[89] *Id.* at 1294 (citing O'Reilly v. Morse, 56 U.S. 62 (1853)).
[90] *Id.*
[91] *Id.* at 1296.
[92] *Id.* at 1297.

In answering the foregoing question in the negative, the Court looked to the content outside the elements that claimed a law of nature.[93] The patent claim was separated into the "administering" step, the "determining" step, and the "wherein" clause that tells what the test "indicates."[94] The Court gave no weight to the physical process of administering, instead saying it "simply refers to the relevant audience."[95] The opinion further said that the relevant audience was already familiar with administering the particular drug and compared the administering step to a claim element that limits the scope to a particular technological environment.[96]

Similar to the administering step, the Court did not consider "determining" to be anything more than a mental process.[97] Again, the Court said the step was already practiced.[98] Comparing the determining step to the post-solution activity of *Parker*,[99] this pre-solution activity was not significant enough to make the concept patentable.[100] Finally, the "indicates" clause was said to merely "tell the relevant audience about the laws."[101] It did not apply the law of nature in a way that went beyond the law itself. Accordingly, the Court held that

---

[93] *See id.* at 1297–1305.
[94] The third step includes the two "wherein" clauses that describe the relationship between the level obtained and what should be done. *See id.* at 1297–98.
[95] *Id.* at 1297.
[96] *Id.* (quoting Bilski v. Kappos, 130 S. Ct. 3218, 3230 (2010)).
[97] *Id.* at 1297–98.
[98] *Id.* at 1297.
[99] *See supra* note 50 and related text.
[100] *See Mayo*, 132 S. Ct. at 1298.
[101] *Id.* at 1297 ("[R]ather like Einstein telling linear accelerator operators about his basic law and then trusting them to use it where relevant.").

the patent claims were invalid because they "effectively claim[ed] the underlying laws of nature themselves."[102]

Following *Mayo*, it was unclear whether this new two-part test applied just to claims involving "laws of nature" or to more than that.[103] In fact, following the Supreme Court's decision in *Mayo*, the USPTO created a test for determining subject eligibility for methods that use natural laws and did not consider computer programs to be affected.[104] This uncertainty remained for more than two years until the Supreme Court again addressed software patentability.

B. Alice v. CLS Bank

In 2014, the Supreme Court granted certiorari on a patent involving computer programs to explain that the *Mayo* framework should be used to determine subject matter eligibility.[105] Alice was the assignee of several patents that disclose schemes to manage certain forms of financial risk.[106] Put simply, the patents claim using a

---

[102] *Id.* at 1305.
[103] *See* Joshua A. Kresh, *Patent Eligibility After Mayo: How Did We Get Here and Where Do We Go?*, 22 FED. CIR. B.J. 521, 521–22 (2013).
[104] MPEP § 2106.01 (8th ed. Rev. 9, Aug. 2012); *see* Bryan Wisecup, *Mayo v. Prometheus: Reorganizing the Toolbox for Patent Eligible Subject Matter and Uses of Natural Laws*, 81 U. CIN. L. REV. 1651, 1666 (2013).
[105] Alice Corp. v. CLS Bank Int'l, 134 S. Ct. 2347, 2354 (2014).
[106] *Id.* at 2352. The patents at issue were U. S. Patent Nos. 5,970,479 ('479 patent), 6,912,510, 7,149,720, and 7,725,375. The parties agreed that claim 33 of the '479 patent was representative of the method claim.
      33. A method of exchanging obligations as between parties, each party holding a credit record and a debit record with an exchange institution, the credit records and debit records for exchange of predetermined obligations, the method comprising the steps of:

computer to track financial data of two parties to determine if the parties would fulfill their obligations. The claims were drafted as method, system, and computer-readable medium claims, but Alice conceded that the "media claims rise or fall with [the] method claims,"[107] and the Court gave no extra weight to the system claims.[108] The dispute began in 2007, when CLS Bank filed suit against Alice seeking declaratory judgment that the claims in four of Alice's patents were

> (a) creating a shadow credit record and a shadow debit record for each stakeholder party to be held independently by a supervisory institution from the exchange institutions;
>
> (b) obtaining from each exchange institution a start-of-day balance for each shadow credit record and shadow debit record;
>
> (c) for every transaction resulting in an exchange obligation, the supervisory institution adjusting each respective party's shadow credit record or shadow debit record, allowing only these transactions that do not result in the value of the shadow debit record being less than the value of the shadow credit record at any time, each said adjustment taking place in chronological order; and
>
> (d) at the end-of-day, the supervisory institution instructing ones of the exchange institutions to exchange credits or debits to the credit record and debit record of the respective parties in accordance with the adjustments of the said permitted transactions, the credits and debits being irrevocable, time invariant obligations placed on the exchange institutions.

Id. at n.2.
[107] *Id.* at 2360.
[108] *Id.* ("Put another way, the system claims are no different from the method claims in substance.").

invalid, unenforceable, or not infringed.[109] Alice counterclaimed, alleging infringement.[110]

In 2011, shortly after the Supreme Court decided *Bilski*,[111] the district court granted CLS Bank's motion for summary judgment, holding that claims were not patentable because they were directed to an abstract concept.[112] A divided panel of the Federal Circuit reversed, holding that it was not "manifestly evident" that Alice's claims were directed to an abstract idea.[113] The Federal Circuit then granted rehearing en banc, vacated the opinion,[114] and affirmed the judgment of the district court.[115] Seven of the ten Federal Circuit judges concluded that Alice's "method and computer-readable medium claims are patent ineligible."[116] Five judges concluded that the system claims are patent

---

[109] *Id.* at 2353.
[110] *Id.*
[111] Bilski v. Kappos, 130 S. Ct. 3218 (2010). In *Bilski*, the Court held that applicants' business method patent was an unpatentable abstract idea, "just like the algorithms in *Benson* and *Flook*." *Id.* at 3231.
[112] CLS Bank Int'l v. Alice Corp. Pty., 768 F. Supp. 2d 221, 255 (D.D.C. 2011) ("The Court finds claims 33 and 34 of the '479 Patent and each claim of the '510 Patent, '720 Patent, and '375 Patent to be directed to an abstract idea under the *Benson, Flook, Diehr*, and *Bilski* Supreme Court line of precedent. Accordingly, these claims are invalid as being directed to patent-ineligible subject matter under § 101 of the Patent Act.").
[113] Alice Corp. v. CLS Bank Int'l, 685 F.3d 1341, 1352 (2012) ("In light of the foregoing, this court holds that when—after taking all of the claim recitations into consideration—it is not manifestly evident that a claim is directed to a patent ineligible abstract idea, that claim must not be deemed for that reason to be inadequate under § 101.") *vacated en banc*, 484 Fed. Appx. 559 (Fed. Cir. 2012).
[114] Alice Corp. v. CLS Bank Int'l, 484 Fed. Appx. 559, 559 (Fed. Cir. 2012).
[115] Alice Corp. v. CLS Bank Int'l, 717 F.3d 1269, 1273 (Fed. Cir. 2013) *cert. granted*, 134 S. Ct. 734 (2013) *and aff'd*, 134 S. Ct. 2347 (2014).
[116] *Alice*, 134 S. Ct. at 2353 (citing Alice Corp. v. CLS Bank Int'l, 717 F.3d 1269, 1273 (Fed. Cir. 2013)).

ineligible.[117] The Supreme Court granted certiorari and affirmed.[118] Justice Thomas delivered the opinion of the Court[119] and Justice Sotomayor wrote a concurring opinion joined by Justice Ginsburg and Justice Breyer.[120]

Justice Thomas declared that the *Mayo* two-part test distinguishes "patents that claim laws of nature, natural phenomena, and abstract ideas from those that claim patent-eligible applications of those concepts."[121] The *Mayo* test first establishes whether or not the claims are directed to a patent-ineligible concept.[122] Part two of the *Mayo* test requires that the claims "contain[] an 'inventive concept' sufficient to 'transform' the claimed abstract idea into a patent-eligible application."[123]

Thomas applied part one of the *Mayo* test to Alice's claims and determined that they were "drawn to the abstract idea of intermediated settlement."[124] Thomas compared the claims at issue to the risk hedging claims in *Bilski* and determined that "intermediated settlement, like hedging [in *Bilski*], is an 'abstract idea' beyond the scope of § 101."[125] The opinion, however, does not elaborate on a definition of abstract concept[126]:

> In any event, we need not labor to delimit the precise contours of the "abstract

---

[117] *Id.*
[118] *Id.* at 2354.
[119] *Id.* at 2351.
[120] *Id.* at 2360–61.
[121] *Id.* at 2355.
[122] *Id.*
[123] *Id.* at 2357 (quoting Mayo Collaborative Servs. v. Prometheus Labs., Inc., 132 S. Ct. 1289, 1298 (2012)).
[124] *Id.* at 2355.
[125] *Id.* at 2356.
[126] *Id.* at 2357.

ideas" category in this case. It is enough to recognize that there is no meaningful distinction between the concept of risk hedging in *Bilski* and the concept of intermediated settlement at issue here. Both are squarely within the realm of "abstract ideas" as we have used that term.[127]

Regarding part two of the test, which requires an inventive concept, the majority held that "the claims at issue amount to 'nothing significantly more' than an instruction to apply the abstract idea of intermediated settlement using some unspecified, generic computer."[128] The opinion describes previous applications of part two of the *Mayo* test, in which *Mayo*,[129] *Benson*,[130] and *Flook*[131] claims failed because they did not have an inventive concept.[132] The exception was the inventive application of an abstract concept in *Diehr*.[133] Thomas asserts that the claims that failed part two merely say "apply it with a computer,"[134] or limit the use of an abstract idea "to a particular technological

---

[127] *Id.*
[128] *Id.* at 2360 (quoting *Mayo*, 132 S. Ct. at 1298).
[129] *Mayo*, 132 S. Ct. at 1298.
[130] Gottschalk v. Benson, 409 U.S. 63 (1972).
[131] Parker v. Flook, 437 U.S. 584 (1978).
[132] *Alice*, 134 S. Ct. at 2357–58.
[133] Diamond v. Diehr, 450 U.S. 175 (1981); *Alice*, 134 S. Ct. at 2358 ("The temperature measurements were then fed into a computer, which repeatedly recalculated the remaining cure time by using the mathematical equation. These additional steps, we recently explained, 'transformed the process into into an inventive application of the formula.'" (internal citations omitted)).
[134] *Alice*, 134 S. Ct. at 2350.

environment."[135] He concluded that the claims at issue were no different.[136]

After determining that the method claims failed the *Mayo* test, the Court stated that the computer-readable medium and system claims were also unpatentable subject matter for "substantially the same reasons."[137] Alice conceded that its media claims rose and fell with its method claims.[138] As for the system claims, the Court held that "none of the hardware recited by the system claims 'offer[ed] a meaningful limitation beyond generally linking the use of the method to a particular technological environment.'"[139] Accordingly, the Court held that these claims were also patent-ineligible subject matter under § 101.[140]

In a one-paragraph concurrence, Justice Sotomayor, joined by Justice Ginsburg and Justice Breyer, said that "any 'claim that merely describes a method of doing business'" is not a "process" under § 101.[141] Accordingly, they too consider the claims at issue patent ineligible under § 101.[142]

IV. HOW THE FEDERAL CIRCUIT CAN ADAPT THE ALICE TEST

Though the Supreme Court left some uncertainty in *how* to apply the test,[143] the Court was clear *when* it

---

[135] *Id.* (quoting Bilski v. Kappos 130 S. Ct. 3218, 3230 (2010)).
[136] *Id.* at 2351.
[137] *Id.* at 2360.
[138] *Id.*
[139] *Id.* (quoting *Bilski*, 130 S. Ct. at 3230) (alteration in original).
[140] *Id.*
[141] *Id.* at 2360–61 (Sotomayor, J., concurring) (quoting *Bilski*, 130 S. Ct. at 3222).
[142] *Id.*
[143] *See, e.g.*, McRO, Inc. v. Valve Corp., No. SACV 13-1874-GW(FFMx), 2014 WL 4772200, at *5 (C.D. Cal. Sept. 22, 2014) ("So, the two-step test

should be followed.[144] The Federal Circuit is bound by stare decisis principles [145] to apply the "framework" articulated in *Mayo* and *Alice* to cases involving "laws of nature, natural phenomena, and abstract ideas." [146] While commentators may protest the *Alice* and *Mayo* opinions, the reality is that courts must follow the Court's analysis. However, because of the ambiguity in the framework articulated by the Supreme Court, the Federal Circuit can formulate a new test as long as it still contains the principles laid out in *Alice*; the new test should be administrable by both lower courts and the patent office.

A. Objective of the Alice Test

In the *Alice* and *Mayo* opinions, the Court repeatedly reiterated concern about allowing patents to claim the "building blocks of human ingenuity." [147] Therefore, when evaluating claims involving algorithms like those described previously, the Court has declared the claims unpatentable according to § 101, [148] rather than

---

may be more like a one step test evocative of Justice Stewart's most famous phrase. . . . 'I shall not today attempt further to define the kinds of material I understand to be embraced within that shorthand description; and perhaps I could never succeed in intelligibly doing so. But I know it when I see it . . . .'" (quoting Jacobellis v. State of Ohio, 378 U.S. 184, 197 (1964) (Stewart, J., concurring)).

[144] *Id.* ("[B]efore *Alice*, it was unclear to some, including the USPTO, that the framework set forth in *Mayo* applied to abstract ideas as well as to the law of nature/natural phenomena at issue in *Mayo*.").

[145] *See, e.g.*, Lighting Ballast Control, LLC v. Philips Elecs. N. Am. Corp., 744 F.3d 1272, 1288 (Fed. Cir. 2014) ("Federal Circuit review, and in particular this Court's application of *stare decisis*, is critical to such uniformity.").

[146] *Alice*, 134 S. Ct. at 2355.

[147] *See Alice*, 134 S. Ct. at 2354; Mayo, 132 S. Ct. at 1301.

[148] *See, e.g.*, Parker v. Flook, 98 S. Ct. 2522, 2524 (1978) ("This case turns entirely on the proper construction of § 101 of the Patent Act, which describes the subject matter that is eligible for patent protection."); Diamond v. Diehr, 450 U.S. 175, 210–11 (1981) ("What I believe does

invalidating the claims for lack of novelty or obviousness. It may be that the patent claims at issue in each of the cases detailed in depth are invalid due to lack of novelty or obviousness.[149] However, the Court's grant of the writ of certiorari in these cases limited the issue to the scope of patentable subject matter.[150] The question presented to the Court limits its holding[151] to § 101 and delays the question of § 102 and § 103 to remand. Though that is a possible explanation, it seems more likely that the Court chose to use § 101 subject matter eligibility to rein in the boundaries of the patent system.[152]

The Constitution grants Congress the authority to develop patent and copyright laws.[153] Congress has

---

explain today's holding is a misunderstanding of the applicants' claimed invention and a failure to recognize the critical difference between the 'discovery' requirement in § 101 and the 'novelty' requirement in § 102.").

[149] *See, e.g., Diehr,* 450 U.S. at 191 ("[I]t may later be determined that the respondents' process is not deserving of patent protection because it fails to satisfy the statutory conditions of novelty under § 102 or nonobviousness under § 103.").

[150] *See, e.g., Alice,* 134 S. Ct. at 2352 ("The question presented is whether these claims are patent eligible under 35 U.S.C. § 101 . . . .").

[151] *See* Mazer v. Stein, 347 U.S. 201, 208 (1954) ("The Court's consideration will be limited to the question presented by the petition for the writ of certiorari.").

[152] *See* Bilski v. Kappos, 561 U.S. 593, 650 (2010) (Stevens, J., concurring) ("[T]he functional case that patents promote progress generally is stronger for subject matter that has 'historically been eligible to receive the protection of our patent laws' than for methods of doing business.") (quoting *Diehr,* 450 U.S. at 184); George R. McGuire & Blaine T. Bettinger, *How the Supreme Court Got It Right in Mayo v. Prometheus,* 10 NO. 1 ABA SCITECH LAW. 12, 15 (2013).

[153] U.S. CONST. art. I, § 8, cl. 8 ("The Congress shall have Power . . . [t]o promote the Progress of Science and useful Arts, by securing for limited Times to Authors and Inventors the exclusive Right to their respective Writings and Discoveries.").

passed legislation directing what is patentable.[154] The statute for subject matter eligibility lists only certain categories that can be patented.[155] The remaining things and concepts in the universe that are not included in Congress's choice of subject matter eligibility consequently are not eligible for patent protection.[156] The categories designated by Congress have been further limited by judicial interpretation.[157] Though Congress did not make the "implicit exceptions,"[158] Congress also has not overruled the continuing precedent of the Supreme Court.[159]

The goal of these exceptions to patentability is to stop those who try to acquire exclusive rights over more than they have actually invented.[160] This occurs when patents are granted for a law of nature, for example.

---

[154] *See* 35 U.S.C. § 101 (2012).

[155] *See id.* ("[A]ny new and useful process, machine, manufacture, or composition of matter.").

[156] *See* Bonito Boats, Inc. v. Thunder Craft Boats, Inc., 489 U.S. 141, 151 (1989) ("To a limited extent, the federal patent laws must determine not only what is protected, but also what is free for all to use."). *See generally* MOY, *supra* note 8, § 5:1.

[157] *See e.g.*, Le Roy v. Tatham, 55 U.S. 156, 175 (1852) ("A principle, in the abstract, is a fundamental truth; an original cause; a motive; these cannot be patented, as no one can claim in either of them an exclusive right.").

[158] *See* Wesley D. Markham, *How to Explain the "Implicit Exceptions" to Patent-Eligible Subject Matter*, 16 VAND. J. ENT. & TECH. L. 353, 355 (2014).

[159] *See, e.g.*, CHISUM, *supra* note 33, § 1.01 ("Despite the controversies at that time [of the America Invents Act] concerning the 'exceptions' to Section 101 for abstract ideas and natural phenomena as applied to subject matter such as business methods, computer software, and isolated DNA, including human genes, Congress chose not to address directly questions regarding patent eligible subject matter.").

[160] *See* Gottschalk v. Benson, 409 U.S. 63, 67 (1972) ("If there is to be invention from . . . a discovery, it must come from the application of the law of nature to a new and useful end." (quoting Funk Bros. Seed Co. v. Kalo Inoculant Co., 333 U.S. 127, 130 (1948))).

The Court, in multiple opinions, has used Einstein's discovery of $E = MC^2$ as an example of an unpatentable abstract idea.[161] If Einstein could obtain a patent on the formula, simply because he discovered the laws that it obeys, it could be used to stop any innovation that harnesses those laws.[162] This outcome would have a deleterious effect on innovation.[163] Harmful outcomes like this are also why the Supreme Court has articulated the implicit exceptions to § 101.[164]

B. How to Square Diehr with Alice

The holding in *Diehr* seems directly contrary to *Alice*,[165] yet the majority opinion in *Alice* took the stance that the outcome of *Diehr* is consistent.[166] A closer look

---

[161] *See, e.g.*, Mayo Collaborative Servs. v. Prometheus Labs., Inc., 132 S. Ct. 1289, 1293 (2012); Diamond v. Chakrabarty, 447 U.S. 303, 309 (1980).

[162] *See Mayo*, 132 S. Ct. at 1297.

[163] *See generally* The Federal Trade Commission, *To Promote Innovation: The Proper Balance of Competition and Patent Law and Policy Executive Summary*, 19 BERKELEY TECH. L.J. 861, 864 (2004) ("[I]f patent law were to allow patent on 'obvious' inventions, it could thwart competition that might have developed based on the obvious technology.").

[164] *See* Alice Corp. v. CLS Bank Int'l, 134 S. Ct. 2347, 2354-55 ("[Claiming] the building blocks of human ingenuity . . . would risk disproportionately tying up the use of the underlying ideas, and [is] therefore ineligible for patent protection." (quoting *Mayo*, 132 S. Ct. at 1294) (internal quotation marks omitted)).

[165] *Compare* Diamond v. Diehr, 450 U.S. 175, 182 (1981) ("It is ['process'] which we confront today, and in order to determine its meaning we may not be unmindful of the Committee Reports accompanying the 1952 Act which inform us that Congress intended statutory subject matter to 'include anything under the sun that is made by man.'"(quoting S. Rep. No. 82-1979, at 2399 (1952)), *with Alice*, 134 S. Ct. at 2352 ("We hold that . . . merely requiring generic computer implementation fails to transform that abstract idea into a patent-eligible invention.").

[166] *Alice*, 134 S. Ct. at 2358 ("These additional steps, we recently explained, 'transformed the process into an inventive application of the formula.'") (quoting *Mayo*, 132 S. Ct. at 1299).

at the language of *Diehr* shows that it actually succeeds on the first step of the framework in *Alice* because, as characterized by the majority, it is not directed to an abstract idea.[167] The *Alice* majority said "[f]irst, we determine whether the claims at issue are *directed to* [a] patent-ineligible concept."[168] According to the Court, the claims in *Diehr* are not directed to a patent-ineligible concept.[169] In *Diehr*, the opinion states the claims are a "process of curing synthetic rubber."[170] Curing synthetic rubber, though probably well-known in the art,[171] is certainly a patent eligible concept.[172] Since step one of the *Alice* test is concerned with the "concept" the claim is "directed to,"[173] the adjudicator need not move on to step two of the framework, which searches for an inventive concept for the process in *Diehr*. Indeed, the opinion in *Diehr* even says it considers the claim "to be drawn to an industrial process."[174] However, according to the dissent's formulation of the claim in *Diehr*, an "improved method of calculating the time that the mold should remain closed during the curing process," the subject matter is likely *directed to* a patent-

---

[167] *See generally* Robert R. Sachs, *How to Correctly Apply the Alice Examination Guidance*, BILSKI BLOG (Sept. 5, 2014), http://www.bilskiblog.com/blog/2014/09/applying-alice-guidelines.html.
[168] *Alice*, 134 S. Ct. at 2355 (emphasis added).
[169] *See Diehr*, 450 U.S. at 187.
[170] *Id.*
[171] The majority conceded that the claims may later be found to be anticipated. *Diehr*, 450 U.S. at 191 ("[I]t may later be determined that the respondents' process is not deserving of patent protection because it fails to satisfy the statutory conditions of novelty under § 102 or nonobviousness under § 103.").
[172] *See, e.g.*, Self-Curing Synthetic Rubber, U.S. Patent No. 2,776,269 (filed Dec. 19, 1952).
[173] *Alice*, 134 S. Ct. at 2355.
[174] *Diehr*, 450 U.S. at 192.

ineligible concept, specifically calculating time.[175] The *Diehr* claim is a prime example of the ambiguity associated with the first inquiry of the *Alice* test. Additionally, once an adjudicator determines what the claim is directed toward, the adjudicator may ignore potential claim limitations.[176]

C. Why the Alice Test is Flexible

The framework handed down in *Mayo* and *Alice* leaves significant room for interpretation.[177] The ambiguity of the test's first step, to "determine whether the claims at issue are directed to a patent-ineligible concept,"[178] creates two questions. First, what is the claim *directed to*? And second, is that concept patent ineligible? The previous discussion regarding *Diehr*[179] illustrates an issue with the first question: the same claim could be interpreted in multiple ways.[180] To determine the second question of this first step, one must know which patent concepts are ineligible. The *Alice* opinion itself gives some guidance on ineligible

---

[175] *Id.* at 207 (Stevens, J., dissenting).
[176] *See generally* Markman v. Westview Instruments, Inc., 52 F.3d 967 (Fed. Cir. 1995) *aff'd* 517 U.S. 370 (1996) (describing claim construction and the use of claim limitations).
[177] *See generally* Eric W. Guttag, *The Broken Patent-Eligibility Test of Alice and Mayo: Why We Urgently Need to Return to Principles of Diehr and Chakrabarty*, IP WATCHDOG (Sept. 25, 2014), http://www.ipwatchdog.com/2014/9/25/broken-patent-eligibility-test-of-alice-and-mayo/id=51370/; Kresh, *supra* note 103.
[178] *Alice*, 134 S. Ct. at 2355.
[179] *See supra* Part IV.B.
[180] With the result that the characterization of the claim is outcome determinative.

concepts,[181] but declines to "delimit the precise contours of the 'abstract ideas' category."[182]

The second step of the *Alice* test, "a search for an inventive concept—i.e., an element or combination of elements that is sufficient to ensure that the patent in practice amounts to significantly more than a patent upon the ineligible concept itself"—leaves open the inquiry about what constitutes "significantly more."[183] The guidance for step two lies in *Mayo*,[184] *Benson*,[185] *Flook*,[186] *Diehr*,[187] and *Alice*.[188] Of these five representative cases, only *Diehr* can illustrate what the Supreme Court considers "significantly more" because *Diehr* was the only case that the Court says succeeded in the second step.[189] Further confounding the problem, the claims in *Diehr* could be considered outside the scope of step two of the *Alice* test since they are directed to curing rubber.[190] Accordingly, the guidance to be gained from *Alice* amounts to "'apply it' [on a computer] is not enough" and "limiting the use . . . 'to a particular

---

[181] *See Alice*, 134 S. Ct. at 2355–57 (holding computing alarm limits, and hedging risk, intermediated settlement as abstract ideas outside the scope of 35 U.S.C. § 101).

[182] *Id.* at 2357.

[183] *Id.* at 2355 (internal punctuation omitted) (quoting Mayo Collaborative Servs. v. Prometheus Labs., Inc., 132 S. Ct. 1289, 1294 (2011)).

[184] *Mayo*, 132 S. Ct. 1289 (treatment of autoimmune diseases).

[185] Gottschalk v. Benson, 409 U.S. 63 (1972) (computer implementation of algorithm).

[186] Parker v. Flook, 437 U.S. 584 (1978) (updating alarm limits).

[187] Diamond v. Diehr, 450 U.S. 175 (1981) (curing synthetic rubber).

[188] *Alice*, 134 S. Ct. 2347 (intermediated settlement performed by a generic computer).

[189] *See id.* at 2358.

[190] *See Diehr*, 450 U.S. at 192. (discussion in step one defining the method as directed to an industrial process versus calculating time for curing rubber).

technological environment'" is not enough.[191] What is enough? Based on the guidance *Alice* provided, perhaps anything more than "apply it on a computer" or limitation "to a particular technological environment" would be enough.[192]

The ambiguity illustrated by the foregoing analysis of the *Alice* framework presents an opportunity for the judiciary to adapt the existing test for statutory subject matter based on interpretation.[193] According to basic patent law principles, claim evaluation should avoid intermixing the consideration of novelty and non-obviousness with the determination of eligible subject matter.[194] The rest of this section sets forth a proposed flow of examination that utilizes the *Alice* test for subject matter eligibility but is in "conformity with the basic principles of patent law."[195] The proposed test postpones the novelty and obviousness inquiry until after a determination of subject matter eligibility has been made.

D. *Proposed Adaption of Alice*

This author proposes a test that could be adopted by the Federal Circuit that is compliant with *Alice*,[196] yet administrable by lower courts and patent examiners. In the proposed test, the first step to determine subject matter eligibility under § 101, similar to the *Alice* framework, is to identify *elements in the claim* that are covered by the implicit exceptions: "[l]aws of nature,

---

[191] *Alice*, 134 S. Ct. at 2358 (citations omitted).
[192] *See generally* Kresh, *supra* note 103.
[193] *See infra* Part IV.D.
[194] *See* CHISUM, *supra* note 33, § 1.03.
[195] Parker v. Flook, 437 U.S. 584, 599 (1978) (Stewart, J., dissenting).
[196] *See supra* Part B.

natural phenomena, [or] abstract ideas,"[197] or those that are otherwise non-statutory under § 101.[198] Note that this is not at all the same as the claim being "directed toward" ineligible subject matter [199] because the proposed test evaluates each of the claim elements independently to identify whether *each* individual element of the claim is statutory or non-statutory. This extra step accounts for the fact that the claim as a whole may not be "directed toward" one single concept.[200] Additionally, determining what an entire claim is "directed toward" can be very subjective and ignores claim limitations,[201] which is contrary to the principles of peripheral claiming. The outcome of determining what a claim is "directed toward" could determine the test's final result. For example, in *Diehr*, the majority asserted that the claim was directed toward curing rubber, [202] whereas the dissent characterized the invention as an improved method of calculating time for the curing of rubber.[203] Both sides made good arguments, but this shows how the characterization of what a claim is "directed towards" can be dispositive.

---

[197] Alice Corp. v. CLS Bank Int'l, 134 S. Ct. 2347, 2354 (2014) (quoting Ass'n for Molecular Pathology v. Myriad Genetics, Inc., 133 S. Ct. 2107, 2116 (2013)).
[198] For example, a poem is non-statutory under § 101 and should instead be the subject of copyright protection. *See, e.g.*, CHISUM, *supra* note 33, § 1.01 ("The general purpose of the statutory classes of subject matter is to limit patent protection to the field of applied technology, what the United States Constitution calls 'the useful arts.'" (quoting U.S. CONST. art I, § 8, cl. 8.)).
[199] *See Alice*, 134 S. Ct. at 2355.
[200] *See generally* Mark A. Litman, *Deficiencies in the Design and USPTO Application of Mayo Collaborative Services v, Prometheus Laboratories, Inc.*, 95 J. PAT. & TRADEMARK OFF. SOC'Y 47 (2013) (noting the difficulty in determining when a claim is directed toward laws of nature).
[201] *See* Freedman Seating Co. v. Am. Seating Co., 420 F.3d 1350, 1358 (Fed. Cir. 2005) (discussing the "all limitations" rule).
[202] Diamond v. Diehr, 450 U.S. 175, 177 (1981).
[203] *Id.* at 207 (Stevens, J., dissenting).

Under the proposed test, an adjudicator would classify elements as either non-statutory or statutory. When an element of a claim is classified non-statutory, the offending element, for the purpose of subject matter eligibility under § 101, is classified "known in the art." The Supreme Court has long implicitly used this step.[204] Another way of saying that an element is "known in the art" is that the element should be left within the public domain.[205] The objective of the proposed test is to avoid granting exclusivity to an invention comprised solely of these abstract elements. As in *Alice*, with enough "additional features" the invention as a whole may be transformed into an "inventive concept" that is eligible for patent protection.[206] The test provides a procedure to determine what precisely is required for this transformation.

After the claim's non-statutory elements are identified and classified, the next step of the proposed test is to determine if there are statutory elements to the claim that are necessary to the invention.[207] This check is meant to prevent patentability from "depend[ing]

---

[204] *See, e.g.*, Parker v. Flook, 437 U.S. 584, 591–92 (1978) ("Whether the algorithm was in fact known or unknown at the time of the claimed invention . . . it is treated as though it were a familiar part of the prior art."); O'Reily v. Morse, 56 U.S. 62, 116 (1853) ("But after much consideration, it was finally decided that this principle must be regarded as well known. . . .").
[205] *See generally* Sears, Roebuck & Co. v. Stiffel Co., 376 U.S. 225, 231 (1964) ("An unpatentable article, like an article on which the patent has expired, is in the public domain. . . .").
[206] *See Alice*, 134 S. Ct. at 2357.
[207] This determination could be considered subjective depending on the technology area. The question to answer is: Can the invention accomplish its purpose without this element? If it cannot, the element is necessary.

simply on the draftsman's art."[208] The necessity determination rules out limitations that are merely "[pre- or] post-solution activity"[209] or are not required for the operation of the overall invention. An adjudicator would then deem these necessary statutory elements to be "known in the art." After all the claim elements have been classified statutory or non-statutory, *Mayo* describes the conclusion of the test for § 101 eligibility: "What else is there in the claims before us?"[210] If there are any remaining statutory elements (i.e. not deemed "known in the art"), then the claim passes the test for statutory eligibility under § 101. Indeed, this can be a low bar for subject matter, but it is far from the end of the test.

Although it is unclear how the *Alice* framework would continue upon a finding that the claimed matter is eligible subject matter,[211] using this test, an adjudicator must evaluate novelty under § 102[212] and non-obviousness under § 103.[213] The test for subject matter eligibility under § 101 merely disregarded the elements that the test considers in the public domain—it does not establish novelty of the invention. The test

---

[208] *Alice*, 134 S. Ct. at 2359 (quoting *Flook*, 437 U.S. at 593).
[209] *Flook*, 437 U.S. at 590 (holding that post-solution activity including "adjustment of the alarm limit to the figure computed according to the formula" did not make the process patentable).
[210] *Mayo*, 132 S. Ct. at 1297.
[211] *See* Samantak Ghosh, Article, *Prometheus and the Natural Phenomenon Doctrine: Let's Not Lose Sight of the Forest for the Trees*, 94 J. PAT. & TRADEMARK OFF. SOC'Y 330, 356-57 (2012) (discussing the boundaries between sections 101, 102, and 103 in determining patentability).
[212] 35 U.S.C. § 102 (2012); *see* Microsoft Corp. v. i4i Ltd., 131 S. Ct. 2238, 2253 (2011) (Breyer, J., concurring) ("Do the given facts show that the product was previously 'in public use'?") (quoting 35 U.S.C. § 102(b) (2012)).
[213] 35 U.S.C. § 103 (2012); *see Microsoft*, 131 S. Ct. at 2253 (Breyer, J., concurring) ("Do [the facts] show that the invention was . . . 'non-obvious'?") (quoting 35 U.S.C. § 103).

sets a low threshold for subject matter eligibility,[214] instead using the other sections of the patent code to block inappropriate claims.

The elements of the claim that are squarely in the public domain, according to the test's § 101 determination are not considered in further examination under §§ 102 and 103. This may seem like a violation of the "all elements" rule,[215] but these elements are still considered if combined with statutory elements in a novel, non-obvious way. Without novel application or combination, these elements should not be protected by the patent system[216] because alone they may "inhibit further discovery by improperly tying up the future use of laws of nature."[217] An adjudicator would consider, for purposes of novelty, the previously excluded elements if those elements add to the functioning of the invention. An example of this is the second step of the 623 patent in *Mayo*, in which a determination is made of the concentration of 6-thioguanine in the blood.[218] This determination step can be used to orchestrate further statutory steps so it contributes toward the claim's novelty.

The test then proceeds by determining novelty under § 102 and non-obviousness under § 103, which

---

[214] Any statutory provisions necessary to the invention would be sufficient for proper subject matter eligibility.
[215] *See* Warner-Jenkinson Co. v. Hilton Davis Chem. Co., 520 U.S. 17, 29 (1997) ("Each element contained in a patent claim is deemed material to defining the scope of the patented invention. . . .").
[216] *In re* Comiskey, 554 F.3d 967, 979 (Fed. Cir. 2009) ("[M]ental processes—or processes of human thinking—standing alone are not patentable even if they have practical application."). *But see Warner-Jenkinson*, 520 U.S. at 29.
[217] Mayo Collaborative Servs. v. Prometheus Labs., Inc., 132 S. Ct. 1289, 1301 (2012).
[218] *See id.* at 1295.

require an examination of the prior art for the statutory elements and a comparison of the invention as a whole against the prior art. Other than this difference, the §§ 102 and 103 inquiries proceed as they normally would. Accordingly, a novel, non-obvious application of an algorithm may be appropriate. But simply applying the algorithm on a computer is not sufficient.[219] The steps below sum up the test.

§ 101: Eligible Subject Matter

1. Classify elements that are naturally occurring, abstract, or not technology as "known in the art."

2. Classify elements that are not necessary to the invention "known in the art."

3. If there exist elements not "known in the art," continue to step 4.

§ 102: Novelty, § 103: Non-obviousness

4. The elements classified "known in the art" are *per se* anticipated, but the novelty and obviousness inquiry can be satisfied by novel combination or application using all the elements.

The proposed test is similar to what is sometimes referred to as the "blue pencil rule," which conceptually

---

[219] Alice Corp. v. CLS Bank Int'l, Inc., 134 S. Ct. 2347, 2358 ("Stating an abstract idea while adding the words 'apply it with a computer' simply combines those two steps, with the same deficient result.").

removes all non-statutory elements of the claim.[220] The examination would then proceed with this purified form of the claim.[221] The difference between the proposed test and the "blue pencil rule" is that the purposed test allows for the non-statutory elements to still be considered, if used in a novel combination or application. In contrast with the "blue pencil rule," no matter how novel the combination of non-statutory elements is, the proposed test will never reconsider an element once it is removed.[222] Another significant difference is that the proposed test does not give weight to unnecessary elements in the § 101 analysis.

To illustrate how the proposed test actually works, consider the following hybrid claim examples. The first example is a novel application of cryptographic security in software.[223] Whether or not the algorithm truly is new, the proposed test would deem the algorithm element to be "known in the art" because it is an abstract concept. The computer system would not be classified "known in the art" since the computer and networking

---

[220] For detailed discussion of the "blue pencil rule," see MOY, *supra* note 8, § 5:67–72. *See also* Diamond v. Diehr, 450 U.S. 175, 189 n.12 (rejecting petitioner's argument that *Flook* requires the "mathematical algorithm [to] be assumed to be within the 'prior art,'" and instead saying that the "fallacy in this argument is that we did not hold in *Flook* that the mathematical algorithm could not be considered at all when making the § 101 determination").

[221] *See, e.g.*, Brief for the United States as Amicus Curiae Supporting Neither Party at 28–29, *Mayo*, 132 S. Ct. 1289 (No. 10-1150), 2011 WL 4040414, at *28–29 (arguing that "[b]ecause the "wherein" clauses of respondent's claims do not recite any physical step to be performed by a doctor (or anyone else), they add no patentable weight to the "administering" and "determining" steps").

[222] Indeed, under this analysis, the draftsman would have no reason to include non-statutory elements because the only effect they could have is to limit the scope of the claim in an infringement action.

[223] *See, e.g.*, System, Method, & Software for Cyber Threat Analysis, U.S. Patent No. 8,601,587 (filed Sept. 3, 2010).

components are statutory and necessary to the invention. The test then continues to the novelty and non-obviousness inquiries. For novelty purposes, the application of the algorithm on the system would be considered since it enhances the functioning of the computer. Evaluating only the allowed elements, the software as a whole would be considered for novelty and non-obviousness. Accordingly, if the entire invention in cryptographic security is novel and non-obvious against prior art, it would be patentable. The second example, which intuitively would be expected to be unpatentable, is a song (or book or poem) on a typical storage medium.[224] The song, novel or otherwise, is not eligible subject matter. Rather it should be protected by copyright. An adjudicator should consider the song "known in the art" for § 101 criteria. The storage medium is deemed "known in the art under the test's necessity inquiry because the song could be stored in some other medium without changing its function, so it fails subject matter eligibility.

V. ANALYSIS OF ADAPTED TEST

The new test should render the same outcome as the Supreme Court's opinions in previous cases; this will ensure that the proposed test is effective and fits the legal landscape as it exists.[225] This section evaluates how each of the previously discussed cases would be analyzed using the proposed test.

---

[224] *See, e.g.*, Compact Disk Musical Jukebox with Digital Music Library Access, U.S. Patent App. Pub. No. 2006/0153020 (filed Sept. 26, 2003).
[225] *See generally* Douglas Lind, *A Matter of Utility: Dworkin on Morality, Integrity, and Making Law the Best It Can Be*, 6 SETON HALL CONST. L.J. 631, 648–49 (1996) (discussing Dworkin's theory of interpretive fit and justification). "Any plausible working theory of legal interpretation . . . must be able to disqualify an interpretation that fails to satisfy the threshold requirement of fit." *Id.* at 648 (quoting RONALD DWORKIN, LAW'S EMPIRE 255 (1986)) (internal punctuation omitted).

A. In re Abrams

In re Abrams involved "petroleum prospecting."[226] The CCPA held that *In re Abrams* failed the point-of-novelty test because the novelty was in the non-statutory elements of "measuring," "determining," and "comparing."[227] Under the first step of the proposed test, these mental-step elements would be considered "known in the art." The remaining elements involving "sinking," "sealing," and "reducing the pressure" are necessary to the invention because the mental steps cannot be performed without them. Because these elements of the claim are considered statutory, an adjudicator should continue the test with the novelty and non-obviousness inquiries. An adjudicator should continue to deem the first three elements "known in the art" for these inquiries, but a novel application may be possible. However, using prior art, it is unlikely that one would consider the application of "measuring," "determining," and "comparing" to the statutory elements as novel. Using the proposed test, one would at least consider this composition of elements obvious because at the time of the invention it was likely known that those steps would reach the expected outcome.

B. Parker v. Flook

Flook involved "updating alarm limits" based on the calculation using an algorithm.[228] Here, the three elements of the claim involve "measuring," "calculating," and "updating."[229] Under the proposed test, since all three elements are abstract and therefore deemed "known in the art," further examination is

---

[226] *In re* Abrams, 188 F.2d 165 (C.C.P.A. 1951).
[227] *See id.* at 169–70.
[228] Parker v. Flook, 437 U.S. 584, 585 (1978).
[229] *See id.*

unnecessary. The claim fails the test under § 101 because each element of the claim is classified "known in the art." The absence of any statutory elements automatically dooms this patent claim.

C. Diamond v. Diehr

Using the proposed test for the § 101 analysis, the *Diehr* claim's analysis would be similar to the majority's analysis.[230] The claim elements involving recalculating cure time would be classified "known in the art," but the portions of the claim involving "curing synthetic rubber" would be statutory because they are necessary to the invention as a whole. Since there is at least something necessary and statutory, it is patent-eligible subject matter. As the majority alluded to, the questions of §§ 102 and 103 patentability are "wholly apart from whether the invention falls into a category of statutory subject matter."[231] The formula used would be classified as "known in the art," so the remaining elements likely would not be novel because curing synthetic rubber is known.[232] Using § 102 or § 103, an adjudicator could easily come to the conclusion that curing rubber was anticipated by other inventions. Since the Supreme Court left this question open, this analysis will not address the question either.

D. Mayo v. Prometheus

To evaluate *Mayo*, the first step is to determine which elements are statutory. The *Mayo* claim is described in three steps: "administering" the drug,

---

[230] Diamond v. Diehr, 450 U.S. 175, 185-87 (1981).
[231] *Id.* at 190 (quoting *In re Bergy*, 596 F.2d 952, 961 (C.C.P.A. 1979)).
[232] *See id.* at 191 ("In this case, it may later be determined that the respondents' process is not deserving of patent protection because it fails to satisfy the statutory conditions of novelty under § 102 or nonobviousness under § 103.").

"measuring" the concentration of the drug in the blood stream, and "determining" what the concentration indicates.[233] The only statutory step of the process is the "administering" step, as the other two are "mental processes," so they would be classified "known in the art." Using the test, an adjudicator should classify the "administering" step necessary to the invention and not merely "[pre-]solution activity."[234] Therefore, the claim survives the § 101 eligibility test. However, this step is the only statutory element, and the addition of two steps that are classified "known in the art" is not enough to create patentability under § 102 or § 103. Note that unlike the majority opinion, using this analysis, the "administering" step is not merely referring to the relevant audience.[235] Using the test, an adjudicator should treat it as a legitimate step because, for eligibility purposes, it can be assumed that it is required in order to make the determinations of the rest of the process. The end result likely would turn out the same because the Supreme Court is correct that the claims at issue "effectively claim the underlying laws of nature themselves."[236] This validates the test because it reaches the same outcome as the Supreme Court, but the proposed test provides more guidance and structure about how to come to that conclusion.

E. Alice v. CLS Bank

Finally, the analysis comes to the most recent case, *Alice*.[237] Technically, the method claim in *Alice* does not

---

[233] Mayo Collaborative Servs. v. Prometheus Labs., Inc., 132 S. Ct. 1289, 1295 (2012).
[234] *Id.* at 1298 (quoting Parker v. Flook, 437 U.S. 584, 585 (1978)).
[235] *See id.* at 1297.
[236] The determination step merely indicates a meaning of the data and does not command any action. *Id.* at 1305.
[237] 134 S. Ct. 2347 (2014).

recite a computer, but assuming the algorithm is run on a computer as the parties stipulated, one would consider the computer statutory using the new proposed test.[238] The computer is necessary, again by stipulation of the parties, so the claim is statutory subject matter.[239] For the sake of § 101, the algorithm steps would be classified "known in the art." For the novelty inquiry, an adjudicator using the proposed test searches for novel and nonobvious application of known elements on a computer. However, the most likely outcome is that with the new proposed test, one would find the use of the algorithm on the computer obvious because there is no other practical use of the algorithm besides "applying it on a computer."

The preceding analysis is not a complete examination of these claims, but rather it is intended to illustrate how the test functions. Though the test appears to predict the same outcome as was adjudicated, the test proceeds with a logical and replicable path. A repeatable procedure is necessary because the examination procedures need to be exercised by thousands of examiners at the USPTO.[240]

VI. CONCLUSION

The Supreme Court's decision in *Alice Corp. v. CLS Bank International*[241] indicates the Court's desire to prevent patentees from obtaining monopoly rights on

---

[238] *Id.* at 2353 (noting that "the parties have stipulated that the method claims require a computer").

[239] *See id.*

[240] *See* John M. Golden, *Patentable Subject Matter and Institutional Choice*, 89 TEX. L. REV. 1041, 1047 (2011) ("No matter how incoherent or tortured relevant judicial precedent is, the USPTO must try to distill it into a set of comprehensible guidelines for several thousand patent examiners. . . .").

[241] 134 S. Ct. 2347, 2352 (2014).

abstract ideas.[242] The holding in *Alice* may align with the greater needs in the patent system, but the "framework" identified in *Mayo*[243] and reiterated in *Alice*[244] gives little guidance for lower courts and patent examiners about *how* to apply the framework factors. This article proposed a test that harnesses the strong points of the framework in a way that guides future examination with articulated steps.

The Federal Circuit will have to follow the framework in *Alice*, and the proposed test is one way to follow it and attain a predictable result. The proposed test is straightforward to follow; it checks each element to determine whether it is statutory and then evaluates whether it is necessary to the invention. The test allows patents for non-statutory elements only when they "'transform the nature of the claim' into a patent-eligible application."[245] Finally, the test isolates the issues of subject matter, novelty, and nonobviousness into three distinct questions.[246]

---

[242] *Id.* at 2354 ("'[M]onopolization of those tools through the grant of a patent might tend to impede innovation more than it would tend to promote it,' thereby thwarting the primary object of the patent laws. . . .") (quoting Mayo Collaborative Servs. v. Prometheus Labs., Inc., 132 S. Ct. 1289, 1293 (2012)).

[243] The *Mayo* opinion never actually refers to its methodology as either "framework" or "test." *See Mayo*, 132 S. Ct. at 1296–97.

[244] *Alice*, 134 S. Ct. at 2355.

[245] *Id.* (quoting *Mayo*, 132 S. Ct. at 1297).

[246] *See* Diamond v. Diehr, 450 U.S. 175, 190 (1981).

www.ingramcontent.com/pod-product-compliance
Lightning Source LLC
Chambersburg PA
CBHW020857180526
45163CB00007B/2537